Sunken Cities,

Sacred Cenotes

& Golden Sharks

Sunken Cities,

Travels of a

Sacred Cenotes

Water-Bound

& Golden Sharks

Adventurer

BILL BELLEVILLE

The University of Georgia Press   Athens and London

Published by the University of Georgia Press

Athens, Georgia 30602

© 2004 by Bill Belleville

All rights reserved

Designed by Kathi Dailey Morgan

Set in Adobe Garamond by Bookcomp, Inc.

Printed and bound by Thomson-Shore

The paper in this book meets the guidelines for
permanence and durability of the Committee on
Production Guidelines for Book Longevity of the
Council on Library Resources.

Printed in the United States of America

08 07 06 05 04 C 5 4 3 2 1

Library of Congress Cataloging-in-Publication Data

Belleville, Bill, 1945–

    Sunken cities, sacred cenotes, and golden sharks :
travels of a water-bound adventurer / Bill Belleville.

      p. cm.

    ISBN 0-8203-2592-9 (hardcover : alk. paper)

1. Belleville, Bill, 1945–—Travel.   2. Voyages and travels.

I. Title.

G465.B435 2004

910'.9163'6'092—dc22   2003020881

British Library Cataloging-in-Publication Data available

For Lisa Kay Roberts

Contents

Acknowledgments

Bob Morris, former editor at *Islands Publications* ("Suwannee"; "Sacred Cenote"; "Amazon"; "Coral Spawning") and later *Caribbean Travel and Life* ("Cat Island"), ought to be recognized for bringing a literate style and class to both publications. Bob encouraged me to write for his "books"—as they are called in the magazine world— and was big-hearted in his support of my ideas, which sometimes must have seemed a bit farfetched. In the same vein, I am much appreciative of the support of Kathy Ely, who as editor of *Destination Discovery* ("Port Royal"; "St. Lucia"; "Trinidad"; "Miskito Coast") stood behind my work in both word and deed. Also encouraging were Don George at *Salon* ("Guyana"; "Everglades") and Marc Smirnoff at *Oxford American* ("Florida Keys"). Many thanks to lawyer-naturalist Clay Henderson and poet-professor Ann Fisher-Wirth for the kind words and thoughtful insights they offered on the manuscript.

At the University of Georgia Press, thanks to Nancy Grayson who shepherded this anthology into print, and Sarah McKee, the project editor whose exceptional grasp of details helped keep me honest. Thanks, too, to Daniel Simon for his careful and informed copyediting.

On the road, I met many kind and courageous souls who allowed me to more fully realize the fine distinctions that characterize their individual places in the world. Some of them are mentioned by name in the various stories, some not. They include Bill Keogh in the Florida Keys, Beder Chávez in the Peruvian Amazon, Chuck Hesse in the Turks and Caicos, Pedro Alcolado in Cuba, Juan Carlos Naranjo in the Galapagos, Gupte Lutchmedial in Trinidad, Paul Butler in St. Lucia, Rene Gómez in Panama, Colin Edwards in Guyana, Sylvia Larramore-Crawford on Cat Island, and Rob Mattson on the Suwannee River.

Thanks, finally, to my brother, Jack Belleville, who was there with me at the very beginning, and to Rick Smith, my old childhood "exploration" buddy who grew up to be a biology teacher on the Eastern Shore. In doing so, he found his own way to create a life in and around the solution that once fashioned our everlasting boyhood dreams.

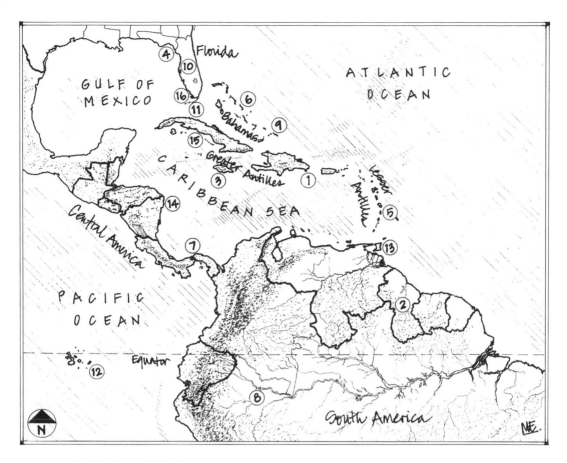

MAP OF SITES

Introduction

In Solution—I Came by It Honestly

I hate quotations. Tell me what you know.

RALPH WALDO EMERSON

The peninsula of my youth, the lower Eastern Shore of Maryland, was veined with the creeks and tributaries and streams of the Chesapeake Bay and, just thirty miles to the east, was edged by the great Atlantic Ocean. My family and my friends and I were surrounded by water, and perhaps more than we knew, our lives were defined by it.

With my mom and dad and brother Jack, I went fishing on the weekends on the little docks of the estuarine Nanticoke River at the hamlet of Tyaskin, or swam in the shallow waters at an old river resort nearby called Waterview. We caught striped bass, which we called rock fish, and croakers and spot. Once, when I was eight, I hooked a rock that was so big my dad had to help me land it. To this day, when I try to define excitement, I think of that moment. I learned that little miracles can happen when you're a small boy facing down a big fish at the edge of a salty river.

Sometimes from little single-lane bridges, we hung chicken necks into tidal creeks that meandered through the vast spartina marshes near Tyaskin. Dad was always ready with the long-handled net to scoop up the blue crabs. At other times, Mom packed a wicker basket with cold fried chicken and we drove to Ocean City, up and over the wide and shallow Sinepuxent Bay. Once there, we played in the great rollers of the surf, exhalant in a mid-Atlantic Ocean that, even by August, never quite seemed warm enough. The enormous granite rock jetties that kept the inlet open were always encrusted with thick clutches of mussels, and the golden sand, hot enough to burn your feet in the summer, created a spacious beach that, farther north, still was corrugated with the swales and berms of giant natural dunes.

Once, when I was seven, I put on a mask and looked underwater for the first time. It was during a visit to Sarasota, Florida, with my family, and my first view of this subsurface reality was in a swimming pool. I saw nothing but legs and torsos and the geometrically perfect edges of the pool—but the clarity of it all! It was as if there were an entirely different world just below the surface, and it was a dimension that someone without a mask could hardly know.

Later, during another vacation, we traveled to Silver Springs, weaving our way across Florida on the blue highways that predated the big interstates. Along the way, we passed assorted Monkey Jungles and Seminole Villages and all manner of pre-Disney, Mom-and-Pop road-side attractions—some with cypress knees carved into totems, some with gator rassling, some just souvenir shops selling turtles and man-atees made out of seashells. At Silver Springs, we boarded one of the glass-bottom boats and puttered off across the water, all of us sitting on benches and looking intently down into the center of the hull.

There, the glass functioned as a giant dive mask, and it allowed us a rare look at a world that was as transparent as the swimming pool in Sarasota. A tour guide with a radio announcer's voice informed us that the springs feeding this large pond were "bottomless" and that its waters were "99.95 percent pure." Under us, bass and mullet and bluegill darted about, and an alligator, so perfectly formed he seemed fake, lolled on the bottom. I longed to be in the water, to see how bottomless this spring really was.

One day, I promised myself, I would learn more about this other reality. Someday I would have adventures, and they would take me across the water and under it.

Back home on the Eastern Shore, my neighbor Ricky and I rode our bikes for miles through the open countryside, across little bridges that spanned creeks, around lakes, and to the edges of the swamps and marshes. We were explorers, and we ranged as far as we could, looking for patches of forest we had not yet seen. The best discoveries of all were the streams we sometimes found nestled down in the underbrush.

Our homes sat atop old pastureland, which in turn was surrounded by fields of corn and soybeans. But there was a remnant swath of natural land at the end of our street, twenty or so acres of pine and oak and maple that had never been cleared for farming. This remnant became "The Woods," and we traipsed through every square foot of it.

Once we found an old well pipe coming out of the ground there, and armed with ropes and shovels and hoes, we set out to dig our way down to where water once fed that pipe. We had been to Luray Caverns across the bay with our parents, and we were sure we would soon stumble on our own miniature Luray, a cathedral of rocky chambers and flowing water. If it were there, we would slog through it and explore it and make it ours. We dug and hacked our way through almost five feet of roots and clay before one of our adult neighbors who liked to snoop came to see what we were up to. When we told him, he laughed and said, "You boys are going to need to dig about another hundred feet, then you might get close."

By the time I reached my last years of high school, I worked on an oyster boat on the Chesapeake Bay on the weekends to make some spending money. On those bitterly cold winter days, our small open boat clank-clanked its way out into the Tangier Sound of the lower bay just after dawn, and we bobbed on the vast sound like a cork. The tongers, men older and hardier than me, pulled their great chopstick-like tongs over the gunnel of our boat again and again, emptying the claw scoops with crusty piles of oysters atop my culling board midstern. Off in the distance, we would see etched into the horizon the sails of the few skipjacks that still worked these same waters. It seems almost romantic now, in the retelling. But then, it was raw and cold and hard. It made me realize I probably wasn't tough enough to make a living that way. I would figure something else out though, and it would keep me near the water.

As a young adult, I moved to Florida—another water-sogged peninsula that, despite its exotic nature, was awash with strong intimations of my own childhood. While I ostensibly came to this Florida to learn to write by working for newspapers, I also came because of the possibilities it offered to be outdoors nearly year round. And there seemed to be water nearly everywhere, in the perfectly round sinkhole lakes, in every low depression in the terrain, around the edges of great cypress bayheads, and in the clear bubbling springs. I was squarely inside a landscape that was tempered by the Gulf and the Atlantic. And a bit farther south, the sea was warm and clean enough to support this continent's only living coral reef.

I was closer to water than ever, and I longed to be more fully inside of it, to find myself in solution with the most primal of all elements. I fished in my little jon boat on a big sandy-bottomed lake called Buffum and swam with my young wife. On spring-fed rivers, I learned to paddle a canoe for the first time, navigating it through the hardwood swamps that cradled the spring runs. I was near the edge of the subtropics now, and my peninsula was rimmed with islands, next to a Caribbean basin that was wholly created from them. I finally learned to scuba dive, and, as expected, I saw there was far more going on below the surface of the water than just the flailing of human legs and torsos. There were fish and alligators and fossils in the springs and, on the offshore reefs, more color and magic than I had ever dreamed. I took lessons in cave diving and found myself inside chambers of limestone, labyrinthine capillaries that held our aquifer, as clear as ether down there. It was all like traveling to another planet, and I became gradually transformed by the experience. I was plumbing the depths of the springs the tour guide of my youth had called "bottomless," and if they were more finite than he let on, they were every bit as captivating as I had imagined.

All the while, I was learning to craft words together and in doing so, found myself able to convince magazine editors to send me places near the water so I could use my newly acquired diving skills. I traveled to islands and to the edges of the sea coast any time I could because, as I soon found, the people and the animals and the plants there were as influenced by the water as I had been. As I cultivated my trade, I was careful to use my travels and my diving as tools and not as ends unto themselves. Islands and remote patches of sea and underwater caves and coral reefs were to be experienced in order to be better understood— they were at the very heart of what mattered to me.

Editors, if not fully understanding of my passion, were supportive. Magazines could afford overseas travel expenses, and most were generous in their fees. For a short while, I even provided "web content," acting as both writer and photographer for the Discovery Channel on what were being called "real-time expeditions." Whatever the medium, it was all about storytelling—about having an adventure, capturing it in print, and then sharing it with others.

Although nearly apolitical at the beginning, I found myself coming to understand the more complete concept of ecology—naturally and culturally. I learned a little of the long-term responsibilities that come with true conservation. Water and islands weren't just one gigantic aquatic playpen. They held magic, enchantment, secrets of life.

And if ecology was the natural kismet of fresh and salt water, then the artifacts scattered on the bottom of these waterways were more than just random coins or stray maritime effects. Shipwrecks, I learned, were time capsules that held secrets to the lives of people who had long vanished from the Earth. They were, in effect, "submerged cultural sites." As I begin to explore shipwrecks, I was introduced to the addled politics that pit treasure salvors against archaeologists—and which frame the traditional urges of us humans to either exploit and consume as quickly as possible or to try to interpret and save as a legacy for another generation. Although I intellectually understood the need for preservation, I also enjoyed the bonhomie and the enthusiasm of the treasure salvors. They could be forthright and unabashedly quixotic.

Flora and fauna special to certain islands caught my imagination, as did the speciated culture of the people themselves. I also began rediscovering all the great writers whom I had either skipped, skimmed, or ignored when I was younger. Charles Darwin was no longer a one-dimensional stiff shirt with curious theories, but a flesh-and-blood man who risked his life sailing around the world in an effort to better understand how the earth came to be. Joseph Conrad, once dense and obtuse and dark, now told maritime tales of people I was actually encountering in real life, Lord Jim types who were every bit as noble—and conflicted—as those who populated Conrad's fictional world. And Jules Verne! My God, in the pre-techno era of the 1800s, Verne imagined a sub traveling to the abyss of the ocean, and long before Peter Benchley latched onto the Jaws thing, he brought a giant squid to life and made it menacing and real and immediate.

As I reconvened with the sensibilities of traditional authors I had missed the first time around, I also begin to listen to the voices of more modern writers, folks who addressed the subtleties of my own world.

Florida naturalist Archie Carr wrote affectionately of the great Suwannee River, and of the warmer latitudes where his beloved sea turtles came ashore to nest. "If you are in the Tropics and have trouble seeing the good in where you are," he said in *The Windward Road,* "work your way to windward where the trade comes in to land." Elizabeth Bishop, the esteemed poet, lived in Key West and in South America, and wrote lyrically of both. Of Florida, she decided it was

> The state with the prettiest name,
> the state that floats in brackish water
> held together by mangrove roots.

In her poem "The Riverman," I learned of the freshwater dolphin that morphed into human form in Amazonia. It gave me a reason to want to go off in search for both *boto* and myth.

I stumbled across a poem by the Chilean poet Pablo Neruda, who lyrically examined the sea and people who would go there in "Oda al Buzo" (Ode to the Diver). In doing so, he suggested the metaphor that linked us rather than kept us apart:

> he seemed
> globular
> king
> of the waters,
> a bulbous
> and secretive
> cuttlefish,
> the truncated
> device
> of invisible
> algae.

And so, after several years of traveling around the globe in pursuit of some odd blend of literary romance and natural history and anthropology, I found myself with a spate of articles and essays that all had to do, not surprisingly, with water. Certainly, from my childhood on, I have come by it honestly.

Of course, that connection was there long before my own existence, buried deep down in our genetic codes. We are, as living animals, made up mostly of water. The planet's surface is three-fifths water. We evolved from sea-things who once crawled upon land and, with the hand of God molding our shape, learned to have choices in our own destiny. Like water and time, we flow and move and change. Now that we have become dominate among all animals, we have the capacity to shape the world for all the other species. There are billions of us on Earth, walking around now, and most of us are imbued with typical human conceits. We forget our origins, forget the medium that, more than any other, has given us life. Maybe it's time to start remembering again, before pollution and demolition of natural systems and a callousness for the aquatic world finally backfires. As Ben Franklin once noted, when the well's dry, we will know the real worth of water.

Will it take that? Sometimes, as a species at the very top of the food chain, I fear we act like giant corporations that use and abuse their resources in the short term until they are bankrupt, then simply walk away, only to do it again somewhere else. The Earth is full of people now, and it doesn't allow that luxury anymore—no manner of spin will make it otherwise. Water was sacred once and—to some people—it still is. But for most of us clever, industrialized folks, it is often a mere utility, a commodity we can consume, exploit, buy, and sell. If water has lost its sacredness, can mere human law ever atone for it?

We may never step twice into the same river, but we can surely revisit the streams and sloughs and coves of our own memories and, by doing so, reanimate ambitions and curiosities and dreams. In our remembrances, maybe we can come to understand how deeply the molecules of water are woven into our substance.

You know, until my father passed away, he and I would still talk about that big rockfish that once tugged so hard and fought so well on the shores of the Nanticoke River one bright Sunday afternoon. On one level, it was just a little boy catching a big fish. Yet it has come to mean so much more. Now, it's forever captured in my imagination, a moment encased in the sweet amber of memory.

The wilderness of my childhood landscape on the lower Eastern Shore of Maryland has been mostly tamed now, but I can still search for it in Guyana, Jamaica, Nicaragua, the Galapagos. While I have traveled to these disparate sites to realize my connection with water, I have also gone to try to recapture the excitement of my own youth, in a place where the earth was veined with the tide, which flowed with the never-ending promise of discovery.

Perhaps if we pay attention to the message of our own genesis, we may even come to a sense of stewardship about this water and its role in our own destiny.

And maybe, if we're lucky, we can have a bit of adventure along the way.

The Sacred Cenote
of the Taino

The Magic Deep Within

The dark and mysterious pre-Columbian Taino cenote of Manantial de La Aleta is preparing to swallow me whole this afternoon, feet first.

It will do so as soon as Tom Hodson, brought all the way here to the wildest jungle gridlock of the Dominican Republic to help with such arcane rigging chores, straps me into a harness, tightens the nylon straps around my waist and thighs, and clips a wire cable to the entire contraption. Tom, an easygoing, sturdy fellow, advises me to lean backward and *swing out over the cenote.* He uses the same tone of voice he might use if he were asking me to pass the butter.

I look down. Some five stories below this trap door in the rock is a patch of spring water which is as clear as a swimming pool where the sun hits it. Floating atop the pool—from my perspective—is a tiny inflatable Quicksilver raft with tiny scuba divers inside of it. My tank and scuba gear are in there with them. When I reach it, I will put on my tank, mask, and fins and, with my fellow divers, flop over the side of the raft and sink into the bowels of the 250-foot-deep La Aleta. Underwater, we will search for artifacts the long-vanquished Taino Indians once sacrificed to their gods, but first I must reach the raft.

"Swing right or left?" I ask Tom, stalling for time, sweating bullets in my wetsuit. Tropical jungles and sacred cenotes don't usually bother me. But heights make my heart beat like the tap-tap-tap rhythm of *merengue*.

"Counterclockwise," says Tom, perhaps figuring he'll allay my fears by simply confusing me. So I swing away—clockwise, as it turns out—and find myself for one brief moment free-falling backward into the same well the Tainos once used to send sacrifices to their gods. And in a split second, I think: here comes a nice hearty gringo sacrifice, a thousand years or so too late.

Thankfully, the slack in the cable snaps tight, and I begin a more steady and gradual descent. As I go, I leave behind the well-lit and safe jungle reality of this century for another dimension—one so little known it can be accurately described as *unexplored*.

As I slowly drop, I fix my eyes on the bowl-like cavern around me and the water below. As I do, I discover that Nietzsche was right. When you stare into the abyss, the abyss does indeed stare back. And it flinches a whole lot less. What the hell, it becomes pretty damn spooky, too. There's no getting around it.

I just arrived in the Dominican Republic yesterday, and this morning I am hiking along a soft, sandy jeep path that parallels the *Mar caribe*. A ridge of coconut palms separates my trail from a sea so blue it seems electrified, as if someone has plugged it in. There is only the scantest breeze, and the water is dead calm and endless, broken only by the churning snow-white wake of a fisherman's wooden pirogue, nets and cork buoys piled up in its pitched bow. My companions and I are headed for a dry limestone cave deep in the forest, a place not just of astonishing geology but, as I will find, one of heartbreakingly graphic history.

Although it is still early yet, the tropical sun here is relentless. As soon as the path narrows and snakes inland through the thick jungle of foliage, the waft of the coastal breeze vanishes and a consuming ovenlike heat takes its place. It is midsummer, perhaps not the best time to be wandering about in a dry tropical forest.

There are four of us, and we are walking single file, Indian style, headed for a cave full of bats and scorpion spiders and nearly forgotten Taino art, a place where the striking geology of time has molded columns and pillars from the ceiling and floor of the soft rock. It is a place where the native pre-Columbians came to worship their *zemis* and to evoke their supernatural powers. Our destination is Cueva del Puente—Cave of the Bridge—and it will give me a preview of what I will be finding here in the jungle during the next two weeks. Its walls are said to be imprinted with pictographs and petroglyphs, its geology incised with the slow flow of calcium and time. Both will have stories to tell, if I listen closely enough.

"The same thing that happened in La Aleta is happening here," Kristen Meier tells me, pushing her short-cropped blonde hair away from her forehead, drenched in sweat like the rest of us. "Except this cave isn't underwater."

Meier is talking about geology right now, and what she means is a small chunk of the cave ceiling has collapsed onto the cave floor, just as it has at the water-filled sink called La Aleta. At the Cave of the Bridge, I can walk into its boulder-strewn collapse; at La Aleta, I will have to dive.

Meier, a young anthropology grad student from Indiana University, is half of a two-woman team that has been mapping Cueva del Puente over the last several weeks. I met Harley (her nickname) and her colleague Kyle Tiernan last night at the Club Dominicus hotel, a coastal resort at the edge of this country's massive East National Park outside of Bayahibe. The Dominicus is one of those all-inclusive Club Med–style resorts catering to large groups of sybaritic-minded European tourists, all of whom are Italian this week, and most of whom are quite satisfied to sip pink drinks, lie naked in the sun, and then—inexplicably—jump up and engage in group calisthenics led by a resort version of a camp counselor. Except for Taino-inspired artwork in the gift shop, most will stay comfortably isolated from the culture for their entire stay. Nevertheless, the manager of the Dominicus has been supportive of the expedition; as a result, the resort serves as a sort of jumping-off point—a base camp, if you will—for the more intensive expeditionary work in the adjacent jungle.

Meier and Tiernan told me the rest of the archaeological team wouldn't be arriving until late tomorrow. Graciously, they offered to lead me to Cueva del Puente today, and I readily accepted.

Tiernan, with three pieces of jewelry studding each ear and a bandanna around her hair, has set the pace in long-legged, energetic strides. She is followed by Meier and then Tony, dark-skinned and affable, a ranger with the Parque Nacional del Este. I bring up an increasingly distant rear, stopping far more than necessary to examine the stunted cycad palm, the starburst-like fruit of the cobey tree, bromeliads fallen from boughs overhead. The cycad, known back in Florida as a "coontie" and here as *guayiga*, has a tubular root that, once pounded, grated, and processed, was the source of the flour the Taino once used as a staple. They turned it into soup, cakes, bread. *Cassava*, they called it.

The pair have been doing postgraduate work here since the first of the year; now, they staff a small field station to support the ongoing archaeology inside the vast 300-square-mile park. A few weeks ago, they spent thirteen days crawling about inside the cave by themselves, measuring the passageways and sketching the art the Tainos left behind over five centuries ago. The women are good-natured, curious, sharp-witted. They are wearing army fatigues, tank tops, T-shirts. Tiernan tells me an Italian tourist back at the hotel spotted them headed out for the jungle one day, dressed in such a manner. "Ciao," he said, eyeing the women closely, "Rambo."

As we travel inland, the trail quickly turns from soft sand to hard, sharp limestone veined with tree roots the size of my forearm. The coastal flatness rises surprisingly up and over a steep ridge, the relic of an ancient coastline. Several of these escarpments trail east-to-west across this dense peninsula, tracing the prehistoric rise and fall of the seas. High and porous, they hold most of the scores of caves for which the region has come to be known. By some estimates, there may be over one hundred limestone caverns, tunnels, and grottos here. But there is no map of them, and even local knowledge is not enough to keep track of where they exist in the landscape. Indeed, caves are being newly discovered—and lost—all the time. Dominican physician and Taino scholar Dr. Abelardo Jiménez only found the cave named José María in 1980; a year later, he found another, Cueva de Romanita—which was promptly lost again. Today, no one is quite sure where it went.

The first of the caves is upcoming, a welcome respite after our four-kilometer march. We step gingerly down a steep ravine to the mouth of Cueva del Puente, turn on our headlamps, hunch down, and walk into the darkness. A ceiling collapse somewhere not too far away has captured a distant breeze, funneling it through the labyrinth. It seems as if the cave is exhaling, and its breathe is sweetly pungent, the scent of centuries of bat guano, damp limestone, sacred exhortations of long-dead Indians.

We shine our lights on the walls, and I see the flowstone captured there, the excruciatingly slow drip of moist calcium forming itself into stalactites from the ceiling, stalagmites from the floor, rocky icicles everywhere, some sparkling with minerals like tiaras broken into shards. Tiernan stops, pointing her beam under a rock, where a small dark thing scuttles. It is a scorpion spider. "They hurt pretty bad," she says. "Be careful where you put your hand." Overhead, there is fluttering. It is the other predominant cave life, brown bats. Some are flying, classic vampirelike wings stretched wide, disappearing in and out of the darkness; others are clustered together inside bowl-like cavities recessed into the ceiling, little furry bodies quivering with thoughts known only to other bats.

Soon we find ourselves in a cathedral-sized cavern, speleothems flowing in stop-time down the walls like organic pipe organs. The flow, moving ever downward, cascades through a limestone hallway, across a ridge, and into another smaller room. Gravity has guided the drip, taking it lower, deeper into the cave. On the floor are the round, marble-sized rocks created by an ancient water flow. *Uvas,* they are called locally, says Meier. Grapes.

The room narrows now, and we are each on all fours, crawling through a tight passage that leads into more rooms, under more bats, down to where the rock is still moist, residual wetness from the flood that once filled it like it still fills La Aleta today. And then I begin to see the visual clues, messages communicated over the centuries. They are petroglyphs—carved into the rock—and pictographs, drawn on it. There are frigate birds and dragonflies, a short-eared owl, something that may be a turtle, and distinctive heads of people—some with happy-face grins. They were created by the Tainos, in the times when the caves were places to seek spiritual refuge, to solicit guidance from ancestors who had passed into the other world, to commune with the *zemis,* the gods who mediated for them with the forces of nature. Later, when the Spanish arrived, the caves became real refuges, places for the gentle Indians to hide when the conquistadors rampaged through the countryside.

Do you know of these Taino? They were among the first to colonize the Antilles, migrating up here from the coast of South America, island by island. Some called them Arawaks, but that was actually the language they spoke. When Columbus first landed in the New World and asked who they were, they replied *Taino.* It meant gentle, kind. It was said they could not tell a lie. Sometimes, when the Spanish tricked the Indians into coming out so they could butcher them, the Taino openly wept in anguish at the deceit.

The Taino crafted dugouts in which to fish and travel, griddles to cook bread, hammocks to sleep and dream. They made up words to describe the things that were vital to their lives, words that have slipped into our vocabularies today. Say these words out loud in their Taino form and hear how they resonate with the place: *hamaca* (hammock), *iguana* (iguana), *manati* (manatee), *canoa* (canoe), *huracán* (hurricane), *barbacoa* (barbecue), *tobaco* (tobacco).

Unlike the more warlike Caribs, the Taino shaped exquisite bowls and pots from clay and wood, vessels adorned with the faces of their gods—a busy pantheon of *zemis* who ruled over rain and sun, storms and fertility, life and death.

We are deep in the cave now, and I look up to where the two women tell me to look. As I do, I see what it is that had chased the Tainos here for the last time. Unlike the other drawings and etchings of natural icons, these illustrations depict the square cut of a sail of a caravel, the flaglike pendant of a conquistador's banner, the distinctive bearded face of a European. Beyond that, there is no more cave art.

It is the picture of the beginning of the end of the civilization of the Taino. As I stand before it, I feel the drip of a stalactite forming itself from overhead, a single drop of calcium-enriched water from the limestone. And I think of it as a tear falling through time, the last touch of a *zemi* left behind now for five hundred years. It is a god seemingly bereft of its mortals, alone back here in the cool darkness of the rock.

What is left are the bats, which—with cave-roosting owls—were believed by the Taino to be the embodiment of the *opias,* souls of the dead. Trapped in the caves like this during the day, the opias would emerge at night to wander the landscape, under the wild orchids and Spanish moss, through the snakelike vines of the copey tree, treading in bare feet above the sharp limestone.

Do the gods really vanish when their mortals succumb? Or do they inhabit another dimension, waiting for the right moment to step again into the collective unconscious of us so-called "moderns"? At what point does newly accrued cultural knowledge reach a critical mass? When it does, isn't there also a critical emotional mass—leveraged by sympathy, awe, respect—that is more than eager to do business with myth?

It is cloudy and early when I finally hook up with Charlie Beeker over breakfast at the Dominicus. I met Beeker a couple of years ago in the Florida Keys, when he had organized a summer field school for Indiana University's underwater archaeology program. His crew was helping to map and excavate a test site on a Spanish wreck they called "El Lerri," one that dated to the era of treasure galleons in the New World. I found Beeker to be stocky, gruff, straightforward, more realist than idealist. He was also one of the few in the archaeology community who could get along with the rough-and-tumble treasure salvors who were demanding full and unrestrained access to any shipwreck they could get their hands on in the Keys.

Beeker's scientific credentials were marginal, however: he had a bachelor's degree and once owned a sport diving shop. Still, he was a natural when it came to finding old things underwater. And he was a bulldog on logistics—he knew how to find the right people and get them where they needed to be. He also could be a bit of a control freak, but that served him well in attending to all the tiny details that could possibly go wrong when people travel to a strange and exotic place and attempt to practice science underwater.

Here in the Dominican Republic, Beeker has assembled a team that includes California senior state archaeologist John Foster; Geoff Conrad, a Harvard-trained anthropologist with IU's Mather's Museum; and a passel of graduate and undergraduate students—most of whom have been specially schooled in the skills of technical diving back in the cold, deep quarries of Indiana. Foster, like Beeker, is a veteran diver; Conrad will deal exclusively with examining the terrestrial sites where the Taino camped or lived.

But no scientific team arrives in a developing country and rushes right off into its interior—especially to a site as remote as La Aleta. There are the logistics of moving shovels and dive gear, compressors and tents, and food and water almost five miles inland. There are tropical storms, always brewing on the horizon—especially now, in the middle of hurricane season. There is the etiquette of gringos making new "discoveries" on ancient turf in which, historically, they have no cultural stake. And there is the delicate and often Swiftian politics of the Caribbean Basin, particularly here in the Latin American country of the Dominican Republic.

Beeker tells me there is only a rough five-mile trail blazed into La Aleta, and it would take two full days to cover if we were to use donkeys to carry our gear. But he has somehow engaged Don Peter Morales Troncoso, the governor of the province, into our expedition. As a result, Morales has pulled the strings to have a Dominican Army Huey fly us in and out. Soon, says Beeker, we will load the Huey with people and gear and soar over the treetops, to the site of the sacred well.

La Aleta is our destination today, and to it we are taking scads of black trunklike crates, scuba tanks and air compressors, shovels duct-taped together, and enough backpacks and freeze-dried food to empower a small revolution. Four tons' worth, all together. Moving and stacking cargo like this draws out scores of Dominicans who live near a barren field in the village of Bayahibe where our helicopter will land. The curious include an earnest, dark-skinned little boy who carries a homemade shoeshine box by a strap around his forehead. In our packing and leaving, we have created a fiesta of anticipation.

From the distance comes first the sound, and then the vision of an old Huey, which thwack-thwacks itself down in a clearing of red clay and limestone rubble. I run to it, lowering my head against the tornado of dust stirred up by the blades, climb aboard, and strap myself into a seat behind the co-pilot, next to an open door. Within minutes we are rising straight up from the ground, scattering everyone below in a melee of red sediment—a herd of horses, remaining expedition members, even the little shoe shiner, who found no solace in a group of gringos shod in hiking boots.

Off we go toward La Aleta, soaring above the dense dry tropical forest, a massive foliage canopy that stretches like a giant platter of broccoli as far inland as I can see. The only relief is to the east, where the Caribbean parallels our progress, a tableau of coconut palms and sliver of sand rimming a vast sheet of blue.

White smoke finally trails up from somewhere inside the giant platter of broccoli and our pilot veers for it. A clear field appears just under us, and our chopper drops down on it like a turbo-charged elevator headed for the basement. As soon as it touches ground, I scramble out the still-open door while the blade swirls overhead, running for the edge of the jungle like a Taino being chased by a conquistador. Two Dominican park rangers have been camping at La Aleta since last May to discourage any looting of the cenote; one of them stoked up a fire of dry wood and guayabi fronds to create the smoke signal that led us here—an ancient but unfailing version of our global positioning systems.

A short trail leads through the jungle, over the same sharp limestone outcropping I have been hiking, a path that winds finally past a series of boulder-lined "plazas" where the Taino once played a ceremonial ball game. Clay pot shards by the hundreds already have been recovered from these sites; a few months ago, rangers stumbled onto a bleached skull of a young Taino girl here, resting half in the leaf cover, half out.

At the end of the path is the mother lode, the cenote I have been waiting nearly a week to see: La Aleta. It appears in the floor of the jungle not as a single dark hole but as nine "eyes" clustered together, dark windows down into the rock and water below. Although brush has now been cleared away from the cavities, when Beeker and Foster first arrived on the site last year, it was so densely overgrown with guayabi and ferns and spindly tropical trees that they came within inches of accidentally stepping into the holes.

I walk up to the edge of the largest hole and, precariously bracing myself with the branch of a gumbo limbo tree, look down inside. There is clear, bluish water there, the water of a spring. Hanging at the edge is a rope attached to a bucket. The rangers have been pulling up water from the well, just as the Tainos did long ago, except their bucket is plastic instead of tightly woven fronds and fibers.

Although Tainos used this well as a source of water, archaeologists say La Aleta was undoubtedly ceremonial, even sacrificial. After all, the Taino attached a profound meaning to caves—in their creation myth, their ancestors emerged from them. And what could be more sacred in a dry tropical forest than fresh water? Taken together, what astounding magic would be expressed in a cave that plunges straight down for fifty feet and then brims with deep water so clear the sun actually penetrates the upper level of it?

Within minutes of my arrival, riggers who have come in with us, men especially trained in the delicate art of stringing rescue lines into remote places, go into action. After two hours, they have crisscrossed the hole with a maze of ropes and pulleys, a spider web of precautions, all designed to safely lower and raise divers into the cenote. An inflatable raft is dragged to the edge of the largest hole, and I help to lower it by a tether down to the darkness below. It will be used as a platform for diving over the next several days.

Soon I will strap on a harness and descend into one of the eyes of the cenote, and with scuba tanks on my back, sink below the water to see what I can find there. Perhaps it will be something a bit beyond the defined edge of science. For now, I pitch my tent not far from La Aleta, back under the cover of another red-barked gumbo limbo, guayabi pushing up at the edge of my thin tent fabric. Just before I zipper myself in for the night against the swarming mosquitoes, two dark-skinned men walk by leading two donkeys. Neither speaks English, but one is wearing a T-shirt that reads Hard Rock Café. It is all a Felliniesque image here in the heart of the Dominican jungle, more details for another god to be assembled by.

In the few days we have been camped here, divers have recovered a substantial portion of whole, ornate pots; exquisitely carved wooden bowls and clubs; human and animal bones; even a woven basket. On a series of deep dives to 180 feet, an Italian named Franco Cotti, who runs a dive shop back at the Dominicus, videotaped scads of calabash-like gourds, still lashed together by twine, lying on the side of the pinnacle that rises up from the 240-foot-plus bottom. This well was surely a source of drinking water for the Indians, but it was much more. La Aleta was also a sacred cenote, a place where the sky met the earth, an underworld where humans communed with the supernatural.

Peter Morales, the provincial governor, visits one day by helicopter with a team of Dominican archaeologists. He is a big-boned man with a barrel chest and a booming, deep voice. Swatting mosquitoes and wiping sweat from his forehead, he pronounces this as the most important Taino site in all of Latin America. Morales brings fresh water and bottles of rum and cigars with him, and later, around the campfire, we pass the rum, smoke the cigars, and revel in what we still may find.

It is July here in the tropics, and it has been too hot to sleep inside my bag, so I have been lying on top of it at night. This morning, I found a segmented worm, the size of a silver dollar, curled up in a bronze spiral on my chest, and what appeared to be an entire colony of ants swarming over one foot. I unzipped my tent flap, shook off the insects, and poured a canteen of water over my head. We are now low on supplies. For breakfast, I ate a granola bar and loaned my pocketknife to photographer Bill Curtsinger who—to the awe of several grad students sitting nearby—peeled a raw potato and ate it.

Today, it is finally my turn to dive into La Aleta. At the edge of the hole, I climb into my full wetsuit, and just as I zip it up, I break into an enormous sweat. I am keyed up and energized despite the oppressive heat, and it finally hits me why I have been so excited about diving into this hole in the floor of a jungle.

When I was a little boy, I once read about American divers who explored and charted another sacred cenote, this one near the Mayan city of Chichén Itzá. I was a sensitive, dweeby kid with microscopes and bug collections and a tank full of guppies in my bedroom. The fantasy of diving into a mysterious water-filled hole somewhere in the tropics grabbed my imagination then and never let go. As I grew up, my dweebiness turned into a healthy curiosity, one I was able to pursue as a writer. And my childhood notion of discovery—of finding very old and secret things in exotic places—never really left me.

But there is more: I have always been sympathetic to the underdog. And there were no greater underdogs than the Indian tribes of Latin America that were bullied and tortured by the conquistadors. While the culture of the gentle Taino was as complex as that of the Maya and Inca, their imprint on their island landscape was scant. I yearned to excavate their memory every bit as much as I wanted to dive back into my own childhood imagings.

At the urging of rigger Hodson, I swing out over the largest hole and rappel downward, twisting slowly as I go. Narrow shafts of surface light stream in from the nine separate crevices above, penetrating the clear spring water where it lands. As it does, it projects an ever-shifting optic show back onto the limestone walls of the cave. It is a reflection that seems comprised of a batch of specters, each vying for space here in the cavern, light-fed geometry squashed and reformed in the wink of an eye, a dance of pre-Columbian remembrance. The effect is mystical, dreamlike. I am half addled with sensory overload, and I'm not even underwater yet.

A massive root from a copey tree trails down all the way from the surface to the water, a macramé of barky veins unsure whether to be a trunk or a root, spreading out like a fat mushroom cap near the bottom. Crawling on its base is a tarantula the size of my palm. Three other divers are in the raft, sorting weights and masks from regulators. Their voices echo softly in the coolness of the massive chamber. Beeker is already geared up, floating in the cool water, patiently waiting.

Bartolomé de Las Casas, a priest who reported on the conquest of the New World, wrote of a place our archaeologists say is La Aleta, describing it as only half a league away from the village of the Taino cacique Cotubanama. Las Casas reported the Taino used a cord of rattan as rope and an earthenware cup to scoop drinking water from the hole. The surface of the well, he said, was about eight arm lengths below the limestone terrain, and cups dipping into it found "sweet water above and salty deeper" below.

I finally land in the raft. We discuss a dive plan, and then I strap on a tank and flip backwards over the side, welcoming the cool snap the spring water gives me as it surges in my wetsuit. I swing my legs down, righting myself and, with the others, descend into the real heart of darkness. More people have been in outer space than have been in this cenote, and there's no telling what we'll encounter.

We pull our way, hand over hand, down a line that will take us to the pinnacle of rock that rises up from the 240-plus-foot bottom. The mercury domes of exhaled air from the other divers rise and effervesce into me. I am descending through the clear spring water when the surface light disappears. I switch on my underwater light and glance at my depth gauge. The numbers inside it appear wavy as the light refracts through the thick minerals in this cloudy middle layer of water, making it seem as if I am looking through an old pane of window glass. I taste sulfur through my regulator, and realize I have left the sweet water of the surface for Bartolomé's salty layer. I shine my light around me in all directions, but reality has dissolved into yellowish silt.

Near the bottom, the sulfur disappears and the visibility turns as clear as a spring again—albeit a very dark one. I hang on the line at 105 feet and watch as the other divers descend to the rock-strewn platform just under me. As they hover over it, they appear as little helicopters with spotlights flying back and forth through the night.

The pinnacle seems made of chunks of limestone and wood, wedged together by muck, punctuated with pot shards. At its edges, it plunges dramatically down into the darkness. From its sides have already come a duho—the royal stool of a cacique, war clubs, two hatchet handles, bowls. All are of wood, a rare organic preserved by the anaerobic darkness of the mud.

The pressure of depth pushing on my wetsuit leaves me with the vague feeling of being shrink-wrapped. Nitrogen fires in my system, and I become fuzzy, lightheaded. My anxiety level is soaring, my heart thumping. It is a very long way to the surface from where I am, and the human conceit that brought me here feels puny, presumptuous. I apologize to the Taino gods, telling them I mean no harm. As I do, my breathing mysteriously becomes more relaxed.

Recovering, I put myself back into the moment, and my senses—which had tunneled themselves into a narrow telescope—open again. As they do, I see Beeker become more animated than the others, finning up and over the top of the pinnacle with something cradled in his hand. He rises up toward me with it and I shine my light beam in his direction. As I do, I see he is carrying a perfectly formed little clay pot, about the size of a squat sugar bowl, rounded sides rising up from a flat bottom. On one edge is the bas relief of the face of a frog—an animal with mystical meaning to the Taino—while on the other is the icon's tail end. Perhaps it is a clue to the Taino belief in the duality of nature; then again, maybe it is just the butt of a frog, a glimpse of it both coming and going, bringing rain or taking it away.

I reach out and touch the pot with my fingers. As I do, I wonder what the Taino potter who once built this piece of art wanted to communicate. I listen closely for the scantest whispers from his time, but all I hear is the exhaust from my regulator. Perhaps the pot is an offering. Except this time it is one made from the distant past—from a millennium ago, from a childhood gone—and then transported to the future. From behind my regulator, I smile broadly, guilelessly. Like a kid.

Up, ever up, we go, our light beams swinging about in the darkness and the bubbles of our exhalations flooding over us. At twenty feet, we stop and suck off a bottle of oxygen hung on the line there; the O_2 helps guard against decompression sickness from residual nitrogen. We also take a "safety stop" here for ten minutes, just in case. I release my grip from the rope and, with an eye on my depth gauge, fin toward the side of the cavern. There's some ambient light at this depth, but I use my flashlight anyway to better illuminate the crevices and slopes in the wall. I am looking for old cave drawings that may have since become covered with water. Instead, I stumble across something even more surprising.

I see a small ledge along the wall, no more than a foot wide. Atop it is a pile of bones. I am still a little fuzzy from the nitrogen, and my first thought is that other divers have stacked fake bones here as a joke. Already, scores of dives have been made into La Aleta, and no one reported seeing anything like this. I shake my head as if to clear my vision, but the bones are still there, mineralized black with age. Hmm. Caveman bones, lost underwater, and now found. I feel as if I'm in a yet unwritten Indiana Jones film. My air is almost gone, and my safety stop is over, so I surface.

I tell Meier about the bones, and no one laughs. They are authentic. I draw a small map showing where they are located, and divers on a final descent recover them. Later I learn that two bones were from the Hispaniolan Sloth said to have gone extinct ten thousand years ago. A recovered rib bone from the stack couldn't be identified, but a tibia found there was human.

This night, I zip up my mosquito net and lie atop my sleeping bag here in the closeness of the humid tropical forest. A refreshing drizzle falls, pelting the tent fabric, lulling me into half sleep. Before I drift off, the metronomic croak of tree frogs fills the darkness, the sound of frog gods happy in the rain. I think of it as the voice of a *zemi* rising from the abyss, the sound of a natural continuum still being forged here in the Dominican jungle night.

Guyana

Seeking Refuge in the Cashew Rains

It is the season of the Cashew Rains, and a sturdy Amerindian in a black cowboy hat is leading me over a trail through the thick tropical bush of Guyana. "Ready to go to the brink?" he asks. We are already skirting the edge of a deep gorge, so I say, sure, why not.

A bank of cumulus steams overhead, sent up from this crown of wet jungle that stretches as far as I can see. The only interruption is the "brink," in which the Potaro River dramatically tumbles off a 740-foot scarp, down into a tumult of misty green. We head for a rock outcropping right at its edge.

These are the Kaieteur Falls, named for a long-gone Patamonas chief who, by legend, paddled himself in a dugout over the scarp to win the favor of the gods in a war against the ferocious Caribs. It worked.

My guide is Mike Phang, half-Arawak and half-Carib, and he is the warden-in-charge of the land protecting these falls. We step across vast crevices in the terrain, dodge hanging lianas, spot carnivorous plants, waist-high termite mounds, and a rare orange bird with a bit of a mohawk, the Guyanese Cock-of-the-Rock. It is no wonder Arthur Conan Doyle's fictional "Lost World," with its time-stuck ape-men and dinosaurs, was set on Mt. Roraima, not far to the west. Or that Sir Walter Raleigh once came looking for El Dorado, the city of gold. It still seems as if almost anything could be hidden here.

Hidden from everyone but Mike. "You are having the bromeliads here six meters high," he says. "You are having the jaguar, the jaguarundi, the puma. You are having the howler monkey." All of this is delivered in stoic monotone, not unlike the cadence I have heard from other Amerindians—the Seminoles back in Florida, the Cocama in the Peruvian Amazon. It resonates with a quiet confidence, the emotional knowledge of place locked timelessly inside each word. "We are also having the bushmaster snake," says Mike. "Step carefully."

A delicate plant the size of a tree looms, nurtured by the vapor plume of the falls. "Look deep into this bromeliad and you will see the golden frog. It lives nowhere else. In its skin is a compound . . . as 150 times as powerful as cocaine." A Scot in our small ragtag group—head shaved clean and an accent like Sean Connery's—squats down, puts his head into the immense green leaves and sniffs.

We have come here from Georgetown, the capital of Guyana on the northeast coast of South America, bouncing down on a dirt strip 140 miles inland via Trans Guyana Airlines. The lone pilot is German; the other passengers are the frog-sniffing Scot, his three mates, and a Dutchman from Aruba. Guyana is a strange, strange place—part Caribbean, part Amazonia. It doesn't much court visitors, and I am thinking that our small white group—individually gathered from around Georgetown earlier this morning by a minivan—may be the country's entire tourism quota for this week.

With a long colonial history that ended abruptly when the British left in 1966, Guyana is not quite sure of its legacy. It is the only English-speaking country in South America. Beyond that, it seems uncertain what unites its people, nearly 90 percent of whom are East Indian–African and live on the coast. The interior forest and mountains and vast savannas are the territory of its nine Amerindian nations. There is wealth here, everyone is certain, in lumbering and mining, but no one is yet sure how much they can take before it runs out.

Folks like Mike Phang sense there is also an interest by foreigners in his country's virgin environment, so he will make a go of it as a warden for now. The traditional Amerindian knowledge of the bush makes it a natural for him. Gold and diamond mining paid much better, Mike tells me, but he got tired of being robbed. "Bandits are the only thing that move fast in this country," says Mike, a slight smile revealing the pleasure in his quiet joke. Mike was robbed nine times; twice, he shot and killed his assailants. But Guyana is a desperate country, and they kept coming.

Tomorrow I will begin a week-long journey that will take me even farther into this odd heart of darkness. It will eventually lead me to a rainforest reserve called Iwokrama—literally, a "place of refuge." It is a million-acre tract tucked away between the Akaiwanna and the Iwokrama Mountains. Set aside by the Guyanese government in the early 1990s, its raison d'être is to preserve a massive oxygen-pumping terrain that helps abate the world's increasingly abundant carbon dioxide load, relieving global warming. I am, well, perplexed that a country like Guyana would attempt something this visionary.

After all, consider Georgetown: It is a place of once-grand cricket stadiums and colonial mansions gone to seed, wood fires scenting the air like incense, and bamboo poles flying Hindu spirit flags. The U.S. State Department warns about violence against "people of wealth" (i.e., tourists) in the streets. After my arrival last night, I read two very curious stories in the local *Stabroek News:* "Ricky Chamatalk, 24, died when, riding his motorcycle downtown without a helmet, he collided with a cow." And, more disturbingly, "Sean Warde, 25, died after being chopped about the body by two men with cutlasses, at whom he had allegedly thrown a grenade." A cutlass, a grenade, an immobile cow all seem so much more *urgent* than global warming.

I was told, however, that that was the frontier capital for you. The interior would be different, rural and friendly. Just watch for the bushmasters and take your antimalaria pills, and you'd do just fine.

A place of refuge could be a very good thing, indeed—especially for a nature-minded guy like myself adrift in an industrialized world bereft of *connection*—and I am looking forward to staking out some space in it at last. Beyond the oxygen benefit, large undisturbed chunks of jungle like this support megafauna rare elsewhere—the tapir, the jaguar, the giant otter, the harpy eagle. Discovery still seems possible here, not by virtue of a remote channel clicker but by your own wits. For me, that is El Dorado enough.

For now, the pre-Cambrian brink awaits. Mike and I shuffle out to its lip. There are no guardrails or warning signs, and we step across a gaping fissure in the rock, graphically leaving solid ground behind. "Years ago," says Mike, "that crack was so small you couldn't get your finger in it." Just meters away, the shallow Potaro begins its long blackwater cascade down into its gorge.

At the bottom, the fallen river maytags furiously, sending up vapor that creates a rainbow in the bright tropical sun. Its energy is potent, producing a muffled echo of thunder that resonates against my skin like sensory riffles. My hair seems to be standing on end, but I am not sure if it is from the upwelling charge—or the realization that one giant step would put me over the edge.

"On February 4," says Mike, with no preamble, "four white peccaries went over these falls." Then, without further explanation, he turns and walks back over the crevice, to solid ground.

Shouldering my single bag and backpack at dawn, I trudge out to the tarmac of the Ogle Aerodrome in Georgetown to catch a flight to the Makushi village of Annai. The plane, a boxy prop locals call the "Flying Coffin," looks like a miniature Spruce Goose. My fellow passengers are mostly Brazilians, headed deeper into their own country. As I board through a port in the tail, a woman hands me a paper box of apple juice and what appears to be a mustard sandwich, crust trimmed off and ensealed in Handi-Wrap.

Up we go, making a U-turn over the Caribbean, which is clouded brown by sediment here and ensealed from Georgetown, like my mustard sandwich, by a massive dike. The Dutch, who settled Georgetown in the 1600s, built the first seawall of wood. Now reinforced with concrete, it opens only to drain the broad Demerara River, an aquatic highway winding inland, beyond the stilt-wood homes and shops of the capital and past a wafflelike grid of cane fields.

We fly into a cloud bank, and when we emerge barely a minute later, there is nothing but green, resplendently wild green, veined by rivers and punctuated with waterfalls. We are squarely atop the equatorial forest and swamp now, the basin between where the Orinoco and the Amazon conflux with the sea.

Guyana is in the middle of the thick swatch of forest called the Guiana Shield stretching across the northern rim of South America. It holds the best of what is left of the tropical forest of this continent: in Guyana, there are 53 forested acres for each person; in Brazil, where the population is taking increasingly larger slash-and-burn whacks out of the forest, the ratio is only 8 to 1. (Up in Central America, Costa Rica—known for its "nature tourism"—has less than one wooded acre per person left.)

Another hour puts us over the Rupununi, the vast grassy Savannah. Before Guyanese Brahmans lost their niche in the world beef market, Makushi cowboys tended cattle on this tropical range. Below, the village of Annai sprawls at the cusp of the Rupununi and the Kanuku

Mountains. The Brazilian border is only twenty-five miles to the west, on the other side of the Ireng River. Down we go onto a narrow strip, dropping like a carnival ride.

As soon as we screech to a stop, there is much shouting. A Canadian photographer and I, the only passengers at this destination, are urged to pick up our bags and quickly exit through the rear. The pilot keeps his motor revved, and as soon as we are clear of the plane, it shoots away from us, leaving us in the prop wash with Colin Edwards, an expat Brit. "Welcome to the Rupununi," says Colin, stocky, barefoot, and convivial. "Breakfast is ready."

Annai, a large village of seven hundred with dwellings of wattle-and-daub (mud brick) and thatched palm, is on one side of the strip, and Colin's Rock View Lodge is on the other. We head to the kitchen, inside a ramshackle two-story stucco ranch house in a grove of mango trees, and settle in. Colin came to South America thirty years ago as a volunteer for the UK's version of the Peace Corps, the VSO, and never left. Fluent in Portuguese from his years in Brazil, he's worked as an agronomist, a gold miner, and a construction engineer. (On contract, he helped build the airstrip at Jonestown for the cult that later perished in a toxic Kool-Aid massacre.)

Now, by leasing this twenty-acre ranch, he is trying his hand at ecotourism. "It is a pet hobby that brings together everything I have come to love about the place," explains Colin. "The culture, the art, the frontier. I do a few hires with the Bedford (four-wheel drive) truck and Land Rover, run the Dakota bar next door, and am also the agent for the airline that flew you here."

I sit on a bench behind a long wooden table full of pitchers of coconut water, passion fruit juice, and hot Brazilian coffee. Here, I meet Velda, Colin's Makushi wife, three of his eight kids, and Shawndell, Velda's twenty-one-year-old younger sister. Shawndell, a quiet beauty in braids, looks as if she stepped from an old Matthew Brady Indian portrait. While Shawndell helps serve, the line between employee and relative is a blur. We feast on platters of eggs, pancakes, wild cucumbers, rice, and hot bread just taken from a clay kiln in the corner of the room. By the time we are finished, most of Colin's great extended family has either joined us at the table or passed through with a friendly greeting.

Wooden shutters and doors are thrown open, and outside in the golden morning light I can see a portion of the lush orchard and garden—cashew, lemon, guava, and almond trees—that feed family and guests. Fenced enclosures nearby hold in-transit local critters— orphaned or injured—that are being nursed to health: a giant anteater, a Brazilian tapir, capybara and spider monkeys. While most guests so far have been scientists going to and from nearby Iwokrama, Colin is optimistic those few hardy tourists who enjoy tropical wilderness and solitude will eventually find their way here. But only a few. "I am concerned it doesn't get out of hand," he says. "There is something peculiar and wonderful about it here. A certain easy rapport. We would like to keep it that way."

Tomorrow we will travel to Surama, a smaller village at the edge of the rainforest, and from there will venture up the wild Burro Burro River in a wooden longboat with local Makushi as guides. In preparation, I join Colin in the living room where he is eager to show me his collection of vintage travel-adventure books from the last century, astonishing old exploits of Brits first venturing into what they knew then as "the Guianas."

On the walls, there is the skin of a twelve-foot-long anaconda— "a small one," says Colin—artistically incised calabash gourds, self-entwining Amerindian sculptures from the latex of the bulletwood tree, a small rack of bush deer antlers, the basketlike nest of an orapendula bird. A chameleon clamps to one wall on suckered feet; a swallow zooms overhead. In the corner is a large green felt card table, where in the evenings one can sit in a chair of woven liana and wood with a cold Banks beer and a plate of homegrown peanuts and have real conversation—for that is what one does in such a place—as the low-voltage lights dim and brighten at the whim of the jerry-rigged generator.

"This is fascinating!" says Colin, effusively pulling *Wanderings in South America* from a shelf and thumbing through its yellowed pages. "In 1812, the British explorer Charles Waterton came here and wrote of Surama! It was famous in the region, along with Annai, for the excellent poison it made. *Curare.* They tipped their arrows and spears with it, and went into the bush and hunted anything that moves." The villagers of Annai and Surama have lost their knowledge to make curare, says Edwards, but the Wai Wai in the deeper south still use it to hunt. "You know, there's so much about this place that hasn't changed in all that time."

Morning comes with the distant scream of monkeys. I jolt awake inside my mosquito-net canopy over my bed. The generators are off and a mild breeze wafts through the windows, no glass or screen to obstruct it. From inside the netting, reality seems gauzy, diffuse. I can smell coffee and warm bread from the nearby kitchen.

After breakfast, we load into a battered, mud-splattered Land Rover, orange foam bursting out of the dashboard, for the hour-and-a-half trip to Surama, traveling over a red clay strip known only as The Road. The Road is a failed attempt by the Brazilian government to build a highway from their interior, through Guyana to the Caribbean ports. You can reach Georgetown, two hundred miles away, in twelve hours over The Road from here, but only in the dry weather. With two wet seasons—a long one in the winter-spring and a shorter one, known as the Cashew Rains, in the summer—The Road is often a quagmire. "You can go halfway by vehicle, and halfway by dugout then," explains Colin, ever enthusiastic.

We pass coconut and papaya trees, ripe with fruit, grind through ruts deep enough to swallow a couple of Honda Civics, watch as tegus— two-foot-long carnivorous lizards—scuttle across our path. Three boys with vine-woven creels and stick poles fish in a ravine. A barefoot man with a machete saunters by on horseback. There is no other traffic. Then we enter the rainforest, bucking and heaving through troughs of mud. The low scrub turns into towering jungle walls studded with red and yellow heliconia. "Adventure travel is going through the jungle in a vehicle without brakes," says Colin, ever cheerful.

Surama is in a clearing just ahead, a modest collection of thatch and wood homes, banana and cassava plants, dark-red chickens and domestic peccaries roaming free. Two larger buildings are set aside as the school ("Be Regular Punctual" written on the side) and the clinic. Barefoot Makushi children surround us, laughing and smiling. Everyone is in western dress, but otherwise the scene might be lifted out of another century. We pile out and walk with them to a benab, a sort of open round house, which serves as the village meeting center. It has started raining. "If the rain is coming from the south, from the Amazon, it will be heavy," says Colin.

An official ceremony has been planned. Camache, the schoolmaster—and the brother-in-law of Colin—introduces the children. They welcome me with two songs which they sing first in English and then in Makushi ("Surama sitting in a valley / Surama you make me so happy / Brown skinned people everywhere / Friendliness is there.") They are holding hands and swaying, their voices ineffably sweet, winsome.

All of nature seems to offer utility, myth, or solace for the Makushi. For instance, the Mutu (the blue-capped tanager) is burned and its ashes rubbed on the skin to relieve a sprain; the Korokoro (the green ibis) is seen as a barometer of rains; if you mock the Arawo (the long-tailed Potoo) by imitating its cry, your hammock strings will burst. Some thirty different species of ants are used, alternatively, to make the bones of babies strong, to cause pari kari (an alcoholic cassava drink) to ferment, to roust a lazy man to work.

The elected village "captain," Sydney Allicock—the cousin-in-law of Colin—stands for his official greeting. Outsiders are welcome here, says Sydney, choosing his words slowly and deliberately. "It is another means of educating our people to the situation in other countries—sometimes you tend to believe the whole world is like this." And then, as if to shatter any shred of ethnocentricity I might have remaining: "Sometimes, visitors bring photographs and you see the concrete jungles and understand what can happen to a place when the people forget what is important . . ."

I ask Sydney what the kids do to amuse themselves, here in this pre-Nintendo world. "They play . . . games. The fruit game—One child will be the fruit, maybe a soursop, and he ripens. When he ripens, his voice changes and everyone runs and hides. If you are found, then you must be the fruit."

With that, we are off into the rain, which is now falling in thick sheets. Sydney, his friend Lionel, and Camache squeeze into the Land Rover with us and the day suddenly seems more festive as we head deeper into the forest, the soggy trail gradually leading us down inside a dark corridor of jungle. "In the rainy season, this trail would be underwater," says Colin. Soon, a narrow stretch of brown water appears. It is Taramu Creek and will lead us to the Burro Burro. On the bank is a long wooden boat, with a motor. We pull the boat into the creek, climb aboard, and head upstream.

Almost immediately, a long silvery fish that looks like a small barracuda jumps into the boat. "Fox fish," says Sydney, admiring its sharp teeth. Later, a silver dollar—an aquarium fish back in the United States—follows suit, rocketing into my wet shirt and flopping about in the few inches of water in the hull. "*Pirae* (piranha) in the river too," says Sydney. "Maybe we will catch one."

In addition to a cooler full of curry-flavored noodles and cassava, Colin has also packed wild limes, a bottle of El Dorado rum, and a mahogany-colored bow with three arrows, each tipped with a slightly different razor-sharp metal edge. "One is for fish, one is for birds, and the other . . . for anything larger," explains Colin, pouring himself a healthy dose of rum. If Guyana has itself been creolized—created from a racial and cultural stew—this British expat has been as thoroughly transformed as anyone. Peppering his conversation with Portuguese and Makushi, he sits barefoot, one arm around his wife, Velda, rain-soaked and happy here at the edge of the Lost World, adrift somewhere between *Swiss Family Robinson* and *Lord Jim*.

Upriver on the Burro Burro we go for nearly two hours, in and out of the Cashew Rains, past keel-billed toucans and macaws, tapir wallows, and a tall ceiba tree with the hollow of a harpy eagle. A flock of green parakeets fly overhead and gigantic kingfishers dive and squawk. We have passed effortlessly through one set of rapids, but there is another array just ahead churning and spitting angrily. Instead of trying to run them, we wedge in between a slew of giant black boulders. By now, we are as ragged as wet dogs.

Just then, the glorious tropical sun returns and all is again right with the world. I climb from the boat up onto a rock the size of a small house, welcoming the chance to stretch my legs. Upstream, through the narrow foliage corridor, the Akaiwanna Mountains materialize from the steamy mist. Howler monkeys bellow off in the distance. "Keep your eye out for a jaguar," says Colin.

We will lunch on the rocks and then drift back, hopefully, by dusk. Noodles, tiny fig bananas, and rum appear—along with thin sandwiches that inexplicably seem to be filled with mustard. Colin tells of his dream to trace the wanderings of the old explorer, Waterton, by reblazing his original trail from the coast, over the mountains and into the interior. "It can be done! . . . Sydney and I will go someday to the mountains. We will do it!"

By the time we cast off, our crew is pleasantly buzzed. The river has swollen two to three feet higher with the rains, and the modest rapids we crossed with ease are now raging. We bounce through them, ricocheting off submerged rocks and fallen trees. My adrenaline is peaking, but no one else seems terribly concerned. Somewhere in here, we lose the mahogany-colored bow.

"My Gawwd," says Colin, a bit later. "Where IS the bow?"

"Fell in the water," says Velda, who seems quite amused by this.

"Gone overboard," says Camache, equally humored by it.

"The water. My Gawwd. The water. O my. The bow is forever lost."

I am headed finally to Iwokrama today. Down The Road I go again, this time in a more modern Land Cruiser with brakes, traveling an hour and a half more beyond Surama, all the way to the edge of the massive Essequibo River. Both vehicle and the East Indian driver are from Iwokrama, funded by a kettle of international environmental aid monies. We pass colorful land tortoises, more tegus, a Makushi man on a bicycle. We rumble over narrow bridges made of fat wooden beams the size of railroad ties.

We stop to reconnoiter a particularly nefarious series of ruts, and I hear the sun bees—large bumble-types—ringing loudly from inside the towering jungle, happy for this luminous rain-free day. I walk to the Congo palms at the jungle edge and listen closely. Just above the ring of the sun bees comes the sweet two-note refrain of the toucan.

A modest wooden sign welcomes us to the Iwokrama Rainforest Preserve. Soon afterward, the jungle falls away to reveal the broad Essequibo. From here, I climb into another longboat for the short ride downstream to the field station of the preserve. As we approach, I notice the station is modeled on a typical Amerindian village—wood structures with thatch roof, up on stilts, both for ventilation and safety from the rainy-season threat of flood.

I stow my gear in one of the huts, take a quick look-around, and see a group of rangers, all Amerindians, assembled on chairs under a tent. I meet Vibert A. V. Welch, a big black-skinned man from Georgetown. Vibert, whose English is accented with a deep Caribbean-African patios, tells me how the scientists from around the world make new discoveries in this pristine landscape just about every time they look. "Iwokrama now has the best documented fauna in Guyana," he says. Indeed, it may be ground zero for snakes and frogs. "Just in two weeks, a team of herpetologists found eleven new species."

As for the tented rangers, they are having their bush knowledge augmented with insight about sustainable use of the forest, says Vibert. In the works is a grand vision—bioprospecting, education, and training, preparation to guide the sort of tourists who will go to the ends of the earth to see rare birds and plants.

Part of the mission, Vibert tells me, is to record and catalog the complex and often mystical bush knowledge—which has been passed along by oral tradition for centuries. There are, after all, some two thousand plants in the wildly diverse Amazon Basin used by Amerindians—both medicinally and spiritually. Ironically, as ethnobotanists revel in the rich cultural-natural texture of the Guyanese interior, the government back in Georgetown is granting large mining and timber leases on indigenous land.

I climb back into a boat, this time with two Amerindians, Rodriguez Anton and Errol McBirney. We will visit some ancient petroglyphs today. Although I am nearly accustomed to the anglicizing of local names here, I have to admit McBirney gives me a start. But both are good traveling companions, easy to smile and eager to share their local bush knowledge. Downstream on the Essequibo we go now in a smaller aluminum skiff, the *Takatu,* one of the field station's official boats, a forty-horsepower Merc pushing us faster than I've been in the last week.

Errol is wearing a plaid ball cap with a Calvin Klein jeans logo, flip flops, a khaki shirt, and pants; Rodriguez, his long black hair curling over his collar, is decked in a black cowboy hat with a tiny miniature horseshoe emblem on the front, long pants, and a long-sleeved shirt. Both are carrying machetes and hand lines for fishing. This time, there are life jackets. "Better put them on," says Errol, "there will be rapids, I think."

And sure enough, there is a set of healthy Class III rapids thrashing just upstream, complete with standing waves. I notice two young boys from a nearby village are riding through them in a log dugout. "They are playing," says Errol. "Something to do."

We run the jungle-rimmed Essequibo for nearly forty miles, bouncing over more rapids, portaging the boat at the edge of others, crossing water that boils, eddies, and swirls. The river mysteriously narrows and widens and I realize we are zigzagging through and around islands. Little white-rumped swallows skim over the surface like jet-propelled leaves; terns with bills as big and yellow as bananas dive and chatter. "The Essequibo comes out of the Amazon, somewhere," says Rodriguez. The entire time, we see no more humans, not a single dugout.

A few white beaches rim the edges of the shore. At low water, says Errol, beaches are everywhere, including sandy shoals in the middle of the river. Most of the rapids become exposed rocks. And the water, seeping from jungle creeks, is tannic black, not brown like it is now from the recent rain.

Finally, immense round boulders rise up from the water with a thin cover of lichens, looking like giant baby heads. Beyond the baby heads, we pull over to another clutch of rocks. Both men hop out and I follow. Rodriguez bends down and traces his fingers over etchings in one rock. They are at least 3,500 years old, he says. "A fox here . . . a scorpion here." I look into an opening where one boulder leans against another and see a finer glyph, a stick-figure of a man, protected down here from the elements for over three millennia.

At lower water, many glyphs can be seen, says Rodriguez. It strikes me that lots more people may have lived along this river at one time, and I wonder out loud where they went. Rodriguez looks at me briefly. "Yes," he says, inscrutably, and then tosses out a hand line, fishing for pirae for dinner.

The rain is again falling, again in sheets. We sit quietly in the boat and drift through the forest to the squawk of distant parrots and the howl of monkeys. I am deep in now, soaked to the skin with the Cashew Rains, but warmed with a feeling of utter security that I seldom feel back in my more efficient civilized world. If Shawndell were here, I'd marry her, and end up years later losing my prize mahogany-colored bow in the rapids and not caring a lick about it. "We make it back by dark," says Errol. "I think."

The Sunken City
of Port Royal

The Pompeii of the Caribbean

I am floating motionless near the once-bustling corner of Queen
and High Streets in the old Caribbean pirate city of Port Royal,
over an ancient brick floor that was painstakingly assembled in
a fine herringbone pattern by some craftsman long ago.

Around me, brick walls with traces of plaster rise two and three
feet from the floor, distinct doorways cut into the bottoms. I move
through one and find a crumbling cistern, round like a wishing well.
Inside, I see a hand-painted pottery shard wedged into the sand,
eggshelled with cracks but still shiny from glaze after more than three
hundred years. I fly weightless over it all, hovering just above the

42

streets, houses, and shops that were once riotously alive with nervous shouts and laughter. In the dim yellow light of surface reality, I'm nurtured not by a deep-sleep REM dream but by a tank of compressed air on my back and a regulator in my mouth.

The notorious Henry Morgan made and spent his fortune here in Port Royal in the late seventeenth century, on a narrow sandy peninsula encircling the Kingston harbor—first as a pirate, then as lieutenant governor of Jamaica. Prostitution was legal, liquor flowed freely, and the merchants, artisans, and sailmakers who serviced the buccaneers quickly became as prosperous as those in the Old World. Flush with its new wealth, Port Royal looked like a well-heeled English shire town on a tropical spit—steep, peaked roofs of clay tile and walls of brick, many as tall as four stories. There was even a House of Correction for Lazy Strumpets, "of which," one observer remarked, "we have many."

This Port Royal was both rich and raucous—the "wickedest city on earth," it was called—until the skies turned copper and a sudden earthquake sunk most of the town, killing two thousand, on a hot June morning in 1692. And under the sea it has mostly remained, hidden beneath fifteen to fifty feet of water and several feet of rubble and sediment, a time capsule breached only by a handful of salvage divers and archaeologists.

I look hard for the nuances of this once-vibrant pirate city, prodding at the edges of the Port Royal mystique. But what I find instead are sponges and lobster, sea fans and bristle worms—and a bright, apricot-colored starfish, knobby legs moving it on a steady crawl over the bricks of Lime Street, the soul of an old buccaneer on an all-night binge.

There are two Port Royals. One is the somnambulant little fishing village built over the pre-earthquake foundations of the old town, the portion that never went under. The other is the "sunken city." Together, they provide what archaeologists describe as a "catastrophic site," where disaster has frozen a moment in time—much as it did in Pompeii. Near the peninsular tip, the Port Royal All Age School and Morgan's Harbour Hotel bookend the entrance to the modest terrestrial village. The sunken city itself lies just offshore.

Getting here is easy enough—just a flight from Miami and a rental-car drive from the nearby Manley Airport, past the roadside stands selling green coconuts with their custardlike milk for fifty cents apiece. But penetrating the enigma of old Port Royal requires some effort.

I begin at Morgan's Harbour, built in the late 1950s on the site of an early-eighteenth-century British naval shipyard. Its clientele is an odd, animated mix of day-tripping locals from Kingston, cheery Germans wishing each other *Guten Morgen!* at the crack of dawn, and transient yachties who moor here inside the protective wing of the peninsula, just as sailors before them have done for centuries.

One such local is Ainsley Henriques, an international businessman and one of the few white-skinned Jamaicans in the country. Over a cold bottle of Ting in the al fresco bar teetering on the edge of the Kingston Harbor, Henriques traces his colonial heritage back through the stormy history of Jamaica with little prompting. It's a history in which adventurers newly enriched from the pirate spoils of Port Royal fanned out over the entire island, setting up country estates. With the sweat of slaves and indentured servants, the estates became plantations, anchoring the sugarcane economy here until well into this century. Henriques's own European ancestors were among the colonists who ran those estates.

Henriques, who chairs the Jamaica National Heritage Trust, views pirates with a sympathetic eye. "Tradition says the English buccaneers were lawless barbarians who robbed the Spanish and burnt their cities. But it is my position that piracy was a legitimate means to break the yoke of the Spanish Main in the New World."

In truth, early British colonials here were isolated and badly outnumbered by their Spanish enemy by the mid-1600s. With their own navy busy back in Europe, the English invited the buccaneers to Port Royal as a sort of private security force—like the Stones hiring the Hells

Angels to police their concert at Altamonte. The outcome was predictable. Legalized with "Letters of Marque" from Jamaican governor Sir Thomas Modyford, the buccaneers commandeered the narrow dirt streets of Port Royal with a renegade verve: the courageous and cruel Morgan, the vicious Frenchman François L'Olonais, and the inimitable Roche Brasiliano, who, when not roasting Spaniards alive, would break out a keg of wine on the street and urge passersby to drink with him, often at gunpoint.

Henriques sweeps both arms wide, taking in all of Port Royal and the vast expanse of harbor beyond. The high-rises and industrial smokestacks of Kingston seem etched into the limestone foothills of the towering Blue Mountains across the water. Night is beginning to fall, and as it does, a black cloud moves down over the city. Amber lights blink on in the lower hills, reflecting in the water like fireflies in the dark mist, evoking a more distant time.

"You literally couldn't get a canoe in this bloody harbor," says Henriques of those buccaneer days. "They did a massive job of fortification." Five separate stone forts and polygon-shaped bunkers were built on all sides of Port Royal beginning in 1656. The ambitions of Port Royal's pirates extended well beyond land, however. Some nine hundred historic shipwrecks, scuttled by battles and storms, now lie at rest under the shallow waters of the harbor. Offshore, near the handful of coral cays and reefs that hug the southern coast, countless galleons and corsairs rest on the deeper bottom. Each has its own tale of romance, intrigue, and violence, dark mysteries still waiting to be told. "The artifacts will tell the story for you," promises Henriques, cryptically. "You can read the lifestyle in them."

Englishman Gary Casson, fresh from assorted jobs in Bermuda and the Mediterranean, is newly arrived to Port Royal. With three studs of gold notched in one ear and rakishly long blond hair, the adventurous Brit looks as if he might have sailed into this same harbor with his own Letter of Marque long ago. Like most here, he speaks in near-reverent tones about the mysterious "sunken city." Casson runs the "Buccaneer Scuba Shop," housed inside the low-slung brick arches of a rustic shed once used to caulk and seal wooden ship hulls. He dreams of one day being able to take visiting sport divers to the nearby site, but national preservation laws now protect the "sunken city" from all but those practicing education and research. And so Casson is content to ferry divers out to local waters around the offshore southern cays.

As a journalist, I have made the plea to Jamaican officials that I am a practitioner of "education" and thus ought to be able to visit the sunken city. They are mulling this one over. As I wait for their answer, I join Casson as he sets out in his rubber Zodiac to dive a site mapped as "Wreck Reef." Wreck Reef is a mélange of ancient iron cannons and an anchor, some ten miles offshore. Casson recently stumbled on it while looking for wrecks and other sites that might be of interest to his tourist divers.

We roar out of the harbor, our dive gear loaded to the gunnels of the inflatable. As we do, a dark squall stews on the eastern horizon, hiding the morning sun. To our left is Rackham's Cay, all low tropical bush and sand. Here, in the early eighteenth century, during a period when piracy was out of vogue in Jamaica, the dashing buccaneer known as "Calico Jack" Rackham met his inglorious end. After being captured while drunk, along with his crew and two women pirates, Rackham was later hung at Gallows Point at the tip of Port Royal. His body, pressed into an iron frame, was displayed as a warning to other pirates on the little cay that today bears his name.

As we approach the Wreck Reef site, I see the remains of a modern ship's rusted old pilot house protruding from the water, stuck where it ran aground on the shallow coral reef. "I usually bring divers to the inside of the reef," says Casson. "It's more shallow and calm there. We see lots of sharks, seven, eight footers." But today he steers the Zodiac out to the trickier, deeper windward slope, where whitecaps froth in from the sea to crash down on the rising coral head. "This is considered very dangerous by locals," says Casson, almost casually. "Fishermen don't even like to come here. Currents are unpredictable."

With that, we anchor a hundred yards from the rusting hull, right where the breakers begin their roll, and fall overboard with our tanks. Sinking toward the bottom, we search for the cannon said to be scattered along the reef, soaring weightlessly over corals shaped into fans, rods, plumes, and pillars. Over time, storms, teredo worms, and rot destroy most wooden wreckage not covered by sand or mud; coral often encrusts any metal remaining. So we are not looking for a Disneyesque shipwreck, skeletons waving from cargo holds, but any sign of geometry—straight lines or angles suggesting the presence of something man-made.

I do this for a good thirty minutes, seeing lots of fish and coral, but nothing at all resembling a cannon or anchor. As the needle on my air pressure gauge edges toward empty, I notice Casson next to a lone cannon-shaped piece of coral rock. I move down next to him in the metronomic roll of the current, and run my hand over its surface, feeling the knobs where it was once held by a wooden carriage. The big gun has been consumed by a thick patina of sea life now, habitat for little gobies and feather-duster worms. We look at each other, nodding and giving the other the "OK" sign. I show Casson my pressure gauge, with its needle edging into the red, and he clasps his hand into a fist with his thumb pointing upward. It is universal diver language: Time to surface.

Back in the Zodiac, we putter a few miles to the natural channel where Casson recently stumbled on an ancient ship's anchor. We change tanks and splash in again. Under fifty feet of water, we swim through a sandy valley in a coral buttress to the outer reef slope. There, a few feet away from a wall of plate coral, lies the encrusted anchor, one tine deeply buried in the sand. Are the remains of the ship that carried it somewhere nearby, disguised by the centuries?

Later, I learn there are no records of historic vessels sinking where we found the artifacts. I wonder then about how something once as grandiose as a warship and its men—pirates or not—can disappear almost entirely from this world.

Regal from a distance with its cast-iron girders and bricks, the old two-story British Naval Hospital was built near the harbor mouth in Port Royal in 1819, abandoned a century later. Having withstood a earthquake in 1907 and a violent hurricane in 1951, it is today home to the Archaeology and Conservation Division of the National Trust.

With scant funds for restoration, it is also condemned. Entire stairwells are missing, plaster is crumbling, and cracks run through the old concrete floor like rivulets. Outside, I count at least thirteen cannons of various sizes and eras, scattered aimlessly under a sapodilla tree.

Roderick Ebanks is the lone staff archaeologist for all of Port Royal. From his battered wooden desk, the bearded Jamaican seems like a besieged captain left behind to steer a sinking ship. In the late 1980s, the Caribbean Development Bank earmarked $6 million to restore the historic treasures of Port Royal. Then Hurricane Gilbert hit, and the money was spent instead for emergency storm aid.

Instead of lamenting his predicament, Ebanks launches a soliloquy on the twisted grandeur of old Port Royal. "Even after piracy was outlawed here in 1681—after Morgan was knighted in England and sent back to arrest his old mates—the city was wild and debauched. There were cockfights and bearbaiting in the streets, reveling all night long. There was one bar for every ten men."

If piracy had created the ambience, the good harbor and fortifications continued to draw traders and merchants. In 1688 some ten thousand ships docked here, unloading linens, silks, gold and silver plates, beef, and African slaves. "New fashions reached Port Royal directly from London, long before they spread out across the rest of England," says Ebanks. Some 1,200 homes, billiard rooms, gambling houses, and taverns stretched roof-to-wall across the sea port.

Today, the best hope for restoration, says Ebanks, lies in a private enterprise plan that would attract cultural tourists to the sites with guided land and underwater tours. The new income would then pay for the preservation and displays that public money cannot. I wander up to the cavernous second floor, stepping carefully around dangling electrical wires. It feels deserted, save for room after room of boxes, sacks, and shelves full of dusty artifacts. This is the repository for most everything brought to light in Port Royal over the past four decades. It includes some one million fragments and twenty thousand whole pieces, from pewter tankards used by pirates to a child's drinking cup.

At a makeshift plywood table in one unlit room, I find Maureen Parent-Brown, a young American graduate student who is piecing together pottery shards recovered from nearby New Street. It is like assembling a giant jigsaw puzzle, except there is no picture to go by, and most of the parts are missing. I ask how much work still remains to be done throughout Port Royal, and she looks up at me with disarmingly blue eyes. "There's enough work here for a hundred archaeologists for a hundred years."

Parent-Brown, who is paying for the New Street project out of her own pocket, was among the last group of undergraduate students from Texas A&M's Underwater Archaeology Field School to dive on the sunken city before that institution wrapped up its work here in 1990. By now, I have received official approval to dive the sunken city, and she offers to join us the next day in our exploration of the site.

After a brief rain shower, a double rainbow arcs between the Blue Mountains and the sunken city, near where we will dive from Casson's Zodiac today. I take it as a good omen. With us is Gauntlet Townsend, a coast guardsman with the Jamaican Defence Force, buzz-cut and shy. Sent along as the official government observer, he is an unlikely watchdog. As a wooden fishing boat roars in nearby to pull a trap full of queen angel fish, we sink under twenty feet of murky water where Lime Street should be.

The water is full of stinging jellyfish, and alive with sharks attracted by the chum of the fishing boats. The jellies we can see; the sharks we can't. While most of the city still remains buried under four to five feet of sand, sediment, and coral rubble, Texas divers uncovered the brick foundations of five buildings, along with timbers of a ship's hull, during their decade here. Parent-Brown, who has drawn a map of the excavated sites, moves next to me. She taps a finger on a circular figure, a cistern, and we move off toward it, across the tops of knee-high walls, forever-open doorways, cinderless hearths, and finally the old cistern itself.

As I stray a few feet away, I quickly lose my dive partner in the murk and run nearly head-on into a giant capstan-like structure covered entirely in coral. I settle near its bottom, flicking on my dive light to peek in the shadow of a dark, rocky ledge. The beam illuminates a thick, nautical-style chain woven into the base of coral. As I look closer, the massive, toothy head of a green moray—as territorial as any pirate who once guarded this city—pokes out to meet mine.

Early salvors called "wrackers" flocked here in the years after the earthquake, removing most of the treasures using primitive dive bells. As late as the mid-1800s, fishermen reported looking through clear water to see some whole buildings intact. But subsequent hurricanes and earthquakes collapsed, and then buried, the remains. Modern pollution and erosion-borne sediment from Kingston have obscured the underwater visibility. By the time American treasure salvor Bob Marx took great chunks out of the sunken city with dredges in the mid-to-late 1960s, he was able to find countless artifacts—clay pipes, human hair, an immense collection of seventeenth-century pewter, and a pocket watch stopped at 11:42, the exact moment of the disaster—but only two caches of silver coins.

Treasure, however, like beauty, is in the eye of the beholder. As I hover over the brick hearth of a house, I spot a clutch of bluish "sea pearls," opalescent bulbs of algae, gleaming like jewels on a pirate's brocaded blouse. Nearby, a lone sand dollar the size of a saucer hunkers next to a filamentous clump of green algae called dead man's fingers.

But the treasure is more than sea life. It's the little truths archaeology delivers by pulling back the curtain of time. In a catastrophic site like this one, pathos is often revealed: children lived in Port Royal, too, and they suffered here at the end like everyone else. This was graphically revealed when Texas divers uncovered a collapsed brick wall and found three small seventeenth-century skeletons, frightened children huddled together in their final moments on Earth.

It's hard not to feel a sense of custodianship for this tableau, a time and place once so violently interrupted and now left to reveal itself, historic voices still whispering to us from under the sea. I am thinking of the profound nature of where I am when I feel something big and modern bump up against my tank. Startled, I suck air more quickly than normal and look to see what has crashed into me. It is Gauntlet, and his eyes are large behind his mask—he is as surprised as I. We back away, regaining our territory. Then he signals me to follow him.

The visibility is bad, and so I trail his rubber fins closely, dodging jellyfish. Soon, we are both atop the black timbers of a ship's hull, timbers nearly hidden with a light dusting of sand. As the streets sank, scores of townspeople saved themselves by crawling aboard a ship known as the *Swan* as it floated over their rooftops. That ship is thought to still be here, near Lime Street where it finally settled. In fact, Parent-Brown has mapped it as so. Gauntlet reaches down to touch a timber, his bare arm as dark as the old ancestral wood, stretching his reach beyond our own time, into the depths of remembering.

Tiny fiddler crabs scuttle in a moatlike ditch next to a crumbling sidewalk in the village of Port Royal. The smell of bammy—pulverized cassava root—frying on an open fire drifts through the quiet streets, mixing with the scent of the salt marsh, superheated in the late afternoon sun. The Taino we call the Arawaks ate bammy before the first Spanish came in the early 1500s, and the English pirates and sailors after them. At the edge of the water, the essence of the frying cassava still drifts to me, over the centuries.

So, too, do the people. As I walk down the street, Frances Fyffe hails me from a kitchen chair, out in front of her modest zinc-roofed house. "This is number 3 Queen Street," she informs me, proud. She is seventy-two, a warm woman with high cheekbones, blue eyes still burning inside a dark face. "I have a Scotch name," she says. "And flowers, I paint flowers on my house." And she has: blue, red, white pansies forever blooming beside the front door.

A few paces away, Queen and Broad Streets join and then descend into the water. At its edge, two young women sit atop wire fishtraps, gutting newly caught snapper. If I were to walk underwater on this street on for two hundred yards, I would run into Fort James. I will do that tomorrow, with tanks, and the fort will rise up mysteriously from a fifty-foot bottom like a wall of coral, old cannon inert under a thick tunic of sediment and time.

For now, I lean back against Mrs. Fyffe's fence near the Jamaican almond tree. Seeing a small gash on my calf from a earlier bout with some coral, Mrs. Fyffe insists on cleaning and bandaging it for me, which she does with a gentle hand. History does speak through the artifacts, as Henriques has told me. Even more surely, however, it endures in the people. Frances Fyffe, a Port Royal native, has weathered modern earthquakes, hurricanes, husbands, and friends long gone. "For everything, you have a time," she tells me, in biblical intimations. "Some days here have been very good, some very bad."

As I go on my way, Mrs. Fyffe's bandage on my leg, she calls to me, a woman used to people and events washing around her and then disappearing forever. "Be careful," she warns, earnestly. It is a heedless refrain, one as old as life itself here on this tropical spit of sand where glory once blazed and then died—where one day the earth sunk under the waves and has never again been fully re-found.

The Suwannee

River out of Time

It is well after dark by the time I push our rented houseboat away from a floating dock near Fanning Springs, leaping aboard at the last minute over a yard's worth of blackwater. We are on the lower reaches of the famous "Swane Riber" and—even for Stephen Foster, the songwriter who once promoted it to the rest of the world—it is an enigmatic waterway far better known by name than by direct experience.

My own nine days on this gloriously wild southern river have so far taken me by kayak, boat, and jeep through a feral karst landscape of rolling moss-draped forests cleaved with transparent artesian springs and plumbed with underground rivers. Insulated by its remoteness, this Suwannee has revealed itself as a slightly out-of-kilter place—Kafka with a southern accent—where cave divers using high-tech gear share the same territory with menacing locals whose only contact with water is in a glass of Jack Daniel's.

This is a Florida far beyond the contrived realm of Disney World and the Ft. Lauderdale fern bars, an isolated place where most anything can happen, at any time. Rivers suddenly disappear into the ground and then, just as suddenly, re-emerge. Prehistoric sturgeon nearly as long as my kayak fire themselves out of the water and then belly flop back down in great explosions. Ghost towns and paddlewheel steamships haunt the thickly wooded shores and sandy river bed, unseen except for a gravestone here, a submerged deck there.

In the dark, I climb the ladder to the roof over our bow as we chug downstream, tiny bits of limestone cave still in my hair from a late afternoon dive. It is rare enough to be able to feel the cool energy of the earth upwelling through these caverns—but rarer still to be wearing the geology of it all in your hair, granules of diatoms and crustacea and whale vertebrae from its twenty-million-year-old oceanic past.

Below, Atlanta photographer Flip Chalfant is at the helm, a brewski in one hand and the wheel in the other. There are no markers or channel buoys on this untamed backwoods river, and at this hour of night, we are the only boat out here. Chalfant is squinting to navigate by the moonlit tree line, aiming for the open space before it falls away into the gloom.

But the blackwater under us is also varnished with the reflections of the vast stars from above, and I can't help but think they create an astral trail through the night. And they do so to a soundtrack of hardcore southern rock and roll—the Allman Brothers and Lynyrd Skynyrd, still alive and wailing from a local station on our boat's AM radio. Down in the cabin, amid the sounds of "Sweet Home Alabama," soggy dive gear, and the half-empty bags of boiled peanuts, our floating home has acquired the distinct scent of wet dog.

To natives, we might be a couple of grungy out-of-towners skirting the edges of their river-driven, retro existence. But to well-scrubbed city folks on day trips here, we may have turned into the very caricatures of the mysteries we have come to explore.

Dave Pharr wrangles his battered van with Chalfant's canoe, my kayak, and four days' worth of food and gear toward the Georgia border, over a lonely terrain of tin-roofed barns and pine woods. Our plan is to spend four days paddling the narrow, shoaly upper river, another three diving spring-cave systems along the middle, and then three more on a houseboat on the broader lower river, right down to where it spills out into the Gulf.

Pharr, an outfitter who runs Suwannee Canoe Outpost, is barefoot and wearing a floppy canvas hat. We might hear the occasion random gun shot, says Pharr in a thick southern drawl, but the Suwannee is otherwise free of *Deliverance*-themed perils. Our van swerves off the country road, down a dirt trail, through a swale of pine and palmettos, and finally out to a fifty-foot-wide sliver of blackwater where a man and woman are fishing with cane poles. Despite our commotion, they do their best to ignore us.

The February-to-April rainy season usually raises the Suwannee by thirty to forty feet, but it has been a dry year and the river is about as low as Pharr has ever seen it. During high water, the earthen furrow we just drove through would have held a surging brook. The rains could start again any day now, however, and Pharr is prepared: back downstream, the cabin that serves as his outfitting store is built atop massive Styrofoam blocks.

Soon we are unloaded, and Pharr's van is rattling away. We have no choice but to climb into our little floating boats and settle into a zenlike rhythm in which the rise and fall of our paddle blades defines our distance. It is a bicep-driven mimic of the paddlewheels of a century ago—a phantom memory that will materialize in a few days when we dive on an astonishingly intact steamboat wreck.

The slow-moving water under us is the color of diluted tea, and when I rake my fingers through it, I taste the detritus of swamp. The river itself is born in just such a place, the Okefenokee, an ancient sea-bottom depression not so far away upstream. Pogo, a philosophical cartoon possum, my childhood favorite, once lived there, poling a little bateaux, and now here we are, driving our own vessels on Pogo's blackwater.

Cypress and Ogeechee tupelo command the banks here, the latter a vision of goitered trunks and Medusa-like roots—a Dr. Seuss tree waiting for nightfall to come to life. I take a few practice casts with my flyrod, hoping for a pop from the disc-shaped red-breasted bream. No luck. From midstream, Chalfant's paddle hits the hard sand bottom. "You could walk down this river if you wanted to," he says, and, for now, he is right.

It is a midweek spring day, sunny and clear with a light breeze, the bugs still not rousted by summer heat. It is a perfect time to be on the Suwannee. We have about six hours of daylight left; by then, we hope to find a shoal of white sand large enough for our tents, maybe a little fire.

Up here, the river does not seem to flow so much as it seeps, barely a knot an hour. At water level, the banks alternate between walls of limestone and the sort of fine, white sand I have seen on Gulf of Mexico beaches. Above, the terrain rises steeply, putting us inside a canyon of rock and earth. In the tops of the highest cypress, I see the remains of a distant flood—massive logs, a lawn chair, a pair of women's panties.

By late afternoon, I hear the sound of running water. We are still a good day from Big Shoals, where the river will drop several feet over an ancient coastal escarpment and create a few raucous moments of whitewater. But here, the resonance is more gentle, and as I round the next corner, I see it is a small waterfall, a spring-fed run spilling down from a rocky ledge. As we continue, the waterfalls appear more frequently, little creeks that would quietly conflux if the river were a few feet higher.

The effect is clearly enchanting. So, too, is that of the water I see trickling out of the walls of limestone, creating little grottos of sphagnum moss and ferns. I paddle over to one such grotto, past the boulder where a large black moccasin is sunning itself, and look closely at the bone-white rock. It is scalloped, with horizontal bedding planes and vertical fissures, much like the walls of underwater caves. It seems as if I'm paddling through a cavern with its lid off. Downstream, we will meet a biologist who will explain how the million-year-old Suwannee likely eroded its way down through the forested limestone terrain—giving us a side profile of the spongelike karst, a sort of geo-hydrological ant farm.

Twilight comes, and we find a deserted beach for camping. Despite state-posted warnings about swimming in the river *(Extreme caution is advised. Steep banks, dark water, swift currents, changing depths, hidden rocks, and trees),* I put on my trunks and dive in to cool off. Refreshed, I join Chalfant near a blazing wood fire, hunch down for some freeze-dried dinner swill, and then, for amusement, I shine my light up and down the now-dark river bank. Three sets of alligator eyes shine back at me, as red as car taillights.

Chalfant wonders out loud where we are, and I tell him I don't have a clue, a fact that strikes us as particularly hilarious. We couldn't find our way out by land if we tried. Above, the stars click on, finally covering the horizon from end to end, undiminished by urban light. Each successive night on our trip, we will measure the grandeur of the Suwannee stars, grown-up Boy Scouts still in awe when nature works, just like it used to when we were kids.

Big Shoals is announced by a sign warning us to portage around it *(Shoals Ahead! 3/4 Mile. River Impassable!).* As we get closer, I hear the distinctive trainlike roar made when tons of water surge over rock. Although barely a "three" by whitewater rating standards, the hidden limestone is chiseled sharp and capsizing could be nasty. Indeed, when the river has been higher and faster, canoeists have drowned here.

We portage our gear, sidestepping groups of half-addled campers who have pitched their tents on the trail, including one sumo-sized teenager who is obsessively chopping at a tree stump with a machete. Then we trudge back up the path, climb in our respective craft and run the rapids. Chalfant's canoe rides high and soars through gracefully; my flat-bottomed swamp kayak bounces, twists, and turns, taking in a gallon of water as it drops an exhilarating yard or so through a gully in the scarp.

The scarp is an ancient sea coast, and the Suwannee is the only river in the region that doesn't go underground when it crosses it. Both the Alapaha and Santa Fe tumble off this Ice Age shoreline and keep on going, down into the soft rock, only to reappear several miles later as springs. Mastodons and camels and, later, paleo-Indians, walked over these land bridges, leaving behind clues to their life in the river basin—fossilized bones and giant elephant teeth and pottery shards. It is no wonder that "artifacting," as locals call it, is a favorite underwater sport.

By late afternoon, we pull over to a concrete ramp just above White Springs, where I have arranged to meet Rob Mattson, a biologist with the government water district that keeps tabs on the river. Mattson is wearing his own floppy hat over a shirt with armored fish swimming across the fabric. "It's a Gulf sturgeon," says Mattson. "A living fossil, left over from the Devonian epoch."

I fantasize catching one on my fly rod, but Mattson explains the imposing fish have tiny mouths for feeding on bottom inverts. When commercial fishermen nearly drove the sturgeon to the brink of extinction a few decades ago, they did so by netting or snagging them. Now, with protection, the fish—a subspecies of the Atlantic sturgeon that seasonally migrates upriver from the sea to spawn—has made a miraculous recovery on the Suwannee.

Mattson takes his shirt off, and I notice he has a tattoo of what appears to be a scorpion on his upper arm. "Stonefly nymph," he explains. "My commitment to a healthy river. . . . During its aquatic phase, it needs particularly clean water, with submerged snags for habitat. The Suwannee isn't dredged, and—despite some problems with nitrates from farm fields finding their way into springs—it really is in great shape."

South of here, says Mattson, the swamplike chemistry of the river changes dramatically as aquifer-fueled springs appear more frequently along the shores. "In a dry year, up to 60 percent of the downstream river is fed by springs."

Indeed, we are at ground zero in all the world for such springs, a place where the magic and ephemery of clear water bubbling up out of forest and rock is so common it's almost routine. In nearby Mayo, a brochure for Le Château de Lafayette Bed & Breakfast advertises such things to do as "browsing the library, going to church, and cave diving." Yet, a new inventory of springs in the Suwannee Basin just revealed an astounding fact—instead of seventy-two, as believed for years, there are nearly two hundred, with the number of first magnitude springs doubling from nine to eighteen. "It's a testament to how little we really know about this river, scientifically," admits Mattson.

Before we pull our kayaks off the Suwannee, we stop at what seems to be a crumbling coquina-walled Spanish fort and go ashore. This was actually a "fashionable" spa called "Suwannee Sulphur Springs" when built in 1890. The sulfur-rich spring waters inside the walls promised to cure everything from gout to insomnia. Today, locals swarm over the old resort, drinking beer, cursing loudly, and tossing each other in the river at random. These are not "ecotourists" come to revel in the legacy of the place and its vanished time. They are locals who are simply using it as a swimming hole. It is the underbelly of the Suwannee River mystique. One buzz-headed, Neanderthalish youth calling himself "Gator" threatens a party of blacks, for no apparent reason. An obese woman in a tie-dyed T-shirt jerks a screaming child around by the arm. There are many tattoos, but none of stonefly nymphs.

I am sitting in the varnished wood-paneled dining room at Jim Hollis's River Rendezvous, the PTL Club blaring from a nearby TV, a photo of Hollis and treasure hunter Mel Fisher on the wall along with an old double-hosed scuba regulator, a display of ceramic angels, and a box of beef jerky. Just out the window, a bulkheaded spring called Convict simmers below in an upwelling of ether-clear water.

We are on the middle river now, a place you can't walk too long without stumbling into a sinkhole or a spring. Many, like Convict, Troy, Cow, and Peacock, are named for some distant half-forgotten story, this one to do with local convicts swimming here for their once-a-week bath. Later today, there will be a wedding at the edge of Convict, bouquets of flowers floating atop the waters. At other times, true believers— including owner Jim Hollis—have been baptized, fully immersed to signify their born-again allegiance to the Almighty. Deep in Convict, a permanent cave-diving line extends for nearly a quarter-mile.

I make plans to have Hollis meet Chalfant and me in a pontoon boat near a wooded shore downstream where he will shuttle us to Troy Springs for a dive. We knock back glasses of cold Convict Spring water, load up a set of tanks, and drive down a deserted country road that leads to the river—passing two Baptist churches and a homemade sign inexplicably reading: *Live Goats. Wigglers. Cold Beer. Ammo.* As Chalfant and I wait for Hollis, I see a swallowtail kite soar overhead, watch as a sturgeon bellyflops like a giant mullet, ancient plates and scutes flashing in the sun.

Troy is just off the river, nestled inside a cypress hollow. Hollis drops us on a sandy shore, sticks a floating dive-flag buoy in the water, and putters off, planning to return in a few hours. Geared up, we fin up the shallow sandy-bottom run, over the wooden ribs of the *Madison,* a scuttled Civil War–era steamship, and then edge out over the deep bowl of Troy. Nearby, a village with the same name once flourished here, but like other nineteenth-century spring towns—Columbus, Suwannee, Charles—it has vanished with hardly a trace. At the edge of the bowl, an endemic Suwannee bass hovers motionless under a patch of phosphorescent-green algae, a diminutive but colorful largemouth with a silvery blue belly and red eyes.

Troy drops dramatically down into the earth, and we drop with it, white sand covering the sloping limestone walls like snow on a mountainside. My depth gauge reads 20, 30, then 40 feet, where I see a boulder with names carved into it. At 70 feet, the chasm bottlenecks into a narrow black hole where the force of 100 million gallons of water a day surges out, forcing me to hold on to the rocky edge just to pull my way another scant yard.

Like other springs, upland rainwater quietly percolates down through the terrain, secretly gains momentum from the alchemy of "conduit flow," and then upwells with great authority in "vents" such as this one. As I turn my head to switch on my light, my regulator is blown from my mouth by the force. I gulp water before putting it back in. It tastes sweet, cool.

The last time I visited Peacock Slough fifteen years ago, it was privately owned, a patch of sinks and springs hidden back in the dense woods under a canopy of cypress, live oak, and southern magnolia. All of us—mud boggers in pickups with Confederate-flag license plates, dope-smoking rednecks, cave divers—were trespassers. Today, the land is "Peacock Springs State Recreation Area." While cave certification is required for "penetrations," a state ranger patrolling the area tells me about the only way to stop untrained divers from entering the conduits is to catch them as they gear up: "They'll be the ones wearing snorkels." Since 1960 at least forty-five open-water divers, unschooled in the redundancies demanded by overhead environments, have died here.

Between Peacock, Orange Grove, and Bonnet, intrepid cave divers have mapped this labyrinthine system for nearly six miles. During my own quarter-mile exploration of Orange Grove then, I traveled through large rooms with vaulted ceilings, linked by winding tunnels. Back in the depths, I watched in awe as peculiar troglobytic fauna flitted under the mercury-like pools of exhaled air in the scalloped ceilings. Speciated by the caves in which they live, they are found nowhere else on earth, subspecies of albino shrimp and amphipods and crayfish with no knowledge of a sunlit world above.

During such treks, the glory for me was never in the distance traveled but in the singular wonder of being inside the living veins of the earth, of feeling a nature-driven force that transcended our puny human conceits. Clearly, not everyone who shares the caves feels the same way. As the late naturalist Archie Carr put it: "Some divers who come now would be just as happy in a system of culverts buried deep in the earth and filled with clear tap water." Indeed, when I walk to the edge of Peacock and ask an exiting diver—one equipped with a cave reel, a set of double full-size scuba tanks, and two small pony tanks—how his dive was, I get a one-word reply having little to do with the poetry I have known:

"Long," he says, curtly.

From Peacock, we drive down another dirt road, snaking our way through the southern woods to Cow Spring. It is what Peacock used to be, a bucolic pool of turquoise-clear water on unposted private land. A half-dozen locals from nearby Mayo are using Cow for a swimming hole, leaping head-first into the boulder-strewn water from the shore.

We drop down into Cow today, planning to stop at the edges of the limestone alcove where the surface light first fades. This is my second dive of the day, and even with a wetsuit, the 72-degree groundwater begins to chill me. I am in awe at how long the swimmers endure it, thrashing about like happy frogs.

As soon as I am inside the cavern, I feel sound vibrations moving through the water, as if some mammoth hand is shaking the landscape.

I slowly fin my way back to full light where I watch as a burly bare-chested man in cutoffs jumps into the clear water and begins to carve his initials on a rock with a screwdriver. Back on the surface, I find the shaking was caused when the screwdriver artist drove his pickup to the edge of Cow, right atop the cavern I was inside, then let it sit there and tremble in great horsepowered fury for several minutes.

We are ready to head out to the Gulf now on our rented houseboat, having just finished a dive at powerful Manatee Springs on the lower Suwannee. Named for the sea cows the Indians used to butcher here, Manatee was first described by naturalist William Bartram in 1774: "The ebullition is perpendicular upwards from a vast ragged orifice through a bed of rocks. . . . The surface of the basin immediately over the orifice is greatly swollen or raised a considerable height."

Today, the waters are not swollen at all, a clear indication the springs are diminishing—as a result of paving over recharge areas and pumping more groundwater. It is proof how ephemeral these natural wonders are, and how manipulation of the landscape, even here in the remote Suwannee Basin, can have unforeseen effects on the health of the artesian "ebullitions."

Before casting off, we rendezvous with biologist Mattson and cruise just upstream. There is a nearly intact piece of the past waiting for us, under the water. "It's the *City of Hawkinsville*," says Mattson, "the last paddlewheel to cruise the Suwannee. It's in such great shape, they made it into a state underwater archaeological preserve."

At the site, Mattson and I put on snorkel gear and fin over from our boat to the old steamship, one hundred yards and a good century away in time. As we fin into her fishing territory, an elderly woman dressed like the Blue Bonnet margarine girl picks up her cane pole and walks up the bank, muttering to herself.

The river's visibility is five to ten feet, and when the steamer materializes under us, I am amazed at how much of its original 141 feet of wooden decking remains. I fin the distance, over rusted steam piping and two enormous piston engines still connected to the remains of a paddlewheel. From inside a hatch, a black shape the size of another person scuttles into the darkness. Bull sharks come this far upstream, but this is more likely a small gator.

I reach down, grasp the edges of the eternally open hatch. Everything before me—fish, Mattson, the ghostly deck, my hands—is in sepia. I feel like I am not just looking at a daguerreotype but have become part of one.

I am way down upon de Swane Riber. Far, far away.

St. Lucia's Parrot Man

On a Wing and a Prayer

A few kilometers down the dense rainforest trail that winds through the mountainous interior of St. Lucia, the man who would save parrots now seems, briefly, to have become one.

Here, on a narrow pathway contoured into the edge of a fern-smothered hilltop, Englishman Paul Butler holds both arms away from his body and—in imitation of this Antillean island's national bird—flaps his palms vigorously. As he does, an odd staccato noise comes from his throat, something between a squawk, a croak, and a cry for help.

Butler is not trying to attract the colorful, blue-headed Jacquot that a conservation program here has coaxed back from the edge of extinction. Instead, he is trying to show me is how this parrot—which today has so far eluded us—is behaving, hidden back there just behind the last towering rainforest tree, out of the range of normal, non-birding sensibilities. "Caaawwwk," goes Butler, lifting his chin sharply with each call, flapping his hands like tiny, plucked wings.

Earnest, bespectacled, and exuberant, Butler may seem a bit like Mr. Rogers on speed, out for a casual stroll in his neighborhood jungle. In fact, he is a man in the midst of one of the most successful campaigns in the world to recast public awareness about the full worth of tropical birds, and of the ever diminishing places in which they must live.

In this way, Butler—whose approach lives or dies with the cooperation of local "counterparts" in the Caribbean Basin in the Pacific—relies on "sexy" avifauna to hard sell down-to-earth conservation ideals in some fifteen countries. After all, the birds hint at the essence of tropical island life—a synthesis of all things unrestrained and imaginative and aesthetically dazzling. If down-to-earth conditions in developing island-states are far more grim, then a green, blue, and red-plumed parrot proudly soaring across the horizon like a color wheel gone mad offers nothing if not hope, a vicarious departure from the murk of daily realities.

To this end there is a bird-laced curriculum, posters, billboards, buttons, puppets, music videos, and even a local bird costume worn to bring the larger-than-life message to school children. "It's like the cigarette companies using a pretty girl to peddle their product," says Butler, whose vision is funded by the nonprofit, Philadelphia-based RARE Center for Tropical Conservation.

Guided by this notion, a number of rare birds found nowhere else on earth other than their native island habitats have all been centerpieces in a strategy that braids national pride with wildlife and habitat protection. The "pretty girls" included Amazona parrots from the Bahamas, St. Vincent, Dominica, and the Caymans; a keel-billed toucan; the white-tailed Sabrewing hummingbird; the Montserrat oriole; the Zenaida dove; and more.

While the individual island campaigns—which all imitate a paint-by-numbers master plan—rely on sophisticated marketing techniques, at the core of each lies the spirit of a grown man or woman who doesn't mind, well, acting like a bird.

"I've dressed up as the bird in all the countries," says Butler. "At least two or three times in each. My wife was the 'Sisserou' in Dominica eighty times. It's bloody hot inside a bird costume, I tell you."

Behind the wheel of a mud-splattered jeep, Butler introduces me to St. Lucia in a lip-biting series of hairpin turns, bouncing over a coastal mountain highway that turns from asphalt to stone to deep, water-filled ruts of clay. The tour is more than a wild ride around a picturesque 238-square-mile volcanic island in the Lesser Antilles; it's a way for a man who never stops being a teacher to instruct: "St. Lucia is a microcosm of the problems facing all the Caribbean," says Butler, swerving to avoid hitting a goat in the road.

Fields of manioc and bananas zip by, grown on land that once was lush tropical jungle. The entire region is being deforested in much the same way—at an average decline of 5 percent a year. "We have four thousand more kids here leaving school needing jobs every year," explains Butler. "Whether they end up cultivating plots of root crops or marijuana, there's simply more pressure on the forests."

Historically, parrots, parakeets, and macaws had once been so plentiful in the Caribbean that Columbus had penned a log entry about "flocks obscuring the sun." Volcanic islands, like Dominica and Jamaica, had been covered with lush jungles that provided nesting cavities, seeds, and fruits. Even the flat, fossilized reefs of the arid islands, like the Bahamas and the Caymans, were thick with low-slung tropical forests that sheltered and fed the birds.

But when Butler first immigrated here from England in 1975 with a newly minted degree in wildlife management, the natural forests were being widely logged for timber and fuel. And the Jacquots (*Amazona versicolor*) were being hunted for food and export as exotic pets. There were less than 159 left on St. Lucia. It was a scene being replayed elsewhere as the region reeled in economic flux, adrift somewhere between a failed sugar-cane industry and the tenuous white hope called tourism. Of the over two dozen parrotlike species Columbus first found, more than half had become extinct.

Serving as the "conservation officer" for St. Lucia's bare-bones forestry department, Butler lived a spartan existence in a cottage in the rainforest with no electricity or running water. There, working under the wing of St. Lucian Gabriel Charles, a veteran forest service officer, Butler soon learned to shed his Eurocentric ideals of "saving" the country from itself. In doing so, he came to understand that wildlife conservation in a poor country like St. Lucia would take more than soapbox oratory.

If the country's rapidly disappearing forest and its remaining birds were to be truly revitalized, there would have to be a grassroots movement that exalted wild things instead of consuming them. But for that to happen, hungry natives who clear-cut forest to plant subsistence crops couldn't be demonized as bad guys—even though the loss of ground cover meant fewer birds, more erosion, and a better chance of seasonal flooding and even mudslides.

"If it's a question between 'Do I starve?' or 'Do I maybe cause a flood next year?' we know what will happen," says Butler, whose intimate knowledge of his adopted country has forged a strong empathy for its people.

Now with a successful campaign under its belt, St. Lucia has stabilized its woodland losses and is even busy replanting. At this time, some 26 percent of the island is forested; half of that is protected in government preserves. Throughout this island, there are still scads of reminders of the original push to "Save our Jacquot" from several years ago. Cars sport old bumper stickers, parrots squawk soundlessly from colorful wall murals, and Butler—who dressed up as *A. versicolor* in front of an entire country of schoolchildren—is widely recognized on the street. In fact, most know him more as "Jacquot" and "the Bird" than by his own name. For the Englishman, it's all a testament to how well conservation has become ingrained in the national consciousness.

At the ocean, Butler's jeep roars past a clutch of expensive, all-inclusive resorts lining the northwest coast here, walled "ghettoes" in which the fun-in-the-sun tourists seldom are exposed to island realities—ecological or otherwise. But as he drives inland at Soufrière, following a local road that snakes up into the heart of the government-owned forest preserve, he passes through the frayed villages of a developing country that, for most affluent tourists, may seem like the other side of the moon.

Indeed, Butler's world is the real Caribbean, the one that exists behind the stage set that has been so carefully erected for tourists. "On small island ecosystems with a limited amount of species, parrots and other birds are the most visible animals we have," says Butler. Many such birds, despite similarities in shape, are actually singularly crafted by genetics and coloration from island to island. "There's a strong feeling of pride now here in the region involving the birds," says Butler. "It's important for locals to know that, maybe you come from a rich country and you have a lot of things—but you don't have their parrot."

RARE's bird campaigns, as detailed in its manual "Promoting Protection Through Pride," show a measurable surge in the appreciation of local nature. But experience proves they work best in places like this, where locals aren't already saturated with marketing pitches. And they do best when the prevailing attitude toward the environment is apathy—rather than politically charged embitterment. "This campaign wouldn't work in the U.S.," says Butler. "There's just too much else going on. . . . And if you dressed up like a spotted owl in the American northwest, someone would try to shoot you."

Butler wheels sharply into a marina on Rodney Bay, where his office is wedged between outrigging shops. It looks like a storage room that a more institutionalized environmental agency might keep hidden behind a locked door—cardboard boxes in the corners, computer wires scattered across the floor, two handmade wooden tables with a thin coat of white paint, posters of birds from RARE campaigns stapled to the walls, and a fax message that is now six feet long and still coming. "We like to spend as little money on administration as possible," says Butler, nonplussed.

At a corner desk in the cramped room is a soft-spoken but articulate St. Lucian named Alleyne Regis, the other half of the entire educational team of RARE. Like Butler, Regis also worked at Forestry, where today's bird campaigns were first tested in a go-for-it atmosphere that was tight on funds but generous and open to innovation. Not surprisingly, RARE itself also functions by the seat of its pants—spending barely 30 percent of its barebones $700,000 international budget on administration.

Today, the bird men of RARE are heading off in vastly different directions. Regis will meet with actors who will bring a radio soap opera to life over the next several months. The drama, disguised with gritty local realism and the island's French-based patios, will expose teenagers to the wisdom of family planning—a core issue in a region wracked by overpopulation and poverty. "It's a more holistic approach to environmental problems," says Butler, smiling. "The more condoms used, the more jungle and parrots we can keep."

Butler, for his part, will drive up into the mountains to perform a far more traditional chore—to investigate the mudslide damage he suspects has been done to a newly opened rainforest trail. Setting up trails like this one are not only a great hands-on way to introduce school kids and tourists to the more sublime values of the country, but they take the RARE mission another step. "It's economic empowerment," says Butler. "These trails can generate a lot of income. It shows both the government and the locals they can make money from the forest and the birds without consuming them."

In fact, before being washed out by a hurricane, the main trail generated $250,000 in fees from visitors. It is that trail, freshly re-opened after a year's worth of rehabilitation, that Butler is now approaching. "Saca fend, garçon?" asks Butler in the fast-paced local patois as he slows next to a rastaman selling coconuts carved into birds at the side of the road. "Can we reach the trail up ahead?" We can, says the bird carver, but the going is slow.

The jeep groans as it pulls its way over deep trenches at Fond St. Jacques, the last village before the trail. Many here used to hunt, eat, and sell the Jacquot ten and twenty years ago. Today, an equal number make money from selling refreshments and crafts to the four thousand annual tourists who visit the trail; during the trail construction, some eighty locals were employed for almost two years.

Butler parks the jeep next to a pavilion with several picnic tables, changes his usual flip-flops for a pair of canvas sneakers, and marches inside the trail entrance. A kilometer away, the side of an immense hill once had collapsed because of heavy hurricane-driven rains. Butler is afraid the same thing may have happened again to the newly shored-up path with a recent spate of storms.

Like RARE's detailed manual on launching bird-based campaigns, Butler has more recently assembled a similar "cookbook" illustrating in detail how to build a local trail. Based on earlier work done by Butler and others in the Forest Service on St. Lucia, the guide covers basic surveying techniques, a cost-benefit analysis equation, and samples of interpretive signs and leaflets. The Cayman Islands, fresh from a success-ful campaign to save its own local Amazona parrots, the Grand Cayman and the Cayman Bracker, became the first to open its own two-mile-long "Mastic Trail" by following the how-to guide. Other countries, from Cuba to the Turks and Caicos, have also expressed a strong interest in the program.

The St. Lucia trail, with narrow, squarish ditches indented on each side to give the twelve feet of annual rain plenty of room to drain, rises quickly up the side of a mountain lushly forested with blue mahoe and mahogany trees, hung with bromeliads and encircled with climbing palms. Butler stops in his tracks, looking up. "That's a very good parrot tree!"

The tree is a *gommier,* a giant that reaches 120 feet. Butler bends down and picks up a tiny orange fruit, rolling it around in his fingers. "See the indentation of the sharp mandibles on it? We know it's a parrot that's been eating it, and not, say, an agouti." Butler walks on, now under a thick canopy of foliage that cools the tropical air. The trail here has not washed out as he feared, and he is happy, if perplexed by its stability.

After another hundred meters, Butler stops abruptly again, head cocked for a distant noise only he seems to hear, like a dog responding to a whistle that is out of human range. "There! There!" He is gesturing toward a distant opening in the thick canopy where a flash of green is quickly disappearing. It is one of the remaining three hundred Jacquots, flying in the distinct parrot pattern Butler earlier had demonstrated.

Butler walks cautiously a few more meters, then stops again, grabbing the arm of his visitor excitedly. The canopy opens up entirely in the place where the hillside once slid down into a ravine. Somewhere down the steep slope, a hundred meters below, water gurgles over rocks. But it is not water the bird man hears. In a tree nearby is an Antillean crested hummingbird, a species endemic to the region. Not far away are a pair of yellowish Adelaide warblers. Butler waits a few more moments. "A peewee flycatcher! All in one spot!" The bird man seems to be in bird heaven.

Still, there is more to be done. Butler calls out, whistling and chirping to another unseen member of the rainforest. It is the rufus-throated solitaire, a bird—like all the rest—that owes its life here to the high-profile role that the illusive Jacquot has played for them. "They call this bird, in patois, the 'Whistler of the Rain Forest,'" says Butler. And then he launches a long rising and falling whistle, one that sounds for all the world like the theme to the *Bridge over the River Kwai.*

"He may answer," says Butler, looking quickly to the left and right.

The little whistler, another native species, remains hidden even to the man who seems to have attuned his eye to seeing just about everything. "Come on you bugger, where are you!" says Butler, as he crouches down and creeps slowly over the trail, occasionally stopping to listen, and then to whistle some more. Finally, he disappears around the corner of the trail entirely, swallowed up by a vast wall of green ferns and palms and hanging vines.

There are only the sounds of cascading water and wild birds in the mountain jungle now—from the shrouded pathway, a human question whistled and, finally, from deep within the forest, an answer.

Cat Island

Tropical Voodoo and

Monasteries in the Sand

It is 10:00 P.M. and we are inside Sylvia's cottage in the tiny village of New Bight on the southern end of Cat Island. Outside, on the one-lane street between us and the warm waters of the South Atlantic, nothing but land crabs move, claws clicking in some small, beastly choreography under the coconut palms. Just beyond, the dark sea mirrors the moon and stars so thoroughly that the horizon seems to have vanished entirely.

We are a long, long way from the bright lights of Nassau and Freeport, with their umbrella drinks and slot machines and pushy T-shirt vendors. I am with Pat, an old high-school friend who now works as a director of religious education in a large Catholic church back in the States. Pat appreciates religious symbolism and a cold Kalik and the little miracles of sand dollars, seen underwater. Pat is cool, engaged in the moment.

Sylvia's last name is Larramore-Crawford, and she was born in Nassau, a busy, sophisticated cruise-port city with a frenetic edginess closer to New York than it is to the isolated "out island" of Cat. She is ebony and chic, straw hat and sandals, necklace of cowries and light summer dress. Sylvia has written a cook book or two and has organized story-telling events and the "Richard Crawford All Male Spelling Competition" here in New Bight, in honor of her late husband.

At this very moment, Sylvia is doing her best to convince us that the local practice of Obeah—a sort of African bush-medicine voodoo—is highly suspect. We are listening. After Sylvia's house was burglarized five times, a well-meaning, Obeah-practicing neighbor gave her a bag of sea salt to ward off future intrusions of evil, she explains. For true believers, sea salt—gathered from salinas, the shallow evaporating ponds—is known to neutralize bad vibes. Got some troubles with evil? Hobgoblins under the porch? Burglars with some devil in them? Spread some salt around the threshold, the neighbor told her. It'll function as a security gate, Obeah-style.

But Sylvia is a skeptic. Before she had a chance to put the magic to the test, someone broke in again—and stole the bag of salt. Sitting in Sylvia's kitchen around a table with wine and good food and rich homemade Bahamian bread, Pat and Sylvia and I have a good laugh at this. Then, we get ready to go drive through a graveyard to hear a guy play music on a saw.

More than most of her fellow islanders, Sylvia understands the value of local tradition in helping maintain a real sense of place, understands how fancy resorts back in Nassau insulate rather than enlighten visitors to what her country is really about. Sylvia is like a big-city American who—wise to the world—moves to the country and, in doing so, ends up with a greater perspective than she would have if she had stayed in the big city or, conversely, was raised in the sticks and never left.

But now she is driving a lonely dirt road past graves of dead Bahamians, taking us to hear a dose of the native "rake and scrape" music at a local seaside bar. Played on a metal saw, rake and scrape is another vestige of the distant past, a sound slaves once made using an African *gambee* of grooved wood. As we go, the raw-edged immediacy of West Indian culture begins to quietly slip beyond the boundaries of anecdotal storytelling. Obeah is easy to make fun of, when you're safe, back in a bright kitchen with a glass of wine in your hand.

Outside, the entire island seems suddenly swallowed by the night. Just moments ago, the stars were covering the sky like Twinkle Lites— and now as we pass through the cemetery, it's as if someone has thrown a thick dark cape over us. As casually as possible, Sylvia admits she would not be taking this road at all if she were alone. "I don't really believe in Obeah," says Sylvia, looking over her shoulder. And then, as if to cover all the bases: "But there are so many stories. . . . There is something, I am not sure what."

Certainly, I am not sure what, either. Cat has no patent on Obeah, a religion said to mediate between the living and the dead. Bahamians elsewhere have likely practiced some form of it since the days of colonial slavery, clinging onto this shard of African-bred faith—a tradition passed over the centuries, like the skills of basketry and gambee playing. But while the more accessible cays have become Westernized and known, the archaic practice of Obeah still has a stronghold on Cat. There are seventeen villages here with 1,700 natives—and only three or four low-profile tourist lodges. The locals are exceedingly friendly and relaxed, their indigenous culture undiluted by swarms of demanding American tourists. They have, simply, been left to be.

Over the last few days, I have already heard astonishing stories about Obeah—both from islanders as well as the few expatriates who live here.

In these stories, shamans have cast spells using disinterred human hearts, the dead have manipulated objects to torment the living, and men have awakened suddenly from a deep sleep believing they are being strangled. Even today, if someone dies in a native home, the remaining family members move out and build a new house next door. The spirit needs a place to be left to be, too.

Not even the devout Father Jerome could chase this Obeah away, and he was a saint if there ever was one. Jerome, a gifted architect and church builder and Franciscan priest, died here in the 1950s after leaving his selfless imprint on the land and the people during the last years of his life. As I will soon discover, his legacy—which includes a miniature limerock monastery he lived in at the top of the highest hill—is every bit as powerful as Obeah. Perhaps Jerome was the yin to the voodoo's yang. Whatever, the story of this departed priest is still very much a part of the spiritual alchemy that drives the mystery of Cat today.

Father Jerome, after all, was a sort of Catholic holy man, a missionary of a doctrine steeped in its own enigmatic symbolism. It is an ancient religion celebrated by a liturgy—the "bells and smells"—full of ritualistic behaviors traced to the earliest practice of that faith. Catholics don't dig up the dead—they just vicariously eat them. If Obeah is to have a Christian counterpart, then Catholicism seems a good contender.

Saw music. Spirit houses. Miniature gothic monasteries. Tropical magic. When you live long enough on a lonely, time-warped slab of fossilized coral reef and sand in the southern Atlantic, you soon find ways of making do. And if making do includes an abiding faith in the unseen, well, who am I to argue?

There are very few cats on Cat Island. What there are—if my vantage point from the patio of our cottage on Fernández Bay is any measure—are Greater Antillean bullfinches and, scuttling in the sand under the sea grape and willowy causarina, curly-tailed lizards. The bullfinch seems like a knockoff of a cardinal—except it is mostly black, just splotches of yellow on its throat and head. Elsewhere, there are also frigates and tropical birds, bonefish flats and coral reefs, and limestone caves with lots of bats. The pre-Columbians known as Lucayans once lived in some of those caves; during hurricanes, islanders still seek refuge there.

Tony Armbrister, the descendant of one of the British colonial planter families of Cat, has told me the island is not named for cats at all but for Arthur Catt, an eighteenth-century British pirate once in cahoots with Blackbeard and Henry Morgan. Buccaneers must have had terrible memories, for Catt—like pirates elsewhere—is said to have buried treasure here and forgotten about it. Maybe it was all that rum.

Pat joins me, and I shoulder a backpack full of drinking water and head out over the sand toward the edge of the cove. There, we stow our gear in a sea kayak and push it out into the shallow, transparent ocean. Already, the rarefied morning light of the tropics is filtering reality, and the horizon seems to be dissolving into cerulean sky and water. Both of us are lighthearted with the prospect of what lies ahead. We paddle out of the cove, and then head inland, following the tidal Armbrister Creek as it winds its way back inside the rugged terrain of hardy scrub and cacti. We are headed for a deep sinkholesque crater called "Boiling Hole," said to roil at the surface during certain tidal changes.

According to a legend retold by Eris Moncur, author of *Mystical Cat Island,* locals consider the holes haunted, inhabited by a raucous "gargantuan creature" who variously swallows up dead horses and live people—even sucks in flotsam and spits it out, far at sea. It is not dissimilar to stories I have heard on Andros Island that have a multi-armed subaquatic creature known as a "Lusca" haunting blue holes there.

The creek is a wondrous meander, edged with the elegant bowlike roots of red mangroves. As it deepens, I see the fins of small sharks coming in from the sea. The water is clear, and under us I see shards of sand dollars and tropical fish, flitting in bright colors of red, blue, yellow.

As we approach the slough leading to Boiling Hole, we find the new tide has not yet re-filled the furrow. Our shallow draft kayak scrapes aground several times until finally it can go no farther. So we tie the bow of it to a mangrove branch and slog the last few hundred yards in ankle-deep water. Suddenly, the tepid sun-heated creek becomes dramatically cooler. The crater and its chillier sea water must be nearby.

Sure enough, just a few feet away, the white sand falls away into a deep blue hole, about the diameter of Sylvia's cottage. My polarized glasses cut the surface glare, and I see just what amounts to a giant aquarium—barracuda and small shark, grunts and snapper, schools of tiny silver fish—all endlessly circling like tigers in a zoo cage.

When the tides are right, the surface over the hole will seem to "boil," for it is connected by a series of underground limestone caves and crevices with the sea. As for the gargantuan monster, well, tale-telling has always been an essential weave of the culture in any rural place. I wonder what story backwoods American southerners would make up if they found a local pond periodically swashing about on its own.

At any rate, both our drinking water and energy are ebbing. We decide to turn back before the Lusca shows up, get back to our cottage, maybe pop open a cold Kalik, put up our feet, and watch the sun settle into the sea. We will consider Obeah some more, consider the monster of the hole, consider Catholicism. Tomorrow, we will head out in search of an abandoned monastery built on a hill.

We have just rented a car and are driving the length of spindly Cat Island on the deserted "Queen's Highway." Our big American sedan sports a huge dent in the driver's side door; stick-on letters smack in the middle of the windshield advise: "——EP RIGH——." At roadside, the rust-colored "love vine" creeps over plants and trees, and tethered goats lay in its shade, on the cool asphalt. We pass the conch-pink Hazel's Seaside Bar, and the First and Last Chance Strawworks. Old men play dominos under mango trees, near where sisal—once a colonial cash crop—now grows wild. Lone chimneys and the shells of plantation manor homes of two centuries ago haunt the thick brush.

The stunted foliage is an Obeah man's medicine kit—as well as a field day for any ethnobotanist who studies the links between culture and the land. Indeed, over fifty different plants are used for "cures"—altor leaf wrapped about the temple for headache, bay vine boiled and drunk to keep a new mother healthy, ploppers leaf roasted and squeezed for "general ill feeling," and gum eleoni branches propped up to ward off snakes. Some have real pharmaceutical value; others skirt the edge of superstition.

We pass sleepy villages with the legacies of the long-gone British Loyalists visible in name only—Orange Creek and Arthur's Town, Dumfries and Tea Bay, Knowles and Port Howe. Historically, Cat had been mapped as "San Salvador," a place Columbus described after making landfall there in 1492. But in 1926 an inscrutable act of British Parliament gave that name to nearby Watlings Island, a fact that still riles locals.

At Old Bight, a church cobbled from limerock sits back from the road, its sculpted architecture making it seem like a chunk of medieval Europe. It is the St. Francis of Assisi Catholic Church, and it is part of Father Jerome's handiwork, an enchanting structure designed with durable materials to withstand the tropical climate—the heat and termites and ever-present hurricane threat. The good father, trained as an architect back in his native England, also hand-built another local church, as well as two on nearby Long Island. We stop, take photos, and then climb back in our sedan and head for the priest's old monastery.

Ten minutes later, and we have parked on a dry chalky jeep path inland from New Bight. There is no interpretive sign, no clearly marked parking area, no formal announcement of the place. It is as if someone simply walked off, years ago, and left it all to be. Here, the fossilized coral ridge that spines the center of the island rises to 206 feet. It is the highest point in all the Bahamas, and the place Father Jerome chose to build his one-man monastery. We will trek up the steep, rocky hill to see what messages he has left for us.

At the base of Mt. Alvernia, there is an arched stone portal to mark the beginning of the ascent. Latin words and keys and crosses are carved here, in relief. I look on in befuddlement. "*Deo* is God," says Pat, an ardent Catholic herself. "*Optimo?* Sounds like a pretty good God." The keys? "St. Pete's, the keys to heaven."

Through the portal we go, past the corridor of wild tamarind shrub, and up the rugged limerock trail. Up ahead, we see the spires and crosses of his little monastery, a Celtic-Mediterranean vision etched into the cumulus of the South Atlantic. As we climb, we pass the various Stations of the Cross, each letter and contour meticulously chipped from stone. Some stations are biblical scripture, some ageless Catholic tradition.

Both the path and the stations are chunks of karst, prehistoric sea animals and plants, part of the soft geology that also created Boiling Hole and the topside caverns of Cat. In these karst vignettes, we have seen Jesus shouldering the cross, watched as he fell, saw soldiers cast lots for his robe—and then finally, at the top, we see a real-life tomb-cave with the inscription: "Blessed are they who die in the Lord." A giant endemic moth flies out, bumps into Pat's bright-green T-shirt, and flutters away. Father Jerome is buried somewhere deep inside. He was more than an ascetic: in the villages of Cat, he ministered to the sick, comforted the injured and homeless.

This mystery man, in fact, was once Monsignor John Hawes, an Anglican priest, a philosopher, a poet, sculptor, and essayist who later in life converted to Catholicism. When he moved to Cat Island in 1939 to spend his last years he had already built six churches, a boys' school, a convent, and a monastery. Eschewing celebrity for meditation—and believing in the need to "mortify" the body to purge the soul—Father Jerome carved each limestone block for his "hermitage" and then carried it to the top of the steep bluff. He named the ridge Mt. Alvernia, for a hill in Tuscany where St. Francis received the wounds of the cross. The trail, with no railings or signs or historic markers to guide us, steepens under a hot tropical sun. "This is good mortification," says Pat, glistening now and flushed from the heat.

Now, at the top of this Mt. Alvernia, we finally see the monastery. We enter, ducking under the open doorway. Room to room we go, me clueless, Pat figuring the original use of each: the tabernacle, the lectern, the holy-water font, the one-man wooden pew. I squeeze into the pew. "He probably knelt," says Pat, and I kneel. In a small room nearby, I see an old slab of slate. On it is written: *Please Ring Bell Before Coming Up.* It was a message to visitors, and a lifetime ago, it was likely posted back down at the bottom of the rock steps, so unsolicited company wouldn't startle this solitary hermit-priest.

Outside, arches and columns open to give a view of both sides of the island—windward whitecaps frothing on the reef, leeward shore as calm as a turquoise pond. A ceramic plaque depicting a lone monk under a magnificent night sky is mortared into an exterior wall. A Latin inscription, translated, reads: *Thank You Lord for the Moon and the Stars.*

I tense and my heart aches: I wonder if I could ever commit as wholly and fully to any one thing as this man once did—to a single idea, a place, a relationship, a god.

In the ovenlike tropical heat of midday, we walk to the silo-like bell tower. Inside, it is cool and dark. There are staggered wooden steps on opposite sides of the round wall, leading up to a bell at the top. "I'd really like to hear the bell," says Pat. Swallowing my fear of heights, I chimney up the tower and grasp the dangling rope. I snap it tentatively, causing a feeble metallic *clunk.* Then I think of Father Jerome, how strong a guy he must have been, in both body and soul.

In his memory, I pull the rope as hard as I can, gonging it seven times, one right after the other. My tension over heights seems to ease. Jerome tried hard, but for him it was likely never enough. His legacy was not one of perfection but of simply having the heart to explore, to be game enough to find glory in the small wonders of island magic, of boiling holes, and atonements of another time. Each ring, fervent and glorious, resonates over the top of Mt. Alvernia, deep heavy gongs that seem to bounce against the sky itself, until each is carried away in the warm Bahamian wind.

Sir Francis Drake in Panama

Questing for El Dragón

Drake's Island, a tiny pinnacle of worn igneous rock tufted with
sapodilla bushes and tropical ferns, rises from the sea just to my left.
The low-slung mountains of Panama's northern coast sprawl in a
cloud-induced, late-afternoon haze to my right. I lie squarely in
between, some three miles off the ancient harbor of Portobelo,
balanced on the gunnel of a small wooden boat, atop twenty
fathoms of remote Caribbean Sea, looking for a pirate.

Sir Francis Drake, for whom the tiny island is named, sailed over
these same waters centuries ago, known and feared by the Spanish
colonists he preyed upon as *El Dragón*. For all the destruction he
inflicted on the Spanish, he might as well have been breathing fire.
But piracy, like beauty, is in the eye of the beholder, and Drake was

regarded by his own countrymen as a hero who plundered and slaughtered his way through the New World only as duty and God required. It all depends which end of the pikestaff you are on, I guess.

I tumble backward off the gunnel into deep blue water, falling in slow motion into the scantly known underbelly of nautical history, 120 feet down to a desolate sea floor. Here, in a requiem of cannon fire and a blare of woeful trumpets, Drake was buried at sea by his men in 1596, dead of battle wounds and dysentery. Down he went into the depths of this lonely cove, ensconced in both a leaden coffin and a luxuriantly rich history. And now, down I go in his wake, fortified with the utterly quixotic notion that I will somehow stumble across his remains.

My pirate of choice was a man to be reckoned with. An expert navigator, he forged the arduous Strait of Magellan to the Pacific in 1578 on a mission for his queen, Elizabeth I. After pillaging Spanish settlements along the South American coast, Drake sailed all the way up to San Francisco, nailed a brass plaque to a tree, and proclaimed that territory for his monarch. Instead of turning around and calling it a day, he then headed west, crossed the Pacific, and became the first captain to circumnavigate the globe. Elizabeth herself came aboard the *Golden Hind* at Plymouth to knight him. Back in the New World in 1585, Drake sacked the rich ports of Santo Domingo, Cartagena, and St. Augustine, ruining the credit of Philip II in the process. In a spare moment, he rescued Sir Walter Raleigh's bedraggled, starving colonists in Virginia, whisking them back across the sea—a true pirate with a heart of gold.

But Panama, the little Central American country best known for its canal or the odd infamy of its former leader Manuel Noriega, may have played the most formative role of all. It was here that Drake—after being badly whipped in battle as a young seaman by the Spanish—began to earn his reputation. In at least four voyages to Panama between 1571 and 1595, he grew from a novice renegade bent on revenge to a rich and famous folk hero. In doing so, he inspired other English captains to launch their own forays all along the Spanish Main. As privateers, they could have both gold and glory and, even better, could function far outside the notoriously rigid routines of the British navy.

Before I left for Panama, I launched my own search for Drake by ringing up Michael Turner in England. Turner, who makes his living as a physical education teacher, has devoted a large chunk of his adulthood to a near-obsessive retracing of Drake's voyages around the world. He first learned of his countryman's heroics as a schoolboy himself. The idea of an Englishman swashbuckling his way beyond the dreary gray countryside of his homeland to some of the most exotic locales in the world grabbed him then and never let go. So far, says Turner, he has visited 350 different sites where Drake was known to have touched land around the world, taking photographs of himself at each place. Turner's dream is to publish a book that compares archival descriptions of these places with contemporary photos—he will call it "In Drake's Wake."

Panama, with its densely wooded rainforests, isolated coastline, and crumbling forts left behind by the conquistadors, has a singular appeal. "It's the most romantic and most elusive of all the places I've visited," said Turner. "Panama is where Drake started and finished his voyages."

Turner, who himself has poked around on the sea bottom off Portobelo looking for the leaden coffin, dreams of raising money to return with a full-scale expedition for a more thorough search. The goal would be no less than to recover the remains and return them to England, where they would finally receive the proper burial and honor they deserve. In the meantime, Turner doesn't have the heart to dash the hopes of a fellow dreamer, however outlandish they may be. "Drake was laid to rest one league off the mouth of the Portobelo harbor," he tells me. "That's 2.4 miles." And then: "Good luck."

After flying into Panama City on the Pacific coast, I rent a jeep and some scuba tanks and, with a photographer, head north on the Trans-Isthmus Highway, leaving the boxy high rises of the capital in our wake. Rene

Gomez, Panamanian dive shop owner, had told us that he had become more aware of his own country's history by poking about underwater off the Caribbean coast. Not far from Portobelo, he recently found the site of a Spanish shipwreck dating to 1581. It was in twenty feet of water, and fifteen of its iron cannon were still aimed outward, as if defending a ship—indeed, an entire way of life—that had long vanished. "Who knows what you can find," Gomez had said. "Ships have been coming here for a long, long time."

As I drove, however, I had to admit to myself that my actual chances of laying hands on Drake's lead casket were not unlike finding a needle in a haystack, albeit a very deep and wet haystack. Still, I knew the quest would allow me to poke around in the ruined colonial ports where Drake and his enemies once warred, and to search for the residual signs of what brought them all here. That would be a search that guaranteed a reward, however intangible.

Today, the Trans-Isthmus Highway is cluttered at first by devilish little cars, trucks, and the wildly painted, gear-screeching, fume-belching buses known for good reason as *diablos rojos*—red devils. As we go deeper and higher into the sparsely populated countryside, the traffic thins and the jungle begins. We're paralleling El Camino Real and El Camino de las Cruces, the two routes the *conquistadores* used to haul their treasure to the Caribbean for shipment back to Spain. The narrowness of this land bridge, the accident of geography, gave colonial Panama its prominence. On the coast where we are headed, the natural harbors of Nombre de Dios and later, Portobelo, provided the most likely depots at the end of the trail. Between them, they helped make Panama the largest center of commerce in the New World in the sixteenth century.

Beyond the Chagres River, the narrow roadway rises up into the continental divide, and the gentle ridge that has hidden the canal falls away into the sea-level flatness of vast Lake Gatún to the west. It is near the end of the rainy season now, and the clouds hang thick in the folds of the peaked hills, giant spritzers of life. Bromeliads the size of the jeep's hood droop from the boughs of gumbo limbo trees and vivid orange bird-of-paradise flowers prick a thick underbrush of green. The rainforest edges in close to the road, then drops back, leaving behind a carpet of wild grass and trees bearing mangos, papayas, bananas, and coconuts.

The Spanish took only material treasure; Panama's natural wealth remains. Jaguars, pumas, and ocelots thrive in the jungle. Rare harpy and crested eagles hunt above the lowland forests. More than a thousand species of orchids and 687 kinds of ferns are scattered like *escudos* spilled from a treasure chest. Drake waded into a jungle much like this one when he led his men down from the Caribbean to stage the first assaults on the overland mule trains, guided and aided by escaped slaves known as *cimarrones.* In a practical split of the haul, Drake's men kept the gold and silver, of little use in the jungle, and the *cimarrones* got the food and clothes.

As I veer sharply east at Puerto Pillión, onto the rugged, winding road that will take me along the coast, I pass little *fincas* tucked into the soft hills, chickens and hogs grazing outside frond-roofed *bohíos.* Sometimes, men wearing *pitas,* the narrow-brimmed native straw hats, walk silently along the road, machete in hand. Most are farmers from the dryer pacific coastal province of Los Santos; several decades ago, they were encouraged by the government to homestead the rich coastal land. (It is not unlike how the Brazilian government has tried to "settle" the vast Amazonia by giving free land to anyone who would clear and farm it—thinking this "progress" to be of more use than wild jungle.) As they slashed and burned their way deeper into the forest here, the farmers left behind barren fields, which are now populated with beef cattle to meet the demand for the American fast-food market. Now, however, unsecured by the roots of trees and plants, the hilly fields and their soil wash freely into the sea and smother the corals just offshore—especially at the mouths of rivers, like the upcoming Río Padres, blanketing the reefs, artifacts, shipwrecks, and, one would imagine, the lead coffins of pirates.

Less than three hours after leaving Panama City, I approach what is left of Portobelo. It is announced by the weathered turrets of the largest of five coral-block fortresses still remaining, Santiago de la Gloria. I look offshore and see Isla Drake shimmering in the amber light of late afternoon at the edge of the natural harbor. Sometime in the late 1800s, long after the rancor of another era had been silted over by time, this little tuft of land came to be named and mapped after the man who—centuries earlier—was known only in epithet.

I continue driving through Portobelo, along a rutted red-clay road that snakes to the older harbor of Nombre de Dios, another hour to the east. My rental jeep and its poorly lubricated undercarriage groans and creaks, and the scuba tanks clank against each other in the back. Here, remnants of an iron cannon—breached when it was used against one of Drake's ships—is reported to be simply lying in the thick grass on a steep bluff behind the bay. Open to the northern winds, Nombre de Dios proved to be a poor harbor; it was finally abandoned for Portobelo in 1597, the year after Drake died. Fort, churches, and homes were built here, battles fought, lives and loves nurtured and lost long before Jamestown or Williamsburg or Plymouth Rock were settled or landed upon. To travel from Portobelo to Nombre de Dios is like going deeper into an archaeological dig, down another square meter into time.

As I reach the edge of the village, I pass the natural harbor where fleets of galleons were once berthed. Except for a huge modern barge recently sunk here as a dock to load stone for shipment as construction material, the waters are empty. There is said to be a path nearby that leads up to where the Drake-era cannon still exists. I park here, and with the photographer, set out for it. Unmarked, and like most of Nombre de Dios, unsung, the path is actually the northern end of El Camino de las Cruces, the Road of the Crosses.

Nombre today is home to descendants of the *cimarrones*, some of whom have mixed with the Antilleans later brought from the Caribbean islands to help build the canal. It is a menage of small *bohíos* of bamboo and fronds and modest, shuttered huts of stucco and wood, all on stilts. The village is divided by the Río Pato, a blackwater tributary that washes itself down from the mountains. We cross an ancient coral-block bridge over it, and as we do, two Cuna Indians paddle under us in a small dugout stacked with freshly cut palm leaves, building materials from another century.

On his second voyage, Drake anchored his fleet nearby, went ashore with seventy-three men, and attacked Nombre at night. The brigade entered the village with "firepikes flaming," trumpets sounding, and drums rolling, according to one report, scaring the wits out of the townspeople, who after a brief, heartless fight, fled into the jungle. In the governor's house, Drake's men found a pile of silver twelve feet high and seventy feet long, a cache that was awaiting the arrival of the annual transport *flota* from Spain. Besides silver and some gold, the treasures stored here usually included emeralds from Colombia, pearls from Isla Margarita, hides, indigo, rare woods, vanilla beans, even natural medicines from the rainforest.

Unlike Portobelo, Nombre was largely built without coral; its original wood homes and fired-clay roofs have long since crumbled into the earth, leaving only a few broken artifacts and pottery shards in the dirt. Not so long ago, the village could only be reached by sea. Still isolated, Nombre remains insular, its people stoic and cautious of outsiders, unaffected by the vagueness of time. The grandiose dreams of Spain once visited here and then disappeared, leaving the *cimarrones* to win the ultimate battle; for now, it is their place alone.

The path meanders near an old cemetery, and a young boy is playing there. I ask him about the Drake cannon, and within seconds, a small group of his friends seem to materialize out of nowhere. They are quiet, diffident, but sure of place. They are all barefoot, and a few are armed with homemade slingshots, used for shooting parrots and macaws. The brightly colored feathers must provide superb dress-up accessories, just as they would for any child, and the birds, well, they are made of meat that can be cooked over fire. They lead us into the jungle, and immediately we are enveloped in a thick tropical heat and set upon by mosquitoes. We step gingerly through a barbed-wire fence, cross a marshy open field, teeter over a precarious single-log bridge spanning a narrow creek, and climb up a steep, rough-hewn path that leads to the top of a bluff. The view from the bluff is magnificent, taking in most of the treetops of Nombre de Dios and the harbor and sea beyond. The strategy of this place is implicit in the expanse of all that lies below, for any approach to the harbor can be easily seen from here. It is twilight now, and seaward, heat lightning flares behind distant cumulus in the twilight, backlighting galleon-shaped clouds on the horizon.

The cannon is not here. At some unknown signal, our young guides lead us back down the hill, through a thick grove of plantain and lemon trees left by the first colonists, and up more rocky footholds to another bluff. Here, amidst the harsh scent of burning charcoal, a young man comes out of a *bohío* with a flashlight in one hand and a machete in the other. After a quick exchange in Spanish, he walks us to the edge of the hill where he casts his dim light down on a three-foot section of weathered iron cannon. It has been here forever, he says, as long as anyone, even the old people, can remember. A beautiful young girl with large brown eyes appears from the darkness holding a rusted ten-pound cannon ball with both hands and, without a word, gives it to me, dropping it into my palm. Giant fruit bats zoom low over our heads. In the distance, lightning flashes, the galleons sail, and far, far off, thunder rolls like the beating of drums.

Back down at the edge of the cove, we find a *fonda* with a tiny kitchen and a thatched roof, supported with thick poles of bamboo and open on all sides. The cook makes us platters of fried octopus, with plantains and rice, and we wash it down with cold *cervezas*. A cool evening breeze has lifted up off the water, and in the darkness we are serenaded by a chorus of giant marine toads, each the size of a softball. Panama City and its bustle and boxy high rises seems light years away. Visitors seldom make it this far, so there is little to cater to them. The dive shop owner had told us that a friend owns a rustic vacation *casa* on a spit of land nearby, and we can string some hammocks and sleep outside it. It is a perfect locale for our exploratory dive into the old harbor in the morning, a prelude for a dive we will make later to search for Drake off Portobelo. But it is dark now and there is nothing but mangroves and water between us and the tip of the narrow peninsula, and we must find someone with a boat to take us there.

We learn of a fisherman who owns a boat with a motor, and so we drive into the village, no street here to speak of, just an assemblage of huts under palm trees, all dark except for the random lantern or candle burning in an open window. A half-dozen wooden boats are dragged up along the shoreline of the Río Pato for the night, some with nets piled in them. We park under a tree and, slinging our dive bags over our shoulders and carrying our tanks, stumble onward. We must look an odd sight. Dogs bark at us, and people begin to stir, raising their voices. Visitors at any time here would be odd; *norteamericanos* in the middle of the night dragging strange metallic tubes must be downright weird. We locate the fisherman's house and negotiate a price for the shuttle, payable only in American dollars and not *balboas*. A big dark-skinned man, he comes out, pulls a new Yamaha outboard motor from under his house, and attaches it to one of the boats. We help drag it down into the river and load our gear. His Spanish is too slurred for me to understand, and when he disappears, I think he has asked us to take the boat ourselves. Within moments, though, another younger man appears, greets us, and indicates he will delivers us and, at a predetermined time tomorrow, come back and retrieve us.

We clatter off down the dark night river, which here is not much more than a mangrove creek, the peaked bow of the dorylike pirogue crashing into clumps of red mangroves on particularly tight turns. Then we are out of the creek and into a wide bay, illuminated by the light of the moon. We cross the bay and land at a beach, under coconut palms. The hut is shuttered and locked, but there are plenty of good places to set our hammocks, and soon we do. I rock gently in a light ocean breeze, just enough to keep down the voracious biting bugs, and then I sleep. I dream of half-seen little native girls with brown eyes firing golden cannonballs into the harbor from slingshots.

Sunrise comes early. We eat some homemade bread we brought with us from last night's dinner, wash it down with water from our canteens, and get in our dive gear. This bay is the original harbor of Nombre de Dios, and not only did the treasure fleets of the earliest European ships anchor in it, the crews also "careened" their vessels here. Careening required them to drag the ships into shallow water, turn them on their sides, and then scrap the barnacles and other marine life from the hull bottom, thus cutting down on drag when back under sail. I have an underwater metal detector with me that might help lead us to the remains of a galleon, and I already feel conflicted over using it. Unlike the avid treasure hunters who use such devices to let them find and then dig up sunken wrecks—often with little regard for archaeological integrity or the provenance of the shipwreck—I just want to use it to help me connect with a piece of the world that was linked to Drake's own experiences here. Shipwrecks are like time capsules, ready to reveal new and rare information about another era, but they must be carefully excavated for this to happen. If archaeologists do one day follow us here, I don't want them to find pages of history missing because I have mindlessly ransacked the library.

We slosh out into the warm water, up to our waists, and then let the air out of our buoyancy vests and descend to the shallow sandy bottom. The plan is a simple one—to follow the bottom as it descends deeper into the bay, listening to the metal detector and watching for any visual clues that might be here: a cannon, the tip of an anchor, a newly exposed slab of wood. Above me, a pair of banded butterfly fish pick at the edges of a clump of dead coral while on the bottom, tiny blennies vanish into their holes like miniature hat tricks. We have heard that sharks routinely visit this bay—a twelve-footer was recently spotted—but for now it's only us, the little tropicals, and the ghosts of *flotas* long gone.

I am sweeping the head of the detector back and forth across the bottom when, suddenly, the needle on its dial jerks to the right, and the headphones I am wearing come alive with loud static. I put down the device and, using the heel of one hand, fan across the bottom with it. The effect is like aiming a gentle propeller toward the sand: the bottom puffs up into miniature clouds and drifts off in the current. Within a few minutes, this technique has created a hole nearly a foot deep. As the sediment clears, I look into the bottom of the depression and see pieces of thinly hammered brass studded with small handmade nails. Shards of old timbers float up and away. Hammered sheeting like this was wrapped around the hulls of wooden ships to protect them from boring worms. Since this harbor was no longer used after 1597, these artifacts likely date from before then—to the time when Drake was still here.

I reach down and touch the metal, rolling the nails over in my fingers and tracing the outline of the sheeting. I try to evoke the musket smoke, laughter, the sound and feel of other lives, but I am not much of a diviner this morning, and the objects remain inert. There are no feelings, just thoughts: it is ancient metal, forged back in Spain. It has been under the bottom of this cove for several centuries. Like me, it is a long, long way from home.

I continue to follow the sloping bottom away from shore, but the needle fails to respond to any more metal. I am almost out of air, so I turn and fin back toward the beach, finally surfacing and swimming the last hundred yards. Ashore, I shake off my gear and, still in my wetsuit, gather up my few belongings from last night. Soon, the boat that brought us here appears at the other edge of the cover, emerging from the mouth of the Río Pato, headed our way. As it approaches, the driver gives us a wave and a hearty *buenos días,* and we are soon loaded and chugging back to Nombre de Dios.

In the village, I strip off my wet suit and put on a fresh T-shirt. It is still morning, and the new light sifts down to the river banks through the fronds of the coconut palms. We quickly load the jeep and head back into Portobelo, finally ending up near its waterfront harbor. The lesson of *El Dragón*'s devastation in Nombre de Dios was taken into account when Portobelo was built: it helps explain the fortress that sprawls along its waterfront, assembled from large blocks of coral into thick walls, archways, ramps, turrets, and rooms with ballast stone floors. Up in the steep hills that rise behind the city, other smaller forts were constructed, and across the harbor, on a narrow sliver of rocky land on the eastern cape, yet another fort the English called Ironcastle was built. Everywhere, cannons face outward, toward the sea, as if waiting for the next assault to come. It would seem that Portobelo was the best-fortified city in all the world. But it was also a place of great wealth, and the presence of such treasure inspired brutal new tactics in the pirates who would steal it.

Indeed, in 1668, the debauched pirate Henry Morgan attacked the nearly impenetrable Ironcastle. Scaling it with ladders meant enduring buckets of hot oil and lead shot from above, so Morgan improvised: he captured local nuns and monks and, using them as shields, went up the sides of the fort. The Spanish oiled and shot them anyway, but enough of the attackers got through to claim the fort. (Later, in the early twentieth century, Ironcastle suffered an ignoble end when American builders of the Panama Canal disassembled it to use as bulkheads and jetties.)

Today, the ruins of Portobelo's once-grand defense system meander along the waterfront of the harbor in a nearly forgotten majesty, consumed with a dark patina of algae and moss. Inside the largest fort of Santiago de Gloria, villagers have built tin-roofed huts; sixteenth-century brick-and-coral walls with the original sapodilla beams abut little *fondas* selling beer and pastries and sodas. *Buitres,* black-headed vultures, perch atop peaked tin roofs, while roosters crow from narrow alleyways.

At the edge of Portobelo is a church, San Felipe, in which a wooden statue of a black Christ, brightly adorned in purple robes, stares out from behind a veil of glass. In the corner, a group of young women are singing a mass in Spanish, and the sweet echo of their voices resonates around us. The glory of Portobelo—once measured in the treasures that sailed from here in the hulls of galleons—is now embedded in the heritage of the worn rock and cultural memory of those left behind.

Normally a quiet fishing village, today Portobelo is swarming with people, and I soon understand why. The annual festival of the Black Christ begins today, and the streets are packed with pilgrims who have come to pay penance. The festival honors the large wooden sculpture of the black Christ that washed ashore from a shipwreck a couple of centuries ago. Villagers tried once to return it, and some natural catastrophe washed over them, convincing them to keep it here and honor it. Now it has become the patron saint of thieves—who, as the dregs of humanity, must suffer similar fates of rejection in their own lives. And today they come—pickpockets, burglars, and other petty thieves, all seeking redemption. Some wear dark-purple dresses and robes, and a few carry heavy wooden crosses on their shoulders. Many have walked here from Panama City, dragging their crosses with them. The greater the guilt to be atoned for, the greater the suffering must be.

By now, I notice that some of the pilgrims have worked themselves into a glassy-eyed, sweating intensity. It strikes me they may have transcended into some higher thief-zen. But then again, the liquor is already flowing freely, and some are likely hammered by the combination of warm tropical sun and alcohol. Either way, I instinctively zip up my bag to keep its contents safe from any backsliders. A pirate, even with penance, may succumb to moral temptation, especially when half-addled. During Drake's time, soldiers and sailors and merchants assembled here once a year for a trading fair, just before the *flota* sailed back to Spain. Portobelo seemed the center of the entire universe, its "fair" a sybaritic over-the-top exhibition that celebrated the wealth of New World exploitation. The spirit of wild abandon was heady, exhilarating, as if it would all never end. This celebration is as close as Portobelo is likely to come to recreating the spirit and raucousness of that time, and I am glad I am here to experience it. A choir is singing, perhaps a hymn, and a procession of some sort is snaking through the throngs, a quarter-size replica of the Black Christ thrust above them all on a stick. Vendors have set up tables in which the icon is sold in nearly every form—as sugar treats, as little plaster figurines, even as refrigerator magnets. *Señor, Protect Us!* they implore in Spanish. *Protect Us All, in Our Lives and in Our Homes.* The singing turns to chanting, the procession to a dance, and the Black Christ bobs and weaves above it all. We are making one final dive this afternoon—the one I have waited so long for—and so I forgo a cold *cerveza Balboa* and instead buy a paper cup of shaved ice with some sweet red liquid dribbled on top. I am in a full sweat myself, sunburned and fatigued from too much time under the sun, and the sugar rush of the treat is welcome.

We are finally ready to search for Drake's actual lead coffin, and given the circumstances of the fiesta, our mission seems encumbered with great irony. With the help of the dive shop owner back in Panama City, I have prearranged to meet with a wealthy Panamanian sport diver who is an amateur underwater treasure hunter. His name is Billy Abundía, and he tells me his family runs a rum distillery called Castilla de Oro, Castle of Gold. "That was once the name of Panama," says Abundía, a history buff who speaks excellent English. "When people would think of gold and treasure, they would think of us." Abundía wears a two-escudo coin around his neck, an artifact he salvaged from some colonial-era wreck off Panama's Caribbean coast. He is clearly anxious about the prospect of hunting for *El Dragón,* that—despite the enormous odds against us—we may actually find *something.* Certainly, his own confidence is pleasantly infectious, and our maritime needle in a haystack actually begins to feel as if might be realized.

We have hired a local boat, another fisherman's pirogue, and Abundía and I load our gear onto it, along with two metal detectors. The photographer, who is convinced that we will find nothing and see nothing worth recording, doesn't bother to come along. Following Michael Turner's original directions, we ask the boatman to head out as close to one league off the mouth of the harbor as we can get. Here, the depth finder shows 120 feet—an astounding depth for an inland cove. We lean backward over the wooden gunnel and plunge overboard, sinking under the same waters where *El Pirata Draque* once sailed. I find the anchor rope and pull my self hand-over-hand down on it, following Abundía's flippers.

Visibility is a scant fifteen feet or so, and Abundía—who is eager to get to the bottom—disappears quickly down the rope, and in moments is well out of sight. I am cocooned inside a narrow bluish reality that I take with me as I descend, losing sight of the hull of our boat and the surface within seconds. There is no up or down, past or present, only the rope that dangles mysteriously toward me from somewhere deeper in the blue, an aquatic beanstalk. And I, a reluctant version of the mythic Jack, follow, going down instead of up, headed to where it leads me and hoping, at the very least, in the muted nitrogen-buzzed twilight of my mind, not to find giants there.

The sea floor finally materializes before me, a moonscape of fine gray silt without a sign of life. It seems like early dusk down here, the silt in the water above us almost fully screening out the bright afternoon light. It is disconcerting in its starkness, spooky almost. *Protect us, Señor, in our lives and in our homes. Protect us all.* I look over and see Abundía stick his arm down into the bottom, all the way up to his shoulder. This bottom is only an illusion; it is nearly liquid; the real hard bottom may be many yards under it. Then the two of us—Spanish adventurer and gringo interloper—sweep across this faux bottom with our metal detectors, back and forth, stirring up thick clouds of mire as we do. I loose track completely of my dive partner, and left with no other plan, simply keep repeating my gesture. If Drake is here, he is somewhere deep, deep beneath us. Even if we get a hit on a detector, it would take more time than we have to actually lay hands upon his tomb.

I think to myself what a wildly delusional act this is, the notion of searching for a dead Englishman and his glory, four centuries old, down here in some dimly-lit underworld. But what is delusion in its highest form if not romance?

If so, it is a bewildered romance, one that looks out blindly now from inside a dark cloud of silt, excising time with each exhalation. I listen closely for the wail of the woeful trumpets, the report of the guns. But all I hear is the sound of my own heart as it pulses the blood against my ears, as rhythmic and loud as the drumbeat of any pirate's brigade.

The Amazon's Pink Boto

The Dolphin That Would Be Man

It is late afternoon in the deepest reaches of the Peruvian Amazon, and the Yacumama—the protective, anaconda-like river spirit that turns nasty when disturbed—is asleep somewhere under my dugout. Stay sleeping, I tell it as I push my heart-shaped paddle down into the tea-colored waters of the Río Samiria. I'm not here to do your critters any harm. Never mind the four red-bellied piranha lying at my feet—I didn't catch them, Meneo the cabin boy did.

I have been here on *El Delfín,* a forever-listing tub of a riverboat, for ten days now with American biologist Tamara McGuire, photographer Layne Kennedy, and a small crew, headed upstream from Iquitos. We are well inside *la selva profunda*—the deep forest—searching for the most endangered of all the cetaceans, the freshwater dolphin known as the *boto.*

Classified as *Inia geofrensis,* it is a peculiar critter, a living ocean fossil with a pinkish cast to its skin, an odd, narrow beak, and an exhalation that can sound a bit like a human snore. It is also considered *encantado,* and its reputation for having powerful magic may have helped save it from extinction: a live boto can change at will into a seductive woman or man capable of bewitching humans of the opposite sex. A dead boto is miserable luck, maybe even fatal. Getting on the wrong side of a boto and its enchanted friends is not a very good idea.

Far less mystical are threats by poachers who covet this wilderness for any living thing in it that can be exchanged for money. Armed with machetes and a hard-edged rancor, they pose their own special risk.

So it is into this steamy equatorial world I have gone this afternoon, paddling away from our boat in my borrowed dugout, through the steep and mysterious corridors of vine-tangled green, past the colonies of spider monkeys and the gold-and-blue macaws soaring overhead in the faint gauzy jungle light. By now, a hull crack not quite sealed by the flattened sardine can tacked onto it has begun leaking several inches of river into the *canoa,* and the piranha are flopping back to life at my feet.

Just as I am wondering what is wrong with this picture, I hear a tumultuous splash a few yards away, a commotion that rocks my unsteady, hollow log of a craft. About fifty feet to my left, I see something large roil just under the surface of the black water and then charge toward me inside a giant V of a wake. Just as it reaches my dugout, it dives deep and under, jostling me precariously in the water and leaving a trail of bubbles on both sides like a giant perforated line, as if showing me where it could have gone.

Adrenaline surging, I put down my paddle and grasp the water-rotted gunnels of the dugout to steady it. Although my informed Western intellect explains this as a startled boto, the atavistic core of my deeper reptilian brain tells me it's a Yacumama, it's pissed, and it wants its piranha back. Just as I am considering this, the primitive, angular back of a nine-foot-long pink boto rises up from the string of bubbles and tannin a few yards away and exhales a powerful *whoooosh* from its blowhole. Then, just as suddenly, its bright rosy color dissolves back down into the sepia abyss of water and magic and time.

There is something going on in this dark Amazon that is far beyond biology. In part, it is the tale of tropical, animistic myths that weave a thin line between the world of the real and the supernatural. But more disturbingly, it is also the story of eco-mayhem—of vengeful and macabre murders of the sort that not even the equatorial jungle, with its piranha and caimans and deadly *fer de lance* snakes, can wish on a human. It is the tragic drama of what can happen when the timeless morality of storytelling loses its power, and the simple greed of humans take its place.

Something is missing from my Aeroperu flight to Iquitos, and it finally occurs to me that it is Peruvians. Most aboard are either ecotourists—earnest folks in earth colors and hiking boots—or soul-saving missionaries, many of whom seem lifted intact out of Peter Matthiessen's *At Play in the Fields of the Lord.* One of the leaders of the latter contingent is a heavy man with a T-shirt reading: Apostle Paul's Full Gospel Travel Service.

We skim the edge of the Andes, flying in the darkness above where streams and rivulets flow out of these mountains to create the genesis of the Amazon. Down we go to Iquitos, some 2,300 miles from the river's mouth. Soon, we are off the plane and into an *al fresco* terminal, the air close and thickly scented with citronella. Once outside, I run a gauntlet of frantic vendors and would-be porters who try to snatch my bag off my shoulder, climb aboard a taxi minivan, and slide back my window for ventilation. Immediately, shards of the rainforest are pushed into my face—stunning blue morpho butterflies and tarantulas under glass, necklaces and headdresses of feathers and teeth, even a pelt of jaguar fur.

Do-lars, everyone is yelling, *do-lars.* The theme for this place is quickly being established, and that theme is desperation.

A night of restless sleep in Iquitos finally takes me to where I need to be: aboard *El Delfín,* a battered *Fitzcarraldo*-era riverboat that will carry me far upstream into the jungle over the next two weeks, back into a pre-Nintendo era of wood fires and yucca root, where river villagers have not yet been lured into the mutant Iquitos version of material exploitation.

Off we go from the shaky wooden dock, our engines clattering against a strong current in the clay-colored water, floating logs and debris pounding into our hull with dull thuds. We pass sawmills carving giant tropical hardwood trees into lumber, families hand-lining for fish from dugouts, an entire waterfront ghetto of thatched huts built on rafts, ready to float with the wet-season flood.

After an hour of this, we are far enough upstream to be free of the city sprawl, out into the vast floodplain of a river just beginning to be fed by the impending rainy season. Low tropical savannas spread out from both sides of the boat, feral shrub and shoals and muddy banks that will soon be swamped when the Amazon—full with upland rain— rises a good thirty-seven feet over the next few months. Great, water-rich cumulus billow around us, a hydrological cycle made vital by the world's largest rainforest.

Soon we pass the confluence where the Marañón and Ucayali surge together to create the Río de las Amazonas, and our intrepid native captain—with no maps or GPS or radar—heads up the main stem, the Río Marañón, intuitively wrangling the ship's wooden wheel to keep us off the shallow bars. We are aiming for the isolated Pacaya-Samiria Reserve, a gigantic protected wetland the size of New Jersey where Peruvians are struggling to preserve the best of the Amazon, a refuge of primal fifteenth-century wilderness in an ever-accelerating modern world.

The fine American poet Elizabeth Bishop first lured me here with "The Riverman," a poem she wrote when she was living in South America years ago. "Riverman" captured the Amazonian lore of the boto, telling the story of how a villager is bewitched when a dolphin arises one night and grunts beneath his window. Enticed from his wife to dolphin cities beneath the water, he meets a tall, beautiful river spirit and falls under her spell, gradually becoming more boto than human. Finally, the Amazon's full utility becomes clear:

> everything we need
> can be obtained from the river.
> It drains the jungles; it draws
> from trees and plants and rocks
> from half around the world,
> it draws from the very heart
> of the earth the remedy
> of each of the diseases.

If this poem-myth stirred the romantic in me, it also touched the conservationist. This was not just a critter with magical powers but a sort of natural guardian, one who protected the sustainability of the river by its enchantment.

Upstairs on the top deck, I hear biologist McGuire setting up her dolphin-watching paraphernalia, tin panels of the uneven decking booming like timpani with every move. With her are five sober Oceanic Society volunteers who are paying their own way to help with the research. Since both the photographer and I will also fill in as volunteers over the next two weeks, we leave our closet-sized cabins—cooled only by screen doors and tiny oscillating fans—and climb the steep metal stairway to see what our duties will be.

McGuire, on her seventeenth visit to this region, is a striking mix—at once tenacious and vulnerable, independent and vivacious. On solo trips, she has traveled by herself hundreds of miles upstream, hitching a ride on one of the river ferries, congested cattleboats where native passengers cook over charcoal fires on the decks and string hammocks in the sweltering holds to sleep. ("Compared to that, this is the *QE II*," she says of the austere *El Delfín*.) A doctoral candidate at Texas A&M, McGuire is also working with a local nonprofit agency, Pro Naturaleza, on grassroots conservation programs in the river villages. Clearly, she is trying hard to reach far beyond the traditional role of the do-gooder gringo from the developed world to become one willing to be changed by the transcendental knowledge of people and place. In a nutshell, it is what sets her apart from the missionaries who leave as rigid and unbending in their strident Western beliefs as they arrive.

McGuire studies both the boto and the tucuxi, a miniature bottle-nose-like dolphin often found in boto territory, but it is clear the boto is the most intriguing for her. "It's a fascinating animal—an oceanic relic," she says of the *Inia*. "They are *plasticoides,* more closely related to sperm whales than to marine dolphins." Although a specimen was first collected in 1790, the boto seems to have been left out of the loop of the trendy, modern field of marine mammal science. Found in murky waters in remote locales, research is difficult—indeed, most of what is known was just discovered within the past decade.

"With river dolphins, there's so few experts to tell you what to do," says McGuire. "It's basically: 'Here's the river, here's the dolphin, go do what you want.'" There are four other groups of freshwater dolphins around the world; while all are threatened by human impacts, the population here in the Amazon Basin is the most remote and thus seems to be in the best shape.

Swift and far more social, the tucuxi *(Sotalia fluviatilis)* could return to the ocean any time to hunt, says McGuire. But the story of the boto is far different—indeed, its prehistoric limitations first chased it from the sea into rivers around the world when the faster-moving dolphinoids evolved some ten to fifteen million years ago. Unable to compete for food with its more efficient oceanic cousins, the boto learned to put its own peculiar body structure to good use in freshwater: today, when the rainforest floods, the boto—with no fused vertebrae to keep it stiff—

weaves in and out of the drowned treetops, grabbing slower and larger fish in its long, teethy beak.

I contemplate this for a while, then suggest the boto may be to marine dolphins what the Neanderthal was to *Homo sapiens.* McGuire agrees—but not before giving me a baleful you-just-kicked-my-puppy look.

By the time McGuire is done orienting us to field observation—recording weather and water conditions as well as dolphin behavior—a bronze twilight has begun to infuse this Lost World around us. Unlike the downstream Amazon in Brazil where the river banks may be miles apart, here the river is only several hundred feet wide, creating a feeling of intimacy with every leaf, branch, and liana vine. This intimacy becomes more profound when our captain steers us out of the channel, noses the bow of *El Delfín* up into the jungle, ties up to a ceiba tree, and calls it a night.

On a battered wooden table in an open-air breezeway of a deck between the cabins and the bath stalls, we feast on a hearty meal of freshly caught river catfish and yucca root and rice. It is a variation we will eat in one form or another for the next two weeks. At dinner, McGuire explains we will soon be entering the reserve, and once there, we will check in at the first "ranger station." There, I will learn more about a giant endangered fish called a *paiche,* and how poachers—angered by enforcement of laws to protect it—recently went on a grisly rampage.

By the time we finish our meal, the jungle is etched with fireflies and alive with unseen rustlings and gurglings. I sip a glass of *masato,* a mildly alcoholic drink made when village women chew and then spit yucca root into a wooden trough to ferment. Overhead, the sky is ablaze from end to end with constellations of the Southern Hemisphere. When I climb in my bunk, the last thing I hear before I fall asleep are the snorts of a boto, exhalations that later seem to speak to me from deep inside my own strange tropical dreams, near-hallucinogenic epics fueled by masato, the strong antimalaria drug Larium, and the luxuriant expectation of what is to come.

Ranger station number 1 appears off our port bow in the morning mist, a ramshackle tin-roofed cabin perched up on stilts in a small clearing cut at the edge of the jungle. *Guardaparques,* paid about U.S.$100 a month, grow their own crops in the clearing, raise chickens, and catch fish so they'll have enough to eat. On the ground next to the station are several giant mahogany logs confiscated from timber-cutters who had intended to float them downstream to Iquitos. Rangers were trained and stations built with critical support from the U.S.-based Nature Conservancy, but the start-up funds are virtually gone, and the Peruvian government—which is in its own fiscal quagmire—seems to be having trouble taking up the slack.

We are on the Río Samiria now, and in contrast to the clay-colored, Andes-fed mainstem, the Samiria and its creeks flow out of local wetlands, creating tannic, tea-colored waters like those I have seen in swamps back in the southeastern United States. The hothouse of biodiversity that spreads out around me is stunning: in the woods, 750 different types of trees have been identified in one hectare (2.4 acres). Throughout the entire river, some three thousand species of fish exist—many found nowhere else on earth.

As *El Delfín* crawls off upriver, photographer Kennedy, myself, and Peruvian naturalist Beder Chávez remain behind with a small motor launch, planning to catch up later in the day. The meager reserve staff, isolated out here at the edge of the world, welcome the chance to explain their dire plight. I notice the boto are literally swarming in the river next to the station, arching out of the blackwater in spectacular displays of pink.

Chávez is a naturalist and anthropologist who grew up in one of the Amazon villages, a former "ribereño" who now speaks five languages, paints, and writes poetry. As we walk into the cabin, Chávez casually points out fresh machete marks left from when six poachers forced their way into the station, hacked one man to death, and then bound the other two and threw them into the river. Chávez shrugs, a typical Latin American gesture of fatalistic acceptance, and then we all sit in a large, shabby room and listen to two rangers who are left to tell the sad details of the story.

The poachers, they say, were angry after rangers confiscated illegal paiche, along with expensive nets used to catch the endangered fish. The paiche, after all, is highly prized for its sweet, white meat in restaurants back in Iquitos. The slow-maturing nine-foot- long adults are prime breeding stock, however; scarce elsewhere, the big, endemic fish has sought refuge in the reserve. And while villagers—most of whom live on rivers at the edge of the protected area—can take subsistence meat from its woods and waters, imperiled critters like jaguars, monkeys, and paiche are off-limits.

Hamstrung by a Peruvian law that doesn't allow them to carry weapons to protect themselves, the defenseless guardaparques were ambushed while they slept at night. The ringleader—who has threatened to return to finish his grisly business—is still at large. Local police, who promised to defend the station, never arrived. I notice little crosses tacked to the walls and doors to commemorate the deaths, and listen to the faint, haunting cry of howler monkeys from deep in forest. Later, Chávez tells me locals believe the station is possessed by restless souls of the murdered men.

I am relieved finally to get into our small launch, which we anchor in the Samiria just offshore from the station. The solitude seems to have appreciable weight, out here on this black Peruvian river enclosed by lush walls of vine-woven jungle, no noise but the exhalation of the dolphins and the odd call of the ovapendula bird, electronic droplets from somewhere in the canopy. For the next three hours, we sit and watch as the boto swim and snort around the boat, sounding deep in great splashes if they surface and find themselves too close.

It is an extraordinary display, made even more so whenever a pink-skinned dolphin raises his great primitive head from the water and looks directly at me. It is the singular glance of an animal alive when dinosaurs roamed the earth. I wonder finally how they must think of us, their new relatives—a species that would mortally wound its own kind over something as transitory and fleeting as a few dollars.

I am up to my neck in the Amazon, just in my swimsuit now, and the tea-colored water in this *tipishca*—oxbow lake—is so dark my lower body seems to dissolve into it. It is midday and, along with McGuire and Kennedy, I have leaped off the bottom deck of *El Delfín* to cool off from the oppressive Amazon heat. The bites I've been enduring from the plague of miniwasps that descend on us daily are soothed by the cool, deep river water, but the swiftness of the current—even here out of the mainstream—startles me.

Before I took the dip, I asked Chávez what perils might await me. "Piranha. Anaconda. Caiman," he said, before breaking into a broad grin. "For the American mind they are great dangers—but only in your movies." I have seen the crew catching piranha over the last few days with cane poles—have even caught a few myself. So I know the muscular little fish sports a set of iron jaws bracketed with sharp, triangular teeth, of the sort that surely looks capable of stripping the flesh off a human leg in a few seconds.

Like sharks, their reputation is mostly the stuff of melodrama, though "Piranha are opportunistic feeders," Chávez assures me. "Their teeth are useful for cracking into hard nuts and fruits that fall down into the flooded rainforest." Anyway, most of the fish stay up close next to the shore, rather than out here in the deeper waters.

After we climb out and towel off, McGuire tells me of another concern, a mythological one: "The crew has asked me, 'If you swim in the same water with the boto, won't they come and take you away?'" Certainly, it is a valid question, especially for those who live on an isolated jungle river, where stories told over a smoke fire have not yet lost their magic to newspaper or television or shopping malls.

I learn more of this two days later, when we land at Enero de Veinte, a small village on the Yanayacu River. As we sit under an open thatched-frond hut at the edge of the steep mud bank, Chávez tells me more about the river dolphin myths he learned as a youngster. Around us, Cocamillo Indian children watch us with alert, almond-shaped eyes. Nearby, I notice a ribereño has tied huge snail shells to the trunk of a lime tree in the belief it will help bear more fruit. At the water's edge, a young woman takes off her T-shirt and washes it along with other laundry, then lays it to dry on the banks.

"This was told to me by my grandmother," says Chávez, in preface:

> The young male dolphin comes out of the water at night and changes into a handsome man, wearing a white suit—with a hat to hide his blowhole. . . . He comes into the village and picks the prettiest girl and dances with her, and she is bewitched—she must follow him.
>
> And they go to the dolphin cities under the river, where the anacondas are the hammocks and walking catfish are the shoes and water snakes are belts. They have great parties, and when the girl returns, she is pregnant by the dolphin.

In many villages even today, Chávez explains, babies believed to have such paternity are named "Delfín."

I am back on the boat and it is groaning and clanking downstream, toward Iquitos, our journey's end. We have counted some 286 boto over the last two weeks, and McGuire seems buoyed by this. But when I ask her about the stories of enchantment, she admits the younger villagers—as well as those who have been exposed to the tarnished glitz of Iquitos—are increasingly forsaking the legends that have kept the jungle hallowed for so long. The vengeful poachers are the most disturbing examples of this, she says. There are more furtive threats, however, like the fishermen who now poison the boto because it rips their nets to get the fish inside.

"The boto is a keystone species in many ways, both in science and myth," says McGuire. "Once its 'magic' is gone and the rainforest becomes less sacred, then only human laws are left to protect it." But such laws, in a poor country with dwindling funding for education or enforcement, have little clout.

It is enough to make me long for superstition, for a condition of jungle magic that is sustained—not by our vague human presumptions—but by our belief in the eternal power of serpent gods who lay sleeping under us in the cool and bewitching Amazon river mud.

Turks and Caicos

Sea Wranglers Herd

Giant Snails

There is pandemonium at the queen conch farm this afternoon.
A killer is loose, and the remains of his victims lay at our feet
under seven feet of clear seawater out here in the southernmost
Atlantic, at the edge of a tropical island cove a hundred miles north
of Haiti.

"Look down," says Chuck Hesse, the head conch farmer, who is
treading water in skin-diving gear, "and you will come face to face
with death." Hesse is only half kidding. I do look down, peering
through my mask to the sandy bottom. Here, I see shards of pink and

amber and white shell gleaming back at me in the late afternoon sun, sure signs of a mollusk crushed to smithereens.

"There's a predator loose here, somewhere," says Hesse, raising his head from the water and looking over his shoulder, as if it might still be nearby, ready to pounce. A predator to a conch—spiny lobster, box crab, tulip shell—is of little danger to you and me. Unless, of course, you happen to have a stake in the survival of the two million conch *(Strombus gigas)* ensconced here in the Turks and Caicos Islands on the world's first commercial farm. And Hesse, who has devoted most of his adult life to that quest, surely has a stake. So too should anyone who cares that wild stocks of conch—a vital local source of high protein for centuries—are now vanishing from the Caribbean Basin because of overfishing.

We sink back underwater, look some more. A small gold and blue damsel fish flits in and out of a hunk of black sponge sitting atop a hard bottom of sand and seagrass. Flat-top bristle bush plants are scattered about like teensy trees. A green moray peeks out from the end of a discarded section of PVC pipe, cautious. Everywhere, conch are grazing like aquatic sheep, their trunklike mouths stretching out from under their pink shells, quietly slurping algae bits from the sand and grass.

If this sea farm has certain links to husbandry back on land, it's no coincidence. After all, the giant snaillike animals are born, raised, and harvested like terrestrial livestock. But there are marked contrasts with cows and chickens—not the least of which is the reality that this "Caicos Conch Farm" is in the midst of our last global frontier, the ocean itself.

Life here in the Caribbean Basin is both flavored by the marine environment and at the mercy of it. Equinoctial tides, northeasterly storms, newly emerging mariculture science, and the whimsical uncertainty of tropical island life and politics all influence survival, for both conch and conch farmer.

"This is all like a floating opera," says Hesse, referencing John

Barth's dark comic novel by the same name. "If you stand here in one place long enough, all the pieces of the plot will pass by, and the whole story will finally emerge."

Hesse is commuting to work on Providenciales Island on a late winter afternoon, bouncing along in a dusty red dune buggy, top down and warm air whipping through his hair and beard. He is barefoot, wearing a flowered shirt and shorts, and has a battered briefcase wedged down behind his seat. The land he drives over is ancient coral reef, now compressed by time into low-profile limestone hills and swales. Educated at the U.S. Naval Academy as an ocean engineer, Hesse worked aboard nuclear subs before taking an early retirement to find out how the ocean was really engineered. In 1973 he sailed eastward across the Caribbean in a wooden sloop with his then wife, aiming to do field studies on the queen conch in Barbados. Along the way, a tropical storm chased them to a safe harbor in the Turks and Caicos, a self-governing British overseas territory he didn't even know existed. When the sun reappeared, Hesse found himself surrounded by conch. And although his wife later left, he stayed.

Providenciales—Americanized as "Provo"—is the biggest and most populated of this archipelago, which consists of eight large islands and forty smaller cays out here in the ocean north of Hispaniola. Until the mid-1960s, Provo consisted of three tiny villages where locals fished and farmed subsistence vegetables. Without electricity, roads, cars, or an airstrip, Provo existed as it had a century earlier, with native fishermen sailing out to the nearby reef and shallow banks in small, hand-built boats. There, leaning over the gunnels, they hooked conch and lobsters and sponges using long wooden poles with iron shanks on the end.

The outside world has since arrived on Provo. On his fifteen-minute ride today, Hesse passes an eighteen-hole golf course, a 230-room Ramada, the heavily guarded entrance to a Club Med, and the upscale Grace Bay Club, where suites are priced at seven hundred dollars a day in the high season. Resort developers have grafted entire south Florida landscapes onto the maritime terrain, importing nonnative date palms and bright shiny grasses, which they keep alive with desalinized seawater.

But Hesse's drive also takes him past The Bight, a native fishing village where modest wood and block homes in pastel colors crowd up to the edge of a limestone bluff overlooking the green-blue sea. Surrounding the little cottages are entire tracts of wild natural flora, endemic island-hardy plants like the stunted silver palm, lignum vitae, sea grapes, and tamarind that require no outside investment to sustain. Elsewhere, in the isolated fishing villages of Blue Hills and Five Cays, it is largely the same. Native families still persevere with the surnames of the British Loyalist planters—Stubbs, Gardner, Williams—who brought them here as slaves after the American Revolutionary War. Closer to the conch farm, the asphalt turns to limestone rut and rubble. Finally, a lone wooden sign with cartoonish conch shells on it announces the entrance to the farm itself.

To a casual observer, it might seem Hesse has history on his side in the aquaculture arena. A Chinese how-to treatise, "Fish Breeding," dates to 475 B.C., and the farming of freshwater catfish, crayfish, and trout are now assembly line–like operations in the United States today. But the ocean isn't always as generous with its gifts: the business of commercially growing saltwater animals—despite success stories like penaeid shrimp, salmon, and bay scallops—is still under development. Marine species simply live more complicated lives, often transmuting through numerous larval stages after birth. More to the point, they live in the ocean, a medium that—even with the advent of the aqualung and the advancement of marine science over the last half century—we have only begun to understand.

Inside his tiny office, next to the rusting file cabinets and the dripping wetsuit, where the trade winds waft in from the ocean through the battered screen door, Hesse leans back in a worn wooden chair and reflects back on his relationship with *Strombus*. "They say it takes fifteen years to bring a species into commercial mariculture production," says Hesse. "I'm a little ahead of the game." Despite Hesse's optimism, the road to running the world's first commercial conch farm has been a long and winding one, with more than its share of roadblocks and culs-de-sac.

Although the queen conch wasn't fully described by scientists until the 1960s, attempts to grow it got underway not long afterward. One of the pioneer mariculture labs was on nearby Pine Cay, funded by a charitable foundation Hesse set up soon after his arrival. Its goal was nothing less than to use mariculture, conservation education, and nonpolluting renewable energy—wind generators—to help establish a marine "biosphere reserve." His hope was to alert islanders to sustainable options before tourism arrived and hooked everyone up to a grid of fossil fuel and the consumptive standards of Westernized materialism—excesses already underway in the Caymans, Cozumel, and the busier islands of the Bahamas.

In an era of unabashed earnestness, Hesse called his nongovernmental organization PRIDE—Protection of the Reefs and Islands from Degradation and Exploitation—and no one even flinched. Flush with a handful of grants and a growing membership of mostly affluent yachties, Hesse's PRIDE became the backdrop for groundbreaking conch mariculture work by a retinue of young and shaggy biology grads from the States. No one seemed to mind living in a tent, on a boat, or in a termite-ridden geodesic dome that had been assembled from a kit. Using a small renovated lavatory powered by a windmill and solar panels, the biologists working with PRIDE learned to successfully hatch conch eggs in captivity and even bring them through to metamorphosis. The initial success rates were small, barely more than a dozen conch, but it was a breakthrough nonetheless. It was as if the Fabulous Furry Freak Brothers had merged with Mr. Wizard.

At the conch farm today, there is a hatchery, a massive postlarval "nursery" for young animals, and a "grow-out" pasture for larger ones. While this sounds practiced and known, there are some wonderful stylistic quirks, as fully unique as the animal itself. As form follows function in the creation of the conch shell—the conch absorbing and then reconfiguring calcium carbonate it extracts from seawater—so does the creation of the farm buildings. Cobbled together by local boatwrights, they appear as a fleet of oddly shaped vessels, arches, domes, and silolike turrets sealed from the elements with fiberglass and white marine paint, hulls up and tops down, topsy-turvy forever.

Inside them, baby conch are hatched in large vats and nurtured through a delicate three-week, free-swimming larval stage. After metamorphosis, they settle to the bottom as fully formed miniature conch about the size of pinheads, then transfer to shallow, sand-filled trays where they're fed a special blend of algae. Seawater, pumped and filtered from the cove, trickles into each tray, creating the sound of a hundred tiny waterfalls, enriching the conch's new world with dissolved oxygen. Outside, larger animals graze in circular concrete ponds, feasting on a special fish/plant blend of "Conch Chow" pellets that workers toss to them by hand.

Older conch, the ones with shells strong enough to survive most predation, get tossed out into the fenced eighty-acre "pasture," which begins just beyond the sun-hardened limestone at the edge of the farm. "We kick 'em out the door at five centimeters," says Hesse. "They have to go out and hack it with the big boys." The shallow pasture itself lies beneath a stretch of vivid, transparent seawater the color of lime gelatin. Studded with white posts and buoys, and walled with fishermen's nylon seines, it stretches from Boy Stubb's Cove to the edge of the scenic tidal cut descriptively known as Leeward-Going-Through.

With the gentle cascading of seawater, the odd, whimsical-looking assemblage of structures, and the ethereal lime-green "pasture"—all washed by the tropical sun and breeze—this customized queen conch farm seems more than just a place to raise livestock for food. It appears almost drug-induced, maybe something conjured up in the nineteenth century by Lewis Carroll, or in the twentieth by Tom Robbins.

Perhaps it's not surprising that, on Hesse's desk, where an anole lizard is in the midst of a hunt for tropical bugs, there is a Robbins novel in which a queen conch plays a major role. Robbins has written of *Strombus:* "A house exuded by the dreams of its inhabitant, it is the finest example of the architecture of imagination, the logic of desire. . . . It is a bonbon pink, a tropical pink, above all a feminine pink. Colored by the moon, shaped by the primal geometry, it is the original dreamboat."

Never one to miss a chance to merge the cosmic with the mundane, Hesse liked the Robbins passage so much he used part of it in his "Business Plan for Investors."

Catherine Dyer is a British marine biologist who grew up around a green turtle farm in the Cayman Islands where her father was marketing manager. Educated in marine science back in England, Dyer came to the conch farm in 1989 to grow the algae used to feed the hungry young mollusks. It was not an insignificant chore: twelve giant 6,000-gallon outdoor vats produce tons of bright green planktonic algae weekly during the peak growing season.

Today, Dyer, blond and tan from the sun, is production manager for the entire farm. In that role, she spends most of the day in bare feet and shorts, supervising a dozen native technicians and checking on the health and growth rate of her animals—often slipping into a wet suit and mask to monitor the herd in the pasture. "It's a fascinating animal," says Dyer, of the giant marine snail. "I enjoy just watching it."

Strombus, as a meal or a shell, has proved to be eminently engaging. A major food staple in the wider Caribbean for centuries, it has also served duty as a cultural icon. Its lustrous shell was used by pre-Columbian Tainos as both a horn and as a medium to carve *zemis,* god icons. Before the thin soils gave out on their sea-cotton economy, the British planters built their manor homes here of cut limestone blocks, mortared with the powdered shells of conch. Today, the government of the Turks and Caicos has incorporated *Strombus* into their official coat of arms. As such, it snuggles up next to a spiny lobster, bookended by two very pink flamingos.

To illustrate how life begins for the conch, Dyer drags some scuba tanks out of a wooden shed on the dock at the farm's edge. "I'll show you where we usually get the eggs," she says, loading the dive gear into a small dory. Islander Ricardo Forbes, who serves as assistant hatchery manager during the breeding season, joins us, and we head off for the nearby reef, some fifteen minutes away. With encouragement from steady northerly winter winds, whitecaps are frothing up over the reef line like meringue, making it an easy navigational target.

During spawning season, up to a thousand breeder conch were corralled out here, fenced in by the reef and a narrow bottom net just high enough to keep the mollusks from wandering off. Technicians like Forbes would routinely dive this site, gingerly collecting the newly laid egg masses from under female conch to fuel the hatchery back on shore, capturing up to four hundred thousand eggs in a single swipe of the hand.

Even though the site has been marked as "off limits" to divers, it is still under open sea and has been badly poached in the past. Both Dyer and Forbes doubt if more than a handful of mature breeder conch remain; today's visit will help confirm their suspicions one way or the other.

Over five hundred years ago, Columbus wrote in his journal of seeing conch shells as large as "calves' heads" in great numbers throughout the region. Arid, dry islands like the archipelago of the Turks and Caicos traditionally sent its natives to the sea for most of its meat. After the strain of native Taino who lived here vanished, the slaves of the British planters—left behind when their owners sailed away in the early 1800s—learned the skills of boat-building, navigation, and fishing. Like the Taino before them, the sea shaped their habits, their heritage. It was their legacy. Yet today, seagoing options for younger islanders like Forbes are increasingly tenuous, thanks to poor conservation of fish and shellfish throughout the Caribbean—courtesy both of overfishing and loss of coastal habitat to development.

Countrywide, there are now less than 150 working fishermen left today. Once they sailed freely in small sail-drawn smacks or waded and snorkeled in shallow waters; today they use motor-powered boats and scuba-diving gear to take whatever they can find. As a result, the harvest consists of smaller, less mature fish—including conch—taken from deeper waters. Fewer mature adults are left to restock the population. As the marine bounty continues to sag, more islanders now take service-related jobs in the burgeoning tourism industry as porters, dishwashers, waitresses. To native "belongers" like Forbes, the conch farm offers another life choice, a spectacularly eccentric one perhaps, but one with vital natural connections nevertheless, unconfined by walls and rich, bossy tourists. It is a vital cultural option in an island-nation that is quickly becoming a country of waiters. Not so ironically, it is self-respect and pride—in an echo of Hesse's long-ago holistic conservation vehicle, PRIDE—that is at stake.

As Dyer and Forbes lead me underwater today, I see a healthy coral reef alive with gobies, damsels, angels, and grunts. But on the adjacent seafloor, the pasture of sand inside the low bottom net is bereft of conch. Dyer's herd of breeders has been rustled, no doubt by someone hoping to cash in on the ten dollars apiece the shells can fetch on shore (conch meat itself is less lucrative booty, usually commanding only about three dollars a pound dockside). This means they'll have to collect several hundred mature conch to restock the egg farm before the next spring breeding season.

As we fin out over the area on the other side of the reef, I spot one lone mature conch, its shell well camouflaged with marine plants, an oasis of life on the white sand. As I move in close, I see a set of beady, stalked eyes protruding through tapered shell groves opposite a spiraled whorl. Mature with its flared pink lip, the mollusk still carries the remnants of its earliest postlarval shell at the tip of its spiral, ancient baggage forever in tow. It is, as Robbins has observed, "a calcified womb, a self-propelled nest."

Slowly, its massive black muscular foot snakes out, gaining traction in the sand with its clawlike operculum. Suddenly, with a herky-jerky thrust, it actually *hops* forward. *Strombus* is on the move, searching for food—or perhaps fleeing the giant bubbling predator that hovers over it. It is this muscular foot that is the conch's undoing: skinned and pounded, it becomes white, seamless meat, tasting a bit like a cross between abalone and sea scallop, tender as veal when fresh, twangy as rubber when frozen too long or poorly cooked.

I move my hand above its eyes, and the animal with the most advanced vision of all the mollusks quickly withdraws. I turn over its heavy shell and see an underside varnished smooth with new calcium. And, yes, Robbins is right again: the color is an astounding pink . . . a bonbon pink, a tropical pink . . . above all, a feminine pink.

Later, back at the farm, I watch as Dyer fills in as tour guide, shepherding a band of tourists from Club Med through the facility, showing them thousands of tiny juvenile conch in the process. And the cosmic, once more, comes face to face with the mundane. "Now I want you to tell me," demands a sunburned woman in plastic visor and fanny pack, "how in the world do you stuff all those things into those little shells?"

On a balmy Caribbean winter afternoon, the tropical sun bouncing off the water over Provo tints the thick cumulus a light but unmistakable mint green, creating a sky of marmalade. Hesse, who spends far more time than he likes with administrative chores, is today making a snorkeling visit to a fenced subsection of the grow-out pasture. Here, some 150,000 three-year-olds graze in aquatic bliss. "This is more than you'll find in the entire Florida Keys," says Hesse, referring to a once-rich environment now decimated by overfishing. Indeed, the great irony back in the "Conch Republic" of the Keys is all the conch served in local restaurants must be imported—usually from Venezuela, the Bahamas, or the Turks and Caicos.

Although thousands of pounds of farmed conch and shells were sold and millions of larval conch released to the sea earlier in the 1990s, the first large-scale harvest of seventy thousand four-year-old animals was delayed until 1997. Today, the farm produces some two million animals a year, not only providing jobs to locals but taking an immense pressure off wild stocks of conch. Hesse has also learned to be a bit of a marketeer: instead of waiting four years for an adult conch to grow to full size, he has begun selling smaller juvenile mollusks in the shell—not unlike clams, oysters, or escargot. And he has found American importers who specialize in seafood that has benefited by conservation. The result is an increased demand for his farmed product and, in turn, a burgeoning conch herd. More conch mean more Crown land needs to be leased, more nursery facilities built. It's always something.

Hesse, always sanguine, is also stoic. His tenaciousness is a large part of what has kept him so single-minded about conch for so long—especially here in the Caribbean Basin, where almost anything goes. Long after other expats have sailed away on the horizon, Hesse remains.

I have been watching Hesse for some time now, and finally, it dawns on me that he is not unlike Conrad's Lord Jim, the once officious and proud officer whose original journey detoured him into a distant corner of the tropics. Here he has remained, vision reshaped perhaps, but always dedicated and unwavering. He will likely be here until the end.

His mission to resupply the region with conch, and thus reaffirm its cultural destiny, has surely been tested. Prime ministers with special political whims come and go. Hesse and his conch farm and conservation ethic are in favor now, but there were some years when they weren't. (During one particularly shaky administration, a scheme to allow an

American company to dump toxic waste on nearby West Caicos was even proposed, to Hesse's great dismay.)

Beyond politics, island life can be capricious all by itself: in the early years, a fall hurricane blew the roofs off all his nursery buildings; another time, a small band of porcupine fish broke into the pasture and ate nearly twenty-five thousand young conch before workers could wrangle them. Once, a star-crossed conch technician, odd man out in a love triangle with a female employee, burned down the gift shop and education dome as well as a nursery building with three hundred thousand young conch, all in a fit of angst.

"No one ever said farming conch would be easy," admits Hesse, grinning at his grand understatement. With that, he sinks underwater, a solitary conch cowboy out riding the range. Off he floats, over his herd of bonbon-pink mollusks, under a cover of lime-green skies.

Blue Springs

Inside the Heart of a Poem

By late May, the warmer weather of the late Florida winter has already
coaxed the manatees out of the thermal protection of Blue Springs
and into the St. Johns River. I have seen manatees underwater before,
have had them actually approach me, since some manatees—like
people—are simply more curious. We have hung there together in the
clear water, briefly studying each other, this giant herbivorous
mammal and I.

I've been struck with how human the animal's eyes seem, pensive
and recessed inside a starburst of deeply-etched wrinkles. It's almost as
if there is a person inside all that insulation. Perhaps the animal thinks
likewise of me—that there may be a manatee hidden in there
somewhere, under all that neoprene.

Today, the shallow run of Blue Springs here in east central Florida is filled with snorkelers, their skin raw and goose-fleshed, splashing among the mullet and bass, gar and tilapia. I watch this from a boardwalk at the top of a natural basin that encircles the headspring.

From up here, the cobalt water below seems to pulse, shimmering with the electricity of the earth itself. I've been drawn to springs like this since I was a child. For me, it's never been enough to simply watch the world unfold. I have always yearned to be immersed in the mystery of it all, to see for myself what's around that next bend, inside that mysterious tree line break in the canopy of the woods or that dark cleft in the rock.

Along with a dive buddy, I gear up with air tanks and, after a strenuous slosh against the upstream current of the run, fin away from the shallow sandy bottom, out to where the spring churns at the surface. Sinking below, I navigate through a giant fork created by two fallen logs. Under me, the cavern plunges sharply, then angles gradually into a black chasm in the limestone. The eighteenth-century Quaker naturalist Billy Bartram once sat on the banks of Blue, and later wrote in wonder of the "diaphanous fountain" that surged below him. Entire tribes of fish vanished into it—where did they go, and why? There was magic here, like nothing he'd ever seen.

His descriptions of springs along this river inspired the romantic poet Samuel Taylor Coleridge to write of Kubla Khan, *where Alph, the sacred river, ran / Through caverns measureless to man / Down to a sunless sea.* I would give all I have if Bartram could be next to me today, could feel the full sway of this natural "ebullition," down here inside of his spring.

As I go, I must fin hard to push against the fierce upwelling of Bartram's ether, cool current pressing my mask deep into the flesh of my face. Looking closely in the soft rock around me, I see subliminal clues to the prehistoric sea that accrued to form, first, the platform and, then, the crust of Florida. The clues are fossilized shells, still ribbed like a scallop, or cupped round like a clam. They are welded together by the dust of Eocene coral, whale skull, oceanic sand, an assemblage of calcium turned white as bone. I am traveling into the cellar of Florida, descending past ledges protruding from the rock, walls sculpted like gentle, vertical waves by a prehistoric water flow. I bump into one ledge, and as I push off, I feel the softness of it, more marly clay than hard rock.

At sixty feet, where the muted surface light fully disappears, a metal sign warns divers without special training to go no farther. It reads simply: Prevent Your Death. I've been schooled in the peculiar behaviors of cave diving, so I turn on my underwater light and let its beam pull me downward. It seems puny, dim, nearly absorbed by the darkness. Scuba tanks, face masks, containers of light—they're all reminders of how unsuited we humans are to travel inside the most primal element of all.

The water I swim against is cool enough to chill me inside my thin wetsuit. I take my regulator out and gulp a mouthful. It is pure, with the vague taste of a sunless sea. Like other springs, Blue is recharged by rainfall seeping down through rocky fissures and fractures upland from here. As the weight of the water in the rock builds from above, the water below seeks out faults and fissures where it might escape. Indeed, if caves are the capillaries and veins of our aquifer, then springs and sinks are the natural incisions through which it most clearly expresses itself.

The journey of water through the rock is not a straight or easy one, however, and the delay between the time rain falls from the sky and when it emerges from the limestone is wondrous. Elsewhere along the St. Johns, hydrologists have dated the age of spring water. At Croaker Hole, a dark, river-bottom vent I will later visit, water has been trapped in the rock for 3,900 years. At Salt Springs, for 7,000 years.

Perhaps the water I taste now once fell as rain when the earliest Native Americans who lived here were still alive, even fell on and around them. The pre-Columbian Timucua had a word for this water. *Ibi,* they called it, and it was cool and eternal and everlasting. They drank it, bathed in it, paddled their dugouts across it. Their reverence for *ibi* was not separate and apart from their life but woven into it—as sure as the rise of the sun and moon over the wild Florida landscape.

It disturbs me that us moderns, with our science and our human presumptions, are convinced we can solve all our problems with just a little bit more technology. But the truth is we are taking out more water from this aquifer than nature is putting back in. Florida is big, driven by growth now, and our thirst is great. For the first time in our history, the liquid energy that once shaped the destiny of this entire peninsula is being shaped by us. We have taken ownership of *ibi* away from the gods and, in doing so, affected the enchantment of the watershed itself. And if water has lost its sacredness, can mere human law ever atone for it?

I often wonder if there is penance for ravaging such inviolability, wonder if we can ever be fully redeemed for mistakes of this scale. I have no easy answers, so I do what I can. And now, all I can do is to breath—slowly in and out—and, down here in the darkness, let the rainfall of the Timucua consume me. I turn myself over to it, promising only reverence.

At 120 feet, the force of the water surging out of the limestone crevice below is massive. Even if the throat of the cave were larger, the power of its flow would keep me from going farther inside. At this depth, the pressure of the water above gives me the vague feeling of being shrink-wrapped. I hold on with both hands to a boulder near the darkest hole and let the energy coming from it blow my body up and away, suspending my torso in the swirling ether, flailing my legs.

I'm deep inside Bartram's diaphanous magic now, my exhaust bubbles rising like domes of mercury and becoming part of the upwelling roil of Alph that swells and—finally—drifts away to the surface. Off it flows, this confluence of springwater and poetry and exhalation, past the tribes of humans and fish, down the spring run, to the river, and toward the sea.

Florida Keys

Beyond the Neon, a Backcountry

The tropical wind is relentless, whipping the bejesus out of the canopy of towering red mangroves and churning the water around this small uninhabited island into surging whitecaps. Here, atop a narrow sandy ridge barely a foot above sea level, I am at once thankful for the shelter and mildly anxious about my condition. Sooner or later, I will have to re-mount my kayak and return to the sailboat from where I came, back in the lee of another islet a half mile to the west—across a deep channel with swells and impressive two-foot waves.

For now, I step carefully through this rarefied environment, looking for natural clues special to the place. As I do, the dark red limbs of the gumbo limbo rub against each other overhead, playing an eerie bass riff, the sound of a string instrument with only one string.

In my mind, I catalog the uniqueness of what I've seen since we put ashore here: the bronze-bellied mangrove snake on the mat of sea grass at the water's edge; the porcelain-like shell of *Liguus,* the tree snail; the hoofprints the size of a half dollar in the wet sand, the track of a white-tailed deer squeezed down to the size of a collie.

This is the seldom-seen face of the Florida Keys, an archipelago where the whimsy and isolation of island life has mutated nature into something apart from what it used to be. Some might say the residents here have been configured likewise, manifesting the glorious eccentricities the mainland works so hard to breed out of the rest of us.

To fully appreciate either, I knew I had to get out of the mainstream, far beyond the tiki bars and the T-shirt shops of U.S. 1, and to ease into a natural and cultural wilderness where animals—and humans—exist wholly untethered to the rest of the so-called civilized world. It's a place where every step or paddle stroke takes me a bit deeper into a territory that is anything but rehearsed and known.

Just as I am wondering about the wisdom of this, Bill Keogh, a local naturalist and outfitter from Big Pine Key, emerges from a tangle of sea grapes at the windward edge of this island. Keogh and I have sailed out here in the Gulf and then, after offloading two sea kayaks from his sloop, paddled to where we are now. He is smiling a quiet smile, which may mean just about anything, since Keogh seems to approach most of life this way. He is also carrying a two-foot-long snake, much like the one I saw earlier. The snake seems to have freeze-framed itself in mid-crawl, not quite sure what else to do. He hands me the snake, and inexplicably, I accept it. The snake tries to bite me—I am not used to handling them—and I drop it.

"Well, it ought to be pretty good going back," Keogh says, brightly. This bewilders me since the wind still seems to be thrashing the daylights out of the mangroves, and the two-foot-high waves still look menacing. I pause, uncertain, as freeze-framed as the mangrove snake. Keogh, a soft-spoken master of understatement, elaborates. "That is, pretty good once we reach the sailboat . . . but maybe not so good for having to paddle to it."

These Florida Keys are slabs of ancient reef and calciferous plants, compressed by time and tide into fine, porous limestone, fringed with sand and mangroves and scattered like green pottery shards along the shallow cusp between the Gulf of Mexico and the Atlantic for almost two hundred miles. Windward, they are mirrored by the living reef, a matrix of hard corals, tunicates, sea fans and sponges that grow atop their fossilized 100,000-year-old brethren in thirty to ninety feet of water.

Nurtured by a complex ecological wet system that once covered much of Florida—from the headwaters of the Everglades just south of Orlando to the vast estuarine swash of Florida Bay—the reef itself is as biologically diverse as a rainforest. It is the northernmost reef in the Western Hemisphere, the only one off our continent. Besides feeding and sheltering gobies and hamlets, lobsters and crabs, rays and sharks, it functions as a magnificent natural sea wall to keep the tiny, low-slung leeward islands and everything that lives on them from washing away.

Throughout history, this reef has also driven the local economy—snagging wooden hulls of sailing ships for pirates and wreckers, growing sponges, conch, and turtle for early fishermen. For the bootleggers and drug smugglers and treasure salvors who followed in the early twentieth century, the shoals of the reef and the maze of islands were every bit as valuable. Rachel Carson, this country's premier environmental writer, spent some time here in the mid-1950s and left in awe. "The world of the Keys has no counterpart elsewhere in the United States," she wrote in *The Edge of the Sea*. "Indeed, few coasts of the earth are like it."

While some 90 percent of the plants and trees of these islands were tropical and water-borne from the Antilles, the animals who roamed the landscape were often continental and temperate. Both had become somewhat transformed by the essential limitations of island life. Some scientists, like Florida naturalist Archie Carr, think the early Keys rivaled Alfred Wallace's Malay Archipelago or Charles Darwin's Galapagos in richness and biodiversity. Maybe the differences in species wasn't as pronounced as the shells of the giant land tortoises or the anatomies of the various finches. But these were still islands, and the more isolated they were from the mainland, the more secrets they were likely to hold. Indeed, biologist Edward O. Wilson, wanting to test his own theory of biogeography, came to these Keys in the mid-twentieth century. Wilson picked one small slab of sand and mangrove, studied it, and came away convinced that biological diversity is limited by the size of any island and by how far it was located from the mainland.

Wilson's point was well-taken: we are, all of us, on an island, a very large one, and it is currently soaring pell-mell through space. When there is less natural land to be had on this global island, there will eventually be less of everything else—including us—to be had, too. Meanwhile, on the true geographic islands that exist, evolution will more clearly transform us into something other than what we used to be. Isolation will adapt, speciate, mutate us. We will prosper in niches, radiating anatomically, to fill them.

As I drive southward from Miami onto the Overseas Highway at the northernmost island of Key Largo, I am keeping my eyes open for signs of this transformation. This archipelago still has a *backcountry*, a place beyond the mainstream where the former chroniclers of local authenticity—from Ernest Hemingway to Jim Harrison and Tom McGuane—might still find a worthwhile reason to exist. It is this backcountry I am looking for, a place where nature is still mysterious and people have a chance to be wonderfully unpredictable.

More to the point, the backcountry here is the territory comprised of eight hundred-odd islands and tiny cays not linked by the Overseas Highway, most scattered westward of it in the Gulf of Mexico and protected inside the boundaries of four national wildlife refuges and one federal park. These are islands stranded, forever out of reach of car or SUV, wondrous in their loneliness and often named for some long-forgotten person or deed: Parjoe, Whaleback, Barnes, Munson, Ballast, Woman, Deadman's. But, as I will soon discover, there is also a sense of backcountry that exists just about anywhere I am willing to look, once I get out of the glow of the neon.

As I travel south, I am following the path the railroad first blazed here in 1912, atop causeways dredged from the limestone and sand, over modern concrete bridges spanning turquoise waters. To the east, shallow-draft sport skiffs with poling towers mounted over the motors cut across the flat water, headed for the flats and a shot at bonefish, maybe some permit. Commercial fishermen hunch over the gunnels of their small boats, hand-pulling wooden slat traps, the ones marked by rounded Styrofoam buoys, hoping for spiny lobster or stone crab but taking whatever they get.

To the west, behind the fringe of mangrove and marl that hugs the road, is Florida Bay, the giant estuarine basin of Everglades National Park, where the freshwater of the upland sawgrass mixes with the salt of the Gulf. The last remaining colony of American crocodiles live here, mean and secretive, sometimes roaming as far south as the islands around Big Pine, my ultimate destination.

I am on Key Largo now, and everything not moving seems to be covered with larger-than-life murals in which angelfish, turtles, and dolphin swim with divers and the mermaids—green, flesh-colored, imbued with sparkles—ever beckon. At a kiosk advertising the Atlantis Dive Shop, a hardy soul known as Capt. Spencer Slate is portrayed in a gigantic photo, preparing to feed a dead fish to a barracuda by holding the bait in his teeth. Nearby, in a cinema-inspired swoon, the Holiday Inn brags of keeping the "Original African Queen" captive at its own little dock. Just down the road, the barnlike Caribbean Club proclaims itself the place "Where the Famous Movie 'Key Largo' was Filmed." This all seems like illusion straining hard for some tangible form.

The Caribbean Club looks rough and tumble, its parking lot full of "Conch Cruisers," rusted and beaten old sedans with local plates, more likely in search of an eye-opening shot and a beer than traces of any *film noir* tryst. Good thing, too, because, only a few brief seconds of the movie were shot here, none of which featured either Bogey or Bacall. Still, myth-making is powerful business: when the Beach Boys first sang "down in the Florida Keys, there's a place called Kokomo" a few years ago, there was no real-life Kokomo to be had. But after the song edged up the charts, several local bars were happy to pick up the slack, shamelessly renaming themselves "Kokomo"—the ultimate act of life imitating art.

It is into these Keys I am going, then, a place where reality is anything if not fluid.

I arrive at Bill Keogh's home at the beginning of rut season on Big Pine, where most of the five hundred pint-sized Key deer left in the world still live. Big Pine is thirty miles and one hour by car north of Key West, but it seems years removed from its glitzier, more sophisticated sister isle. Maybe that's because much of the island is taken up by the Key Deer National Wildlife Refuge. There is simply more room for nature to be.

In the last quarter of the twentieth century, the 110-mile-long road-bridge link connecting forty-three of these keys with each other and the South Florida peninsula became wider and safer. Cruise ships began to dock in Key West and air service became more routine. Between the early 1970s and today, tourism exploded from one to six million visitors annually. Land, always a premium on islands, became more expensive, chasing the characters and the raw Keys raunch back into the shadows. The Keys were transformed into an upper-middle-class playground. Virtual reality, safely defined by caricatures of dead writers and overpriced umbrella drinks and some guy with a lounge-lizard voice playing Margaritaville for the five hundredth time, became the Keys for most of its visitors. This self-proclaimed "Conch Republic," originally intended as a haven for the iconoclast, has mutated into something more packaged and marketable and safe. I have to search hard for the edges not yet rounded off.

Keogh is a naturalist, a photographer and a friend, and whenever I drop in, he always seems to have time to just hang out for a few days, with little notice. His modest frame house, which teeters on stilts next to the opening of a canal on an isolated spit of land called Doctor's Point, is down a road of finely ground coral rubble, past stacks of crab and lobster traps.

Outside are weathered boats, motors, stacks of kayaks. Inside is a collection of old topwater fishing plugs, a clutter of found nautical things, two mongrel dogs, a photo of a naked woman with a paper bag over her head standing in knee-deep swamp water, and unaccountably, a mean-looking five-inch-long centipede in an aluminum pot that, for reasons unclear, a neighbor brought by. "Maybe they think I can identify it," says Keogh, shrugging. He looks at it more closely. "Guess it's a big centipede." This could be Cannery Row, slightly updated and moved to the Lower Keys.

The few other homes, simple wooden structures, are also up on stilts, ready for that special day when the next hurricane churns the Atlantic and Gulf waters until they rise up and meet each other over the flat landscape, as they did here in the mid-1930s. Ernest Hemingway was living seasonally in Key West then. After that tumultuous storm, he wrote to his editor, Max Perkins, about drowned bodies hanging in palm trees, and how Henry Flagler's railroad, which first linked these islands, was washed into the sea—train, tracks, passengers, and all. For those living here today, the probability of another killer hurricane is regarded in a way that Californians must regard the San Andreas Fault. It is not something they much want to think about.

Keogh, who moved down from Maine some twenty-five years ago, does some nature photography, some teaching at a local summer camp, some backcountry outfitting and guiding with his small fleet of kayaks. Like most residents who are not retired or independently wealthy, he makes do by cobbling together his own lifestyle, gathering a few bucks from each job. As Clark Gable once said in *The Misfits:* "It beats working for wages."

A few years ago, Keogh worked by himself as a commercial lobster diver, scuttling along the bottom of the deep channels around nearby Cudjoe Key, pulling his boat along behind him on the surface with a rope like a giant bobber. In the course of poking into dark crannies to catch spiny lobsters by hand, Keogh would sometimes stumble across the forgotten, often mysterious jetsam of other's lives down there on the sea bottom. "I found an intact airplane wing, a children's swing set, old boats no one seemed to know about," he says. Once, Keogh finned around a corner and ran straight into a giant loggerhead turtle—with both its head and one of its front flippers freshly chewed off by what must have been a massive shark. "It could be a little scary, sometimes," says Keogh. He reports his lobstering experiences in a gentle monotone, like he reports most of life, in a cadence that never seems to rise or fall too far, whether he is sipping a high-octane cup of café con leche or knocking back four or five beers.

Soon we are in Keogh's pickup, headed out into the deepest reaches of Big Pine, to those tropical hardwood hammocks and pine rocklands protected on this sixteen-square-mile island as part of the Key Deer National Wildlife Refuge. Unlike parks, federal refuges are set up more for animals and the places they like to live than for people. As a result, there are few interpretive signs or marked trails, and even these are closed at dark. The best window to wildlife, says Keogh, are some twelve miles of firebreak roads, straight and narrow jeep paths that crisscross the refuge in some arcane grid. In all his time on Big Pine, Keogh admits to not having seen them all. We are looking for Key deer today, but we are likely to find most anything.

We pull over and stop next to a symmetrical pond known locally as the "Blue Hole." The hole was excavated for fill from a smaller "solution hole," a depression naturally carved in the soft rock by slowly decaying, acid-rich detritus. Alligators, far more freshwater dependent than their crocodile relatives, are concentrated on the island around places like these. "Let's see what's here," says Keogh.

I stand at the edge of the hole, noticing it is, in fact, very blue. I use binoculars to scan foliage around the entire shore. Nothing. When I put down my scope, I notice Keogh is fixated on something just a few yards away, next to a brace of limestone boulders. It's a man-sized gator basking in the sun, the primitive schutes along the ridge of its back glistening like wet rubber. Other big reptiles are likely here as well. Keogh tells me about one of his neighbor's boxer dogs running off one night and attempting to swim across the Blue Hole—for what reason, no one seems to know. "Of course," says Keogh, "he was eaten by one of the gators."

We drive on, deeper into the island, headed for the sprawling Watson Hammock in the heart of the refuge. The road we travel is increasingly desolate, surrounded by acre after acre of Caribbean slash pine. The island looks more like Andros or any of the remote Bahamian Out Islands I have seen than any of the other Keys.

Suddenly, Keogh makes a turn off the main road, then another. Finally, we come to a stop next to a lone sign (*Area Closed for Fawning April 1–May 31*) at the edge of the tropical hardwood hammock. Here, we duck under a horizontal metal pole designed to block vehicles and set off into the underbrush. The trail leads us first across a pasture of skin-pricking needle grass, then into a waist-high field of saw grass, just like the sedge of the Glades. On the soft gray marl, I look closely and see the neat piles of scat left by the tiny deer, watch as a scorpion scuttles around them as if dodging boulders. Everything seems smallish, like the dime-sized blossoms of the sky-blue Bahamian morning glories growing here in profusion.

Stunted by North American standards, the trees around us are dense, heavy tropical woods that entwine like the tortuous rigging of an ancient galleon. Under the shade of the foliage canopy, it is almost gloomy, the giddy, sunny ambience of the tourist-driven Keys dissolving with every step. As it does, a true sense of place gradually begins to emerge.

The air is full of the sweet if delicate pungency of a tropical forest being parboiled by the sun. Even here in winter, something fresh is blooming. When I stop and look around, I spot *Liguus,* one of the spectacular little tree snails. It is up high on the trunk of a Jamaican dogwood—busy gumming algae and fungi—and it looks for all the world like an ornate two-inch cone of porcelain. Collectors who prized the stylization of these shells once rampaged through these islands, snatching all they could reach. I can't help but wonder if snails that today graze up out of pluck-range have been spawned by generations of other mollusks who are similarly inclined.

Tree snails like this are found throughout the West Indies, where they speciate as they do here, changing colors and adding stripes depending on the forest in which they live. When these Keys arose from the sea after the last ice age, *Liguus* accidentally immigrated—riding flotsam on favorable currents. Unable or unwilling to crawl between hammocks, they now live out generations of their lives in a single place, coloration and shell thickness added or taken away by the algae, the bark, the moisture special to each. They are Darwin's Galapagos tortoises, in miniature.

As we near the mangrove rim of the island, our path becomes covered with several inches of water, tiny isopods swarming madly to get out of our way. One of the richest zones for trees on this continent, this tropical woods is a Whitman's Sampler of trees—as many as 120 different species in a single hammock. Stunted in size when compared with a North American forest, the jungle around me is a fretwork of Jamaican dogwood, sea grape, poisonwood, and the elegant, reddish-barked tree known as the gumbo limbo. Towering above them all is a massive buttonwood, a highland mangrove, two-hundred-year-old boughs sagging from the weight of time and a crusting of spiky green bromeliads.

Suddenly, less than fifty yards away, I see a tawny buck with a large rack scamper and bound, his white tail erect and wagging, until he disappears in the thick foliage. He is no taller than a collie-shepherd mutt I owned as a boy, but not nearly as bulky. Earlier, back at the refuge headquarters, I saw a young fawn stuffed and mounted, curled forever in a diorama of twigs and a bed of grass. She was the size of a house cat.

These "Key deer" migrated down from the mainland during the last ice age as full-sized mammals, back when the water levels were three to four hundred feet lower than they are now and a land bridge extended all the way to the Tortugas in the west. Stranded here when the seas rose, the whitetails learned to live with less on island environments, downsizing themselves into the miniatures I see today. Other critters marooned here also evolved into subspecies: the marine raccoon; the ringless ring-neck snake; and the Lower Keys marsh rabbit, inimitably classified as *Sylvilagus palustris hefneri*—for *Playboy* founder Hugh Hefner, who helped fund research on it.

It was geology that helped make all this so. The flat limestone outcroppings splotching the soft earth here—what locals call "caprock"— signal the underpinning of a terrain vastly different from the fossilized coral of the Upper Keys. I look closely at the caprock underfoot and see how this dense, ghostly pale "oolitic" limestone naturally holds water in little pockets, when the more porous coral simply lets it drain like a rocky sieve.

If this oasis of geology fed unique plants and animals here, it encouraged settlers too, lulling them into thinking the thin soil of these Keys could be farmed just like the mainland. And for a while, it could. Keogh tells me there were almost as many people on adjacent No Name Key around the turn of the century as there are today, fifty or sixty. All the heads of the household were Bahamian, except for one lone Russian, a hermit with a green thumb who grew sapodillas "the size of saucers" and trip-wired his property with guns to shoot trespassers.

The drug smugglers who followed were just as enterprising and reclusive. Throughout the 1970s and into the 1980s, drug running was so common that jettisoned bales—dubbed "square grouper"—were routinely found snagged on mangrove bushes. Windward of Big Pine is what remains of the "Pot Wreck"—a trawler scuttled in ninety feet of water, its holds jammed with salt-saturated bales of cannabis. In a clearing in the woods, I look westward toward Stock Island and see "Fat Albert," the DEA's snow-white radar blimp paternally hovering, lurking for the occasional low-flying renegade plane that might still arrive from the Bahamas and Central America with no flight plan.

Back on the trail, I notice the water that a few minutes ago I was splashing over is now about calf-deep. I also notice the mosquitoes are so thick they have blanketed Keogh's legs. As I alert him to this, he stops, twists and looks down. But instead of going into a slapping frenzy, he swings his Nikon around and focuses it on the carnage taking place. "We're in the thick of it now," says Keogh, clicking happily away. Oddly, the water here is fresh, rain-driven, and the giant marine mangroves around us seem to have acclimated. After particularly heavy rains, says Keogh, the water actually flows through here like a little river, creating riffles as it cascades over rocks and the spindly red mangrove roots.

Finally, we come to a large depression where the water reaches mid-thigh, an enchanted natural alcove ringed by a fretwork of foliage, where nearly every square inch of trunk and limb is covered with pineapple bromeliads. Nearby, something large splashes and then V's away, disappearing under the tannic, tea-colored water. A gator? "I've seen them back here before," says Keogh, nonchalantly. "There's one who likes to sit right out in the middle of the trail and let the water flow around him."

As we slosh back upland to where the marl reveals itself again, I see black, runic-like slashes at the trunk base of a poisonous manchineel, the marks of a buck rubbing the velvet off his tiny antlers. Or maybe just sharpening them up for the rut battles soon to come. "They'll be ready to fight soon," says Keogh, who has heard the young studs loudly clacking antlers together in heated battle before, off in the woods. "They'll be defending territory, chasing down the babes."

Under threat from loss of habitat and speeding cars, ninety-four Key deer were killed last year, leaving a wild herd that will always be a step away from extinction. Ironically, the pro-growth faction here—mostly retired military and real-estate salesmen—would rather see the little deer fenced in on the refuge than abide by any restriction to make them drive slower or build less. Some have even suggested the deer herd can be managed and bred, and its meat sold as gourmet fare. This is the underbelly of the Conch Republic, where iconoclasm has also become speciated into something that right-wing radio blowhards would revel in.

Much later, soggy and insect-bitten, we climb back into the truck and drive off, stopping finally by a ramshackle structure half-hidden in the woods. This is the No Name Pub, which advertises itself as "A Nice Place, If You Can Find It." Inside, the off-plumb walls and ceiling are papered with stapled and taped dollar bills, each of which holds virtually unreadable felt-tipped inscriptions, wisdom which must have seemed terribly clever after four or five pitchers of cold beer.

"One night some guy stole a handful of them," said Keogh. "He went outside, passed out, and then came back in and tried to spend them." Perhaps he figured the amnesia of alcohol would erase his deed as well as the felt-tipped scrawlings on his booty. Even in the No Name Pub, it didn't work.

A low-pressure front is blanketing the Keys with dark, ominous clouds and a hurricane named Lili is on its way here from Cuba—an event that has all the real-life makings of the climatic storm in *Key Largo*. In keeping with the plot, we fall into our roles as half-addled islanders: we plan to spend a couple of days sailing and kayaking.

Taking advantage of a slight break in the weather, we head out to *Lolita,* Keogh's twenty-six-foot hand-built sailing cat at the edge of Big

Pine. With the strong wind filling our sail, we are soon cutting across the green clear water at a nice six- to seven-knot clip. We are headed for Bird Island, a colony of magnificent frigates, and who knows what else.

As our boat's pontoons slice easily through the waves, we pass a moored cabin cruiser, a battered live-aboard where a wizened vision who looks like Neptune himself waves to us from the deck. This is Dwayne Hope, a former electrical engineer from New England who somehow found his way to this anchorage, and then just never left. "The first year he was here," says Keogh, "I just knew him as 'Z.'" With its stern awning, its jungle of potted plants and strings of sponges, Dwayne's maritime home seems as if it may have been set adrift from Gilligan's Island, the Professor finally making a clean break on his own in some alternative universe. I ask Keogh how Dwayne supports himself, and he points to a handlettered sign on the stern that reads: Pinfish for Sale. "Low-tech living," says Keogh. "His needs aren't great."

Within a half-hour, we reach the edge of Bird Island, deserted except for a colony of magnificent frigates and a few scattered cormorants, orange throat patches the color of papaya flesh. Tonight will bring a clear sky, a great star-studded amphitheater to sleep under, out here on the tarp strung between the bow pontoons, not far from the rookery. For now, we offload the two sea kayaks we've brought along. Our plan is to skim the edge of Bird Island, then cross the channel to a much larger key, aiming for a place where the dark-green wall of foliage cleaves in on itself like a natural foyer. In the cleft of trees, Keogh says, there will be a creek leading to the island's interior.

Keogh soon disappears into the froth where the standing waves formed by the outgoing tide and incoming wind are white-capped. By the time I cast off, I have lost sight of him completely. I forge ahead anyway, crashing through the tops of the waves with the wind to my back, headed across a deep channel for the Newfound Harbor Keys. Surging with adrenaline now, I ride the crest of every roller I can, until finally my rhythm abandons me and I slide down into the vast, terrifying gully in between. In a split second, the next green wave crashes over me, filling my kayak with water and turning me sideways.

Windmilling my paddle for all I'm worth, I realign my heavy sea-filled hull and track onward with just a little more finesse than a chunk of flotsam. Finally, I reach the opposite shore just in time to encounter a surprisingly dry Keogh, who asks me why I was paddling so furiously. I ignore this question, bale all the water out I can, and then we paddle single file through a tight foliage corridor leading to an inland slough.

The water back here is glass-clear, with small barracuda and mangrove snapper hanging motionless over a hardbottom community of small corals and sponges. The clouds part just enough to let a plume of sunlight through, and every animal and plant in the water under me responds by becoming incandescent. The moment burns itself forever into my memory, one I will paddle through again and again, until the day comes when I can remember no more.

For now, a peregrine falcon soars overhead in the wind, and a frigate bird swoops and dips like a Chinese kite. I am at once sweating, soaked with sea water and still half-buzzed from the rush of crossing as I push the bow of my kayak ashore. I'm not sure yet what I'll find on this island, but I'm almost positive it won't have anything to do with a tiki bar or an umbrella drink. Keogh disappears in a thicket of red mangrove and, dutifully, I follow.

Galapagos Journal

An Expeditionary Wink

in the Eye of the Cosmos

Evolutionary Arrival

Eden first appears to me in a cloud bank over the Pacific, some six hundred miles off South America. It is Isla de San Cristóbal, all volcanic craters and lava-inspired flatlands, a vision that seems on the edge of dissolving completely into vapor, somewhere between distant past and the ever-evolving now. No wonder the Spanish first named these islands "The Enchanted Isles," and noted on the earliest maps that they may not actually exist at all.

Minutes later, our Ecuadorian jet bounces down on the runway on the island, next to a lonely little al fresco hut of a terminal, cobbled together from rich tropical wood and cut volcanic stone. Behind a battered counter, an Ecuadorian shopman smiles inscrutably next to his hand-lettered sign advertising "cerveza, whisky, dollars, and Queso, Jr." It is a strange slogan to find here in the Galapagos Islands, a place scientists regard as a Living Laboratory of Evolution.

Isolated from the mainland since they erupted from the ocean a few million years ago, these islands are now widely recognized as a classroom for the study of natural selection. That's because plants and animals—whether they drifted here from the mainland as seedpods or larva or floated atop mats of seaweed—produced generations of offspring that were visibly changed by their environment. And they became so without the influence of pre-Columbian man or large voracious predators, surviving and adapting in a virtual Eden where wildness also meant tameness.

Ironically, when a young naturalist named Charles Darwin sailed here aboard the HMS *Beagle* in 1835, he did so as a "creationist." But in his five weeks in the Galapagos, he found sharp differences among the finches and the giant land tortoises. He hung baited lines over the gunnels of the *Beagle* and hauled in fifteen species of fish, all unknown to science. By the time the *Beagle* set sail to continue its five-year journey around the world, Darwin had begun to assemble the first few crucial pieces of the puzzle known as natural selection. Thanks to the Galapagos, Darwin's "theory of evolution" became the crucible by which the shaping of our world is now explained by mainstream science.

We are here as an expedition to look for these same signs—except we are searching beneath the sea and underground, looking for new life in places where Darwin could never go, and where no one since has ever been. In doing so, we hope to show that evolution is not a done deed but a vital, ongoing process in which humans are now playing a mighty role. What we do to our environment today in the Galapagos—or anywhere, for that matter—will surely reshape future generations of all of us, from tortoises and finches to fish and humans.

There are four biologists, all eminent in their field, with us to direct the search, as well as a crew of filmmakers to record each step of the way for a two-hour documentary that will be called "Galapagos: Beyond Darwin." I am along to write journal-style "dispatches" and take digital photographs, which I will whisk back to the United States, one satellite-bounce away, as part of related coverage of the expedition on the Internet.

Our launchpad will be a deep-diving research sub and an oceanographic ship equipped with scuba gear, now steaming down from Ft. Pierce, Florida, to rendezvous with us here tomorrow. Instead of riding vehicles of sail and wood in our quest, we will be riding technology that is part steel and part silicon. It is also part ether, too, with the unknown still weighing as mightily as it did in Darwin's day.

I write this from a stone bench on the waterfront Avenida Charles Darwin, awaiting the arrival of our ship. As I do, a small yellow warbler flits about at my feet, while several magnificent frigate birds soar high overhead. A gaggle of sea lions loll at the edge of the frothing, turquoise surf, sometimes squirming up into the moored, brightly-painted fishermen's pongas to bask in the sun. I am getting ready to venture out into the wilds of Eden, but Eden, apparently, is already swelling about me.

Finally Underway

By morning the *Seward Johnson,* a 204-foot research vessel from Harbor Branch Oceanographic, appears on the horizon, a splotch of snowy white against the patchwork quilt of brightly colored fishing boats here in Wreck Bay. On its stern, under an A-frame crane, rides the Johnson Sea-Link (JSL), a custom-built submersible capable of diving to three thousand feet. Next to the sub is a crated-up ultralight plane, which, when assembled, will give the filmmakers an aboveground perspective of this wild environment. It is all a welcome, if bizarre, sight here at the edge of the world.

Soon we are loaded—not a small chore when you are traveling with an entire film production crew and scientists with dive and field gear. We are seventy large cases of luggage strong, over 3,500 pounds worth, and we have hauled each piece on and off of trucks, airport conveyors, and hotels here and back in Quito at least eight times in the last two days. Everyone pitches in, including myself and our two Florida-based scientists, David Steadman and Grant Gilmore.

Steadman, thin and intense with an offbeat sense of humor, is the curator of ornithology with the Florida State Museum and a veteran of over a year of cumulative Galapagos field work. As our lone land scientist, he's explored the lava caves on these islands more thoroughly than anyone in the world, searching for fossils there. Gilmore, a quiet, earnest man, is a marine biologist with Harbor Branch who specializes in deepwater bottom life off Florida and in the Bahamas. Although he has logged far more time in the sub than any of the others, this is his first trip to the Galapagos. "Anything is possible in this environment," says Gilmore, who has discovered new species of marine life on every Harbor Branch expedition he's ever made.

With the ship underway, we assemble on the deck for a safety drill given by the ship's captain. To demonstrate the thick, red neoprene cold-weather suits we will don if the boat sinks, Steadman crawls into one and, looking like a giant foam cutout figure, holds his arms out to the side. His voice is muffled by the hood covering his head, but the words from the esteemed scientist are still clear: "Gumby Lives!"

Filmmaking in the Lost World

The rolling hills of the Galapagos highlands rise in front of me, lushly carpeted with ferns, lichens, and mosses, and dotted with a half-dozen massive black shells of the mammoth tortoises. From my vantage point three thousand feet up, I can see the Pacific on the horizon, next to the volcanic hump called Cerro Gallina, where the female tortoises go each season to hide their eggs under its soft earthen base.

With the chilled mountain breeze and ethereal lay of the landscape, we seemed to be squarely in a lost world, a Jurassic Park of a place in a remote back slough of time. The ancient tortoises here lumber in slow motion, and when I approach, withdraw their heads into their shells, hissing out a sound that seems to have been born in another millennium.

When Darwin put ashore, there were fourteen different kinds of giant tortoises, each with a shell shaped slightly different as the result of living in a slightly different island habitat. Today, three have become extinct, and the Pinta Island tortoise is down to one remaining animal. Early sailors gathered the tortoises by the thousands to eat. The vermin they left behind—rats, goats, donkeys—either feasted on the eggs, the young, fragile tortoises, or the plants that were their traditional food source. Long ago in Florida, giant tortoises much like these once lived; but the appetite of pre-Columbians for the tasty tortoise flesh drove the lumbering herps to extinction by the time the Europeans arrived.

I have come ashore on our own launch today with Dave Clark, a veteran documentary producer from the suburban D.C. area and his topside film crew, including camera assistant Billy McCullough of Miami. There is no new scientific ground to be broken today, only some routine shots of some very unroutine wildlife to set the stage. We are in the *garua,* the season where each day brings a spritzerlike misting of rain. As the cameraman sets up to film two giant tortoises in a shallow duckweed-covered pond, McCullough pops open a brightly colored golf umbrella and stations it over the camera.

By day's end, we will have traveled over rugged mountain roads and hiked in the mud and rain with cases of gear for hours. We will have done so to capture what will eventually amount to a few seconds of final-cut footage, transporting this Lost World vision back to the comfort of the American living room, where it will be subject to the whims of the clicker. This reality has already stood the test of time. But I worry how this lesson of evolution will play next to the mania of prime-time sitcoms.

Up from the Ooze

I wake to a start this morning at 5:30 A.M. as the ship's engines rumbled to life and the anchor was hoisted, clanking against the hull like the chains of Marley's ghost.

At first light, I walk out onto the stern to watch the ship bulldoze its way through the steady chop on the slate-gray sea, paralleling a rugged, uninhabited shore chiseled from the lava of prehistory. We are shadowing the easterly coast of Santa Cruz, aiming for the "Plazas," an outcropping of rocks where the island seems to have been pinched into a point by some giant hand. It is here we will make the first deep submersible dives of the expedition.

Don Liberatore, the chief sub pilot, gathers everyone in the tiny conference room to brief us on today's sub dives. Liberatore, a small, wiry man with a wild tangle of hair and a left earlobe studded with shiny gold things, has the confident and easy demeanor of a true adventurer.

By tomorrow at this time, we all expect to have a brand new species of marine life on board, and to witness another piece of the evolutionary jigsaw puzzle being fitted into place. I think that each day creates itself from yesterday's promise, wild possibilities turning into reality overnight. Just as I am thinking this, John McCosker, our chief scientist from the California Academy of Sciences, walks up. The evolutionary biologist is wearing a T-shirt that depicts a nasty-looking paleo-fish crawling from the murk onto land. The inscription reads: Up from the Ooze, Born to Cruise.

Last night, I stood alone on the stern of this Florida ship, so many miles from home. Several hundred yards away, a rusted Ecuadorian freighter rocked in the folds of the sea, its deck lights ablaze like a magician's parade. From here, I watched the moon burn through the thick clouds, the sea lions and pelicans feeding in the clear tropical waters, chasing tiny fish, just as they've done here for centuries.

I thought of the HMS *Beagle* then, and of its captain, Robert FitzRoy, and Darwin and all the men who rode her to these oceanic isles, not really that long ago, coming for discovery, just like we are. We are surely more modernized, but the essential spirit of adventure remains, a thread woven through time.

Underwater Mountaintops?

We are out of sight of land today, bobbing and weaving in the ever-moving sea, with only the frigate and tropic birds soaring overhead like untethered kites to remind us of the tenuous link we still have with the islands themselves.

By Wednesday, we will pick up Steadman on Floreana, where he has been exploring an isolated lava cave over the last few days, searching for fossils never before recorded. For now, we continue our own ocean exploration, on the relatively shallow bottom of six hundred to nine hundred feet in the JSL, looking for living fossils that may still be swimming or crawling about.

If we were elsewhere in the ocean at these depths, the little sub would merely hover alone in the deepwater column, an aquatic butterfly lost in the clouds of an infinite blue sky. But since we are atop "drowned mountain tops," we have the chance to putter up and down volcanic slopes that may once have tasted sunlight, places where Mother Nature perhaps experimented with the genesis of today's animals before sinking her lab back into the sea.

It is this world that I visit today, curled up in the aft compartment of the sub, face pressed against a ten-inch-wide porthole for the duration of the three-and-a-half-hour dive. Sub tech Charlie Ridler, a sturdy, athletic-looking young man whose job sometimes requires him to leap into the bucking seas to connect a thick wench cable to the surfacing sub, shares my compartment. Ridler, of Jupiter, Florida, gives me a quick safety briefing. Then he hands me a headset so I can chat with Dr. Bruce Robison, our midwater specialist from the Monterey Bay Aquarium, who is riding inside the Plexiglas dome up front with pilot Liberatore.

While early scientists have dredged animals here up from the depths since Darwin's visit, that heavy-handed collecting only hinted at the true nature of the deep underwater world. "It was like we were trying to study a forest from a blimp by dragging a butterfly net through the treetops at night," Robison had told me earlier. "You'd get a few acorns, some feathers, a butterfly wing." Now, with the submersible, we have a first-ever chance to "walk down in the forest and look around."

If this is indeed the ancient island the scientists anticipate, we will find rounded basalt rocks, which could only be eroded by surface waters, and wave-cut rocky terraces far beneath the surface. I hear Robison's voice crackle in my headset: "Keep an eye out for sand and some very old beach umbrellas."

After the hatches are secured, the A-frame crane lifts the sub off the stern and swings it gently down onto the sea, mechanically unhooking the wench line back to the ship, giving my stomach a few swings of its own. As we sink easily into the green, late-afternoon sea, Ridler gives me the comforting news that we have enough food, water, and oxygen to survive five days on the bottom, should that be necessary.

We lose our light quickly as we drift slowly down like a rock dropped into a very deep barrel of oil. Our descent seems to take us through a virtual no-man's-land, somewhere between the lush poles of Up and Down, a zone with no definition, like being stuck between floors on an elevator that plays only Barry Manilow music.

Finally, we hit rock bottom, with its tiny, sparse forests of white, treelike corals atop flat volcanic rock, the sort of vision I might have if I flew in a plane high over a fire-ravaged woods back on land. Long ago, when author Herman Melville sailed to these islands aboard a whaling ship, he longed for a chance to know more about the strange world on the other side of the looking glass. "Below the water-line," he wrote, "the rock seemed one honey-comb of grottoes, affording labyrinthine lurking places for swarms of fairy fish. All were strange."

And now here I am, down to where only the whales Melville helped to hunt could go, a magical forever-dark netherworld even the great writer couldn't imagine. I push my face to the port and see a bottom carpeted with layers of brittle stars, odd reddish fish darting under ledges, scarlet crabs hoisting white sponges on their backs, and strange little eels slithering away into crevices.

A peculiar fish darts by, a half-foot-long creature with exquisite spots and stripes on the back of its body. Robison sees another from his dome, and captures it on the underwater video camera that is bolted to the front of the sub. "It looks like a *serranus* [grouper-seabass family]," says Robison. "But what genus and what species? It's probably never been seen before." Not only will new fish like this one help to continually refine our knowledge about all marine life, it provides valuable new information about how the dark, cold depths influence evolution.

Around us, the bottom becomes a series of terraces, rocky steps leading to the mountaintop. We slowly ascend this slope, finally reaching a wide plateau, an ancient volcanic crater that seems to be filled with sand and small rounded rocks. I look around. There's not a beach umbrella in sight.

Unlocking Fossilized Secrets

The seas are calm as a lake this morning, the sun is shining brightly, and a hundred yards off the bow of our ship, a giant cetacean is exhaling a geyser of ocean spray far into the air. A mile away, off the southerly coast of Isabela, the twin volcanic peaks of Cerro Azul and Sierra Negra maintain what seems to be an unremitting pact with the clouds.

Steadman has been literally sifting away layers of history from the past. Back on board after four days digging into the sediment of a lava-tube cave on Floreana, Steadman stands next to a chest-high gunnel, carefully screening dirt through a brass sieve, revealing a trove of Lilliputian fossils, like sifting sand through the hourglass of time.

Steadman has finally had the chance to return to a cave he first started to explore fifteen years ago. There, he dug a yard-deep pit, closely recording the strata every centimeter of the way with a grid-like string. From the pit, he filled bags with earth that had washed down into the cave over the centuries, preserving the tiny mealtime bones left by predatory barn owls nesting there. Now, in the greatest of ironies, the little endemic owl itself is extinct, a victim of man's impact on the island.

Still, the work of the departed owl has opened new portals in the history of these rare island environments. As a result, Steadman has now penetrated a layer of detritus that carried him and his imagination beyond the red, organic sand of the 4,000-year-old Holocene, down into a cindery deposit that signaled the end of the last ice age.

"It's the first time anyone's been able to cross that boundary in the Galapagos," Steadman tells me excitedly. "Now we can see what the major fauna changes were then. Did the finches have shorter beaks? Did the tortoises have a differently shaped shell? We're taking the evolution in the Galapagos farther back in time than anyone ever has before." This is especially important because it provides more evidence on the life of other extinct animals, like the Floreana ground finch, which became extinct just ten years after Darwin's own visit, a victim of voracious rats from the HMS *Beagle*.

In a science lab on the ship, Steadman lifts a round tin canister off a table to show me some of the fossils already recovered. The tin, which once held cookies, has little rabbits dancing on it under a label that says: The World of Beatrix Potter. Inside, the bones are as small and fragile as slivers of very old wood, and in the palm of one hand, Steadman holds ten thousand years of newly excavated history, a chapter to a long-lost book, teensy femurs of birds and reptiles never before seen by man.

If there is elation about the find, there is also a confirmed suspicion as well, a replay of an extinction scenario Steadman has seen in

Polynesia and other once-isolated oceanic isles. "Creatures can adapt to even harsh changes in climate, temperatures, sea level rise and fall, and still survive. But the arrival of man is just too catastrophic for them, especially on island environments like this where the number of species are small to begin with." As in earlier digs here, Steadman has found that man—and the livestock and vermin he introduced—was tragically fatal to a number of birds, mammals, and reptiles, creating an accelerated extinction rate from one hundred to four hundred times as intense as in the prehuman world.

Back out on deck, I look out over the railing again, to where Isabela rests on the horizon of the blue-green seas. And as I do, the very tip of the truncated cone of Cerro Azul emerges from the thick cumulus, making it seem to float in the rarefied air atop the clouds. On the surface nearby, another whale blasts a tall stream of exhaled water and mammalian breath, and I think of how ephemeral the beginning and end of life is for us all, of how we each carry the fossilized records of our own rarefied visions around with us, perhaps in anticipation of excavation and light.

If we're lucky, maybe we'll end up in a cookie tin with cartoon rabbits on it a thousand centuries from now, being picked over gently by a person who cares enough to restore us to life with the vehicle of his own dreams.

A Sea Full of Stars

It is no secret that most of the underwater footage you see in documentaries recreates discovery already made in a given expedition. To perform pure science is to poke and to prod, to spend endless hours underwater merely observing, an act that is as exciting as watching paint dry for most viewers. To "sex up" this experience, it is necessary to turn the cameras around and go after the "megafauna" at the edge of the haze—the bull-necked Galapagos sharks, the Honda-sized manta rays, the scores of giant barracuda. For viewers, as well as for participants, this provides what our underwater producer Al Giddings only half-kiddingly refers to as the "sphincter factor."

While dives that hunt for this megafauna have surely provided lots of thrills, I've found it personally more rewarding to be around when the science itself takes place. To this end, I put on my wetsuit and neoprene hood and climb down into the Zodiac tonight, headed out to search for marine animals that glow in the dark and a fish that groans underwater. Leading the way are Gilmore, McCosker, and Robison. A dive like this has little cinematic appeal; the filmmakers stay aboard ship, drinking coffee in the galley or resting in their bunks.

We putter out of Tagus Cove, the broken-down volcanic crater where Darwin once anchored, into the edge of the Bolívar Channel, running next to the steep cliff wall of Isabela Island in forty to fifty feet of water. As soon as we leave the ship and its cascade of lights behind, the great vast bowl of a sky comes alive with tiny dots burned into a velvet curtain, stretching from the tops of the surrounding mountains across the entire night sky. I look up during our brief ride and see two stars fall, watched Orion lying on its side, Venus and Jupiter blazing atop each other like vertical headlights.

Darwin walked these mountaintops after breakfast early one morning, picking his way through the ghostly Palo Santos trees and the stubby cactus, all the way up to where he found a crater lake. "The day was overpoweringly hot and the lake looked clear and blue," Darwin wrote. But when the thirsty young naturalist hurried down to drink the water in the crater, he found it to be saltier than the ocean itself.

I plunge into the water just on the other side of the crater where Darwin drank, sinking slowly down into eighty feet of pitch-black water. We have all agreed to keep our underwater lights turned off for at least the first several minutes so we can adjust our eyes to the bioluminescence in the plant and animal plankton in the water.

As I descend, flippers first, I hear the static crackling of the little bottom shrimp. A few minutes before the dive, I had listened to this sound on a hydrophone Gilmore had dangled over the side and it seemed remote, under control. Now it consumes me, like an atmosphere full of thousands of tiny, repetitive sonic booms. In front of my mask, the glowing organic sparks of life are so thick I can't see anything but green flashes flickering like fireflies on and off, all the way to the bottom.

At eighty feet, I look for my dive buddy, McCosker, in the ebony waters, but I see nothing but the bioluminescence. Finally, as he exhales, the upwelling of his exhaled air tears through the plankton over his head, outlining each tiny bubble with a rim of blue-green.

Finally, we turn on our flashlights and shine their beams under the ledges, down into places where the molten flow from the craters of Isabela ran long ago. Here, marine life has done a fine job of carpeting the lava over the centuries, covering it with a fabric of coral and worms, sponges and tiny invertebrates, all united here by their isolation from the mainland.

Holding his light in one hand, McCosker reaches back under a ledge with the other. Out swims a hornshark, a spotted bottom dweller the length of my forearm. It is not the shark McCosker wants, but a little fish that was sharing its space, the Galapagos drum, a dark-hued little fish I heard groaning like a foghorn on Gilmore's hydrophone

The drum stays hidden, as does a jeweled moray, another small specimen-to-be that was too quick for McCosker's collection bag. As we head back to the boat, my light beam illuminates a nudibranch atop a stubby rock, a marine slug that, in its iridescence, has taken the notion of hallucinogenic art as far as it can go. Locals call it *El Tigre,* the tiger, because of its dramatic stripes. Scientifically, it is virtually unknown. By studying the nudibranch, we can only add to our knowledge of shallow-water invertebrates—especially about how they have evolved in isolated environments like this. With that information, we can then compare their form and function to similar critters in other oceans and coastal shores where man's presence is far more dominant. As one tiny animal, the existence of the tiny nudibranch is of little consequence; but when seen as part of a larger pattern of evolution and survival, it is vital to understanding our natural world and what makes it tick.

We bag the little nudie and head up, lights off and bioluminescence twinkling around us, thicker than I've ever seen before. On the surface, another star twinkles, falls, and then vanishes forever from sight, and for a moment I wonder about redefining the boundary where the glimmering sky ends and the glimmering sea begins, all of it so alive now with isolated grandeur and ever-changing light.

Thanksgiving

Our sub has logged more than forty dives by today, including one that took me down to a 3,000-foot bottom and collected several invertebrates "new" to science. Classifying animals at sea is tricky business, and it will take months after we return to fully confirm real discoveries. At this point, we have aboard over two dozen fish species—including conger and moray eels and scorpion fish—and another couple dozen anemones, shrimps, and gelatinous animals that are, so far, unknown. Together, they make up quite a menagerie, providing brand-new ways for science to continue to define the never-ending tale of evolution. After curation back in the United States, many will return to Ecuador to help that country more fully realize its own natural legacies.

Our visit has been about more than just new species and the specifics of natural selection, however. I ask McCosker about this higher meaning, and he looks over at the churning green water beyond our stern for a few moments before he answers. "It's not just that there are new animals to be named and tagged," he says. "It's about the fact that no species stands alone on the planet, that we're all connected here. And a society that doesn't understand evolution is setting itself up for a great fall."

In another week, I will be headed back to Quito and then to my home in Florida, while the rest of the scientists and the film crew will scatter to the four winds. A few months ago, I barely knew where these islands were—or what the players in this expedition would turn out to be. Now, I have seen sides of them all in a way few ever have.

After dinner, I walk out to the bow, where a pod of dolphins are skirting back and forth in the pressure wave of the moving ship. As they weave through the plankton in the black water below, they create a macramé of blue-green light, an image that dances like mercury across the walls of darkness around us.

Immersed in the odd fauna of the Galapagos, I realize, finally, that I am probably the oddest bird of them all—an animal who's entire existence in this place is owed not to my race's own skills of adaptability but to our newfound technological cleverness.

Like some Swiftian character, we arrive at places bigger and smaller than us, expecting all of reality to be defined in proportion to ourselves. But in these strange shadow isles, the definition is woven far more deeply into the configuration of life itself, bleeding deep into our own souls. Ultimately, we are as marked by it as are the shells of the ancient tortoises, the beaks of the finch.

Coral Spawning

Sex on the Rocks

It is just after dark in the Florida Keys, about six miles out in the Atlantic, on our continent's only living coral reef. I have been under the ocean here for over an hour and my skin is as wrinkled as a prune, just like it used to get when I would sit too long in the bath as a little kid, rubber ducky bobbing somewhere nearby. It is late August now and the sea is as warm as my boyhood bathwater. As I look up, I see the hull of the boat that brought me here gently sloshing on the surface a couple dozen feet overhead, comforting somehow, like the dark underbelly of a giant rubber ducky.

My dive light is starting to dim, so I flick it off to save batteries. Thusly situated, I squint in the darkness for some sign, flush with anticipation, like a kid waiting for Christmas. So far, the sparkle of bioluminescence from floating plankton is all I see, and it mystifies me as it always does, like some underwater circuit board firing itself at random—perhaps sending out signals known only to those who can breathe down here without tanks of surface air.

I have traveled worldwide in quest of underwater mysteries—giant tridacna clams in Australia, sea turtles in Nicaragua, marine iguanas in the Galapagos. Now, here I am in Florida, at the edge of a slab of coral called Key Largo Dry Rocks, in search of one of the tiniest and most elusive of the ocean's secrets.

That secret is the reproduction of living coral—more to the point, sex. And when an animal built like a rock so engages itself, the brief and rare spectacle of its own genesis is rare, indeed. It is so unique and short-lived, in fact, that no human had even photographed coral spawning in this hemisphere until witnessing it on the Flower Garden Banks in the Gulf of Mexico in 1990. Tonight, there are only five of us—photographers, writers, and conservationists from throughout Florida—virtually alone in the dark sea, watching closely as the reef prepares to begin its own once-a-year tango with procreation.

Very soon, some coral heads will synchronously erupt with millions of tiny egg packets, creating an underwater snowstorm of pink-orange pellets. Others will smoke furiously with sperm, as if on fire. And the twain, somewhere, will meet, providing the nexus for another generation of reefs yet-to-be, the pioneers of underwater cities of stone and flesh that nurture a multitude of fish and shellfish that range throughout Florida's waters and beyond.

Meanwhile, back in the tiki huts and Kokomos and Holiday Inn bars on land, the dim light of sexual reckoning of my own species is likely underway: foreplay has already begun and, if it seems rehearsed, it is far more uncertain than what the coral will eventually reveal to me here tonight. After all, we humans have been groping about with each other in the dark for a relatively short time; in contrast, coral has been in the colonizing business for over two hundred million years.

* * *

In T-shirt and swim trunks, a deeply tanned and barefoot Laddie Akins pulls the throttle back gently on a forty-foot dive boat, spins the wheel, and moves the vessel away from the dock with a practiced deftness. It is nearing dusk here on the ocean side of Key Largo, and Akins is taking a small group of friends and colleagues out to watch the coral engage in sex. Akins is the head of a marine conservation program called REEF, which is to marine life what Audubon is to birds back in the terrestrial world. REEF volunteers take waterproof survey slates with them on their dives, identifying and counting all they see. In this way, they help augment the poorly funded work of government biologists who try to keep a handle on the health of the underwater world. As veteran fish counters know, there is no better place to observe fish than on a coral reef, for it is a valuable oasis of life on an otherwise featureless sea bottom. Although reefs cover far less than 1 percent of the sea bottom, they support 80 percent of its marine life. A single healthy reef system may include some three thousand different species of fish, reptiles, mollusks, sponges, and plants. Tonight, there will be no inventory of fish to be made. The reef is the holy grail of the ocean, and we simply want to see how it all begins.

It is seven days after the full moon in August, and the coral is said to be literally bulging with promise. When it does climax, its moment of ecstasy will be brief—probably less than an hour. That means just being on the water in a boat tonight is not enough: if we aren't under the sea, right next to the action when it happens, we could miss it entirely. (Indeed, another boat out here to witness the same spectacle tonight will pull anchor prematurely and go home, as it were, unconsummated.)

Unlike happy hours and last calls here in the Keys, the rites of coral do not dance to the drummer of man's clock. Instead, it listens for something distant and internal, waiting as it has waited over the millennia for all the natural clues to present themselves at once. To do any less is to court disaster with its continuing existence. "To survive as a coral is very risky," Dr. Alina Szmant had told me before my trip tonight. Szmant, a leading coral scientist with the Rosenstiel School of Marine Science at the University of Miami, has studied coral behavior in the wider Caribbean since 1982, particularly on the reefs off La Parguera, Puerto Rico. "All the natural conditions have to be just right." Water must be warm, and the tide must be weak to keep from washing everything away too suddenly. The half-full moon, which is at its neap, rises later in the evening to give the eggs a head start over predators who hunt by vision. Even then, survival is probably less than .001 percent, which explains why millions of eggs flood the water during a spawn, and why the spawn takes place all at once: synchronicity improves its odds for survival. Most will be eaten by fish, will wash away in currents and tides, or will simply go unfertilized. Szmant says an early spawn of elkhorn a couple nights ago released countless eggs over the reefs in Biscayne Bay. But a sudden rain storm fell afterward, diluting the surface-riding eggs with fresh water and bringing their short if profuse lives to an abrupt end.

Nevertheless, the urge to spawn all at once is a mighty one, genetically encoded deep down in the Jurassic origins of the coral itself. Scientists who keep living corals in aquariums—even inside of buildings with a roof and no natural connection to the wild sea—report their corals spawn at exactly the same moment as those on the reefs.

We reach the reef site called Key Largo Dry Rocks just before sundown. Here, Akins ties the boat to a mooring buoy and we gear up for the first dive. With us are Ned DeLoach, co-founder of REEF and a publisher of marine-life identification guides in Jacksonville, his wife and partner, Anna, Deena Wells, a British-born conservationist who does consulting work for REEF, and Dan Wagner, a veteran underwater videographer from Indialantic, Florida.

I twist open the air knob on my tank, hoist on my gear, and do a penguin walk to the stern dive platform, where I bend to put on my fins. Wagner, my dive buddy, is already in the water, and I lean down unsteadily to hand him his video camera. He takes it and then slips fully under, an upwelling of exhaust bubbles taking the place of where he had been. I look over my shoulder once at the now-empty boat, glance briefly back at the silent shore of Key Largo six miles away, and then leap feet first into the flat, mirror-like ocean.

Once here, I breathe steadily as I adjust my eyes—and my attitude—to this world. As always, entry brings with it an exhilarating, emotional rush. But that is soon replaced by a reverence, a deep and almost spiritual caring for this seldom-seen reality. Unlike all the topside wonders of nature, this hidden marine world is neither readily accessible or easily understood for us air-breathing mammals, which explains why we've been watching birds and bees procreate forever—while the phenomena of coral spawning has remained a mystery until recently.

Tonight, we are on the lookout for several species of star coral. As one of the major reef builders, the star is also one of the most common corals we're likely to find. Seen up close, the rocky cups of the star coral seem, well, starlike. Inside each lives a tiny anemone-like animal that usually extends to feed under the cover of darkness.

Once thought to be a plant because it is anchored to the bottom, corals are living colonies of animals that live in symbiosis with an algae called zooxanthellae. The animal snatches tiny shrimp or the early larval stages of other reef animals with its tentacles—not unlike its cousins who share the same phylum of *cnidaria,* hydroids and sea anemones. While the polyps provide food, the algae uses the classic plant trick to harness energy from the sun by photosynthesis. It is also this algae that gives corals their colors. When under stress—from superheated seas, for instance—the reef will expel its zooxanthellae, not unlike a tree dropping its leaves in a drought. Although corals are found worldwide—even in polar waters—it's only those that live in the shallows of the subtropics that grow fast enough to create the great blufflike reefs. Upward they grow, toward the light, sometimes even breaching the water's surface. For early mariners, they could be a nightmare, rising abruptly from thirty feet and more of otherwise navigable water to poke a hole in a wooden hull. For that reason, great Spanish treasure fleets today lay scattered along the reef tract of the Keys, most of them now consumed by the same colonies of corals that first brought them down.

To a diver, corals appear soft, like sea fans, whips, rods, and plumes, or they seem hard, like the descriptively named elkhorn, staghorn, brain, and star. On healthy reefs, there may be over sixty-five different species of coral, and they all share the same needs: seawater that is warm, clear, and shallow—fed by plankton and oxygen in a steady swash of currents and tide. While attacked by natural predators like parrot fish, snails, and sea urchins, the biggest threats are man-made. Indeed, this John Pennekamp Coral Reef State Park was first established in the 1960s after men blasted away huge chunks of it to sell for roadside souvenirs. Now, threats are more sublime and come in the form of land-based pollution and bleaching caused by various El Niños. Global warming, as it continues, will surely factor into the equation.

By now, darkness has descended over the reef like a thick blanket. The moon has not risen yet, and although we are in barely thirty-five feet of clear water, the world here is as black as the deepest trenches. I pan with my underwater light, and its beam illuminates scads of normally secretive glassy sweepers swarming atop the reef. Have the little fish been clued in somehow to the impending event? I think of similar spawns in western Australia where massive whale sharks are drawn in by the chumlike scent of the eggs, and I wonder what other predators we might encounter here tonight.

Wagner flicks on the strong lights of his video rig and moves quickly to a small, cabinet-sized mound of great star coral, *Montastrea cavernosa.* The DeLoaches are already there, with their own cameras, hovering a few feet off the bottom. As I approach, I see the gumdrop-shaped mound is smoking, as if on fire. The white puffs of sperm, which seem to be fired out of the coral in strong jets, dilute and thin a few feet from the mound and then, nearly invisible, float away to the surface. It is as if a very little person is inside the coral head, puffing madly away on a García y Vega.

Unlike some bisex corals, which eject tiny packets containing both eggs and sperm, the great star creates itself in colonies of the same sex. This one is all male, and it is reacting to the release of eggs by a female colony, somewhere out there in the darkness. We hang suspended in the water in a little circle around the hump of great star coral for the next half hour, filming and carefully watching until the smoking sputters and then, finally, stops altogether.

I flipper away, investigating other mounds of coral nearby for any other signs of activity. As I move across the sea floor, I see a yard-long porcupine fish with puppy-dog eyes scuttling into a little coral cave, a Spanish lobster prancing under a school of Caribbean reef squid, a six-foot nurse shark resting with its head under a coral ledge. The world down here is alive with life, but the isolated smoking seems to have come to a halt. One by one, we ascend to the surface.

Back on deck, we change tanks for the next dive while Akins moves the boat a few hundred yards to the shallow lee of the reef. It is later now, closer to the 10 P.M. window when Szmant predicted the action for most of the star coral would begin. Like other years, though, this one could produce a "split spawn." In this scenario, some coral heads would erupt tonight, while others would wait for the same lunar cycle in September to begin their tiny work.

Under the dim amber light on the boat, we share tales about other spawning rites we have encountered in our underwater travels. Anna tells of diving in Roatan in midsummer and seeing a throng of tiger tail sea cucumbers entwined, atop a reef, busily releasing eggs. Akins says he saw brittle starfish spawning not long ago off Key West. I mention I saw sponges smoking in Bonaire last September. Unlike tonight's expected event, the other experiences were pure serendipity for us all, a matter of blundering onto the right place at the right time.

Back under the dark sea, I turn off my light to save batteries. Looking up, I see the hull of our boat gently crashing down into the surface, outlined by blue-green bioluminescence on each rise and fall. The water is more shallow here, only ten to fifteen feet, and if I am careful, I can stay down for over two hours with my single tank. I breathe carefully in the dark, awed by the natural flashes of light, which seem to mirror my own slow-release bursts of adrenaline.

Conditions for the spawn, as Szmant predicted, are at their very best: the half-full moon is not yet above the horizon, so nocturnal predators who hunt visually by its light have no advantage. The neap tides of the midlunar cycle are not strong enough to separate the eggs and sperm or to send them out to deeper water. Nor are there any pesky winds that might do the same. Finally, the sea is as warm as it will ever get, creating a natural incubator for the temperature-sensitive tropical polyps. Unless the individual corals suddenly develop stage fright from all this attention, a spawn should soon be underway.

Despite the widely reported problems with this reef tract—a marked decline in water quality, overfishing, boat groundings, and scars from heavy sport diving—the good news is the coral can still procreate. "Active sex," Szmant had told me before the dive, "is always good for survival." In this way, spawning can be viewed as a sign of good health. The more sex, the better.

At this very moment, however, I am not pondering anything that intellectual. Instead, I am simply floating in the dark womb of what amounts to a giant isolation tank, feeling all warm and transcendentally fuzzy, watching the underwater fireflies flash on and off. All I need is some Windham Hill music to numb me out entirely. And that is about where I am when something big and tangible suddenly thumps into my tank.

After swallowing a mouthful of seawater, I turn to see Wagner, with his big walrus mustache splayed out from above his regulator. The underwater videographer is hovering over me like some mutant sea creature with his black neoprene hood, lights blazing from his camera rig.

He motions me to follow him and we fin a hundred yards across the sea bottom, between the haystacklike mounds of boulder star, *M. annularis,* spooking an octopus into an emotional flash of iridescence as we go.

In the distance, I see the other four members of our team fluttering about a single coral head, their light beams crisscrossing like search strobes on miniature helicopters. As I approach, there seems to be no signs of a spawn. Then, I move in closer. As I do, I see that each polyp on the surface of the coral is nearly bursting with its own pink-orange BB-sized "egg."

These eggs, in fact, are often not single embryos at all, but podlike packets called "gametes" that contain sperm and hundreds of miniscule eggs. Unlike the male colony of great star that jetted out cloudy sperm, and females of other species that extrude eggs, this colony of boulder star is hermaphroditic—a nifty trick that seems somehow to eliminate a lot of guesswork from the process.

If we think of the other corals as the freewheeling singles, sending their male or female DNA out like ships passing in the night, we can see *M. annularis* as a natural high-rise condominium chock full of fertile married couples. And the stork—indeed, an entire flock of them—are on their way.

I look at my dive watch. It is 11:00 P.M. I have been in the water for most of the night, and I'm beginning to doubt if the spawn will take place after all. And then, without warning, it happens. The pink-orange packets begin to shoot out from the surface of the coral, as if being fired by teeny popguns. First comes one handful, then another. Within seconds, thousands of packets are released, almost at once. I am literally surrounded by a snowstorm of Technicolor pellets. Christmas has surely arrived. And it's not difficult to reach into myself and remember how it really felt as a kid to be thoroughly and deeply surprised by an event, to be awed by the eternal magic of it all.

As the egg packets swirl about us, it strikes me how far we humans have come: the notion of sharing in a natural phenomenon of the sea—instead of spearing it, netting it, or filleting it for dinner—seems somehow redemptive, reinforcing our own long and immutable links to the ocean itself. The spawn continues as I move from coral mound to coral mound, watching as the ocean around me becomes filled with the eggs. Tiny crustaceans called copepods swarm in my lightbeams like mosquitoes, and tropical fish dart frenetically through it all.

At last, just after midnight, the spawn stops as suddenly as it started. I look closely at the surface of the coral heads and see the tiny polyps there, bereft of their gametes. Somewhere above, the packets will rupture and the fertilized eggs will float away with the current. Szmant had told me the eggs will hatch into free-floating animal plankton and, after three to five days of metamorphosis, will settle down to the bottom as tiny coral polyps—which is where they'll spent the rest of their lives, secreting their little castles of calcium from the seawater. But exactly where they end up and why is still a puzzle.

Vital questions like this still remain about the life cycle of the coral, and more careful reporting of the spawns may help answer them. For instance, reefs in the Keys and off the South Atlantic coast of Florida may be still healthy enough to support a spawn of mature corals—but are they healthy enough to nurture the highly vulnerable baby corals?

Time, and more field research, will tell. For now, I check my air pressure gauge, and seeing the needle has moved over into the red, flipper gently up to the surface. I hang here, with my mask on my head, breathing in the sweet, fresh, night air now. The other divers are still submerged, and it seems as if I have the entire sea to myself.

Off in the distance, I hear a fish jump and then splash back down again. I can barely make out the shoreline of Key Largo and its muted lights six miles away. The ocean is so placid it could be a big pond, a great pool of water with gentle, subtle swells. I tilt my head back and watch as the half moon begins its slow rise above the horizon. It is pink-orange tonight, a giant astral gamete, and it seems to be bursting with promise.

Trinidad

Shark, Where Did You

Get That Gold?

Just offshore Trinidad's Manzanilla Bay, beyond where the little
chip-chip shells softly gurgle on the varnish of the wet beach and sand
dollars lie bankrupt in shards, three dark-skinned fishermen in an
open pirogue are up to their waist in gill net. I am in the bow, quietly
watching. To the east, the new sun rises up out of rolling seas that
stretch uninterrupted, all the way to Africa. To the west, the quarter
moon, as faint as an old memory, seems to teeter atop a grove of
coconut palms.

Set in shallow waters here late yesterday, the monofilament seine
has quietly done its work throughout the night. Its rewards emerge

now as the fishermen pull the heavy net up and over the stern gunnels of the boat, straining in the cool air of the early tropical morning with the weight of net, fish, and seawater. Up come small mackerel and catfish, bonnethead and smalltail shark, all whitish and glistening, adeptly yanked from the net and tossed into a box built into a hollow seat.

And then, in a flash of brilliant color, up comes something else altogether. No more than two feet in length, it is an economy version of some made-up sea creature, twisting and bucking in the seine. With its angry little mouth and splayed-out head lobes, the hammerhead seems patched together from bits of an early morning dream: it is a goldfish with an attitude, grimacing like Peter Faulk on a bad hunch. This is *Sphyrna tudes,* an elasmobranch like none other—the only shark scientifically known to acquire the color of what it eats.

"Yellow *chapeau,*" the captain says to me in a thick patois, pulling a French word from distant Trini history to describe the shark by the hatlike hammer it wears. Then he snatches it free of the net and tosses it unceremoniously atop the other fish in the cold box. And there it lies, a shiny doubloon among a phalanx of dull quarters. Whatever status the golden hammerhead may have in the scientific world, here on the southernmost island of the West Indies—where it has been found more often than anywhere else—it has a far more down-to-earth manifestation. Seined and hooked, filleted and salted, cooked into native dishes of accra and buljol, *S. tudes* is, most of all, sustenance.

It is the end of the dry season and Trinidad is burning. From the air, I see the glow of brushfires smoldering like Christmas lights in the dark night foliage. As soon as I step down onto the tarmac, I smell the sweet, pungent scent of charred tropical hardwoods, fruit trees and flowering shrubs, the aroma of natural incense.

I have come to Trinidad in search of the golden hammerhead, an animal little known to the rest of the world, but one which thrives here in the murky plume of Venezuela's Orinoco River delta. The freshwater

Orinoco, a river that begins deep inside Brazil 1,600 miles away, surges out into the Caribbean around Trinidad, transporting bits of its rarefied Amazonian environment, sediment, and organic nutrients far to sea. Corals, which grow best in clean, clear waters don't do well here, preferring the more oceanic waters of neighboring Tobago twenty-two more miles to the northeast. So, too, do the tropical fish that traditionally inhabit Caribbean reefs. But for the golden hammerhead, the silty waters around Trinidad are its briar patch, chock full of shrimp and catfish, its favorite foods.

Before my departure, I talked with Dr. José Castro, the noted shark biologist who did the first thorough study of the animal in 1987, making the startling connection between the orange pigments in its diet and its vibrant colors. Today, Castro works with NOAA's U.S. Fisheries field office in Miami.

Castro, who was awarded a special year-long contract with the U.N. Food and Agriculture Organization between August 1985 and 1986, came here to determine if the entire shark population that ranged off Trinidad and Tobago was healthy enough to support a fishery. Based in waterfront government offices at Chaguaramas on the northwest tip of the island, the Cuban-born scientist regularly traveled to the roughshod fishing villages around the coast of Trinidad—immersing himself in an authentic environment few tourists here ever see.

Sometimes rising before dawn, Castro rode out in the open pirogues with the Trini fishermen, often fighting seasickness in the rough, near-shore waters. Aboard, he watched carefully as they pulled in their long nets and baited hooks, identifying some eighteen different sharks before the year was over. The haul included larger elasmobranchs like the bull, tiger, and spinner, as well as four species of hammerhead. Of them all, the blacktip, the smalltail and *Sphyrna tudes*—then known as the "smalleye hammerhead"—came over the dripping gunnels in the nets most often.

Later, after preparing a local shark identification guide and authoring a report urging that the biologically vulnerable shark fishery be carefully regulated, Castro turned his personal attention to the golden hammerhead. "There was hardly anything known about it," he told me. "Some thought it was found in the Mediterranean. Many reports of people capturing the animal didn't even mention the coloration. And most preserved specimens had lost their colors. The first time I saw it when it was fresh, I said: 'Whoaaa!' It was a very intense color."

Castro, who knew the local villages well, had suggested Manzanilla Bay on the northeast coast as a good starting point for my hunt. Here, he said, I will find a rustic fishing village where the wooden pirogues routinely return with catches of a variety of sharks, including the little golden hammerhead.

And so it is this village that I am off to from Port-of-Spain, driving across the single-lane roads that wind over the hilly jungle terrain at the edge of the 3,000-foot-high northern mountain range. Situated little more than eight miles off the South America coast, Trinidad shares many of its plants, animals, even its topography—mountains and waterfalls, coastal plains and seashore cliffs—with the mainland to which it was once attached. With a culture compressed from the descendants of African slaves and indentured East Indian servants, the island seems a potent staging ground for all things exotic, tropical, and unknown. The golden hammerhead couldn't have a better home range.

As I approach Manzanilla Bay, the thick tropical roadside tangle of lobster claw heliconia, sapodilla, and calabash trees is abruptly replaced by a vast, wild grove of coconut palms hugging a hard-packed gray-brown beach. Here, I leave the pavement and drive northward over a jeep trail to the village, dodging fallen palms and a road-kill caiman as I go.

The broad bay stretches south for miles from here, fading into a thick haze. Although its waters have the distinctive green hue associated with the tropics, I look closely at the waves as they curl and see the underside of the sea is thick with brownish sediment. The jeep trail narrows as it winds onto a small, sandy peninsula wedged between the bay and a tropical river. Here, a dozen shacks of sun-weathered planks, plywood, and tin line both sides of the road, which is now comman-deered by little reddish chickens. An old woman sweeps the dirt with a broom made of twigs. At the edge of the river, two men unload a long seine from a battered wooden pirogue. Nearby, a handful of fishermen rest atop an overturned hull under a tin-roofed palapa that has collapsed on one side.

Charcomas, ominous-looking black-headed vultures, feed on fish scraps in the mud, and yellowish bannaquit birds chatter in the mango trees overhead. The sweet smell of burning marijuana hangs thickly in the air.

On one make-shift table of corrugated tin, newly cut shark fillets are drying in the sun. On another, several sets of shark jaws and sea turtle shells are scattered about. It is not yet the season for the turtles, says one fishermen, but they get caught in our nets and die, so we can keep them now. There is no golden hammerhead to be seen in any form.

A Trini fisherman with the unlikely name of Charlie Chapman tells me he will be catching some of the little sharks in the next couple of days. Chapman is the owner of a fiberglassed wooden pirogue he has named for himself. But now the moon and tides are bad, and the mud-dier, more shallow waters where they set their nets around the protective rocky point are too rough. Maybe tomorrow.

After driving my rented jeep northward to the "fishing depots" of Balan-dra and Salybia and finding no sign of the shark, I return to Manzanilla by late afternoon the next day. The new moon is still not good, but the surf is better. "Plenty much calm," says Charlie. He and his men will set some nets now, and he invites me to join them.

Although I have come with the half-formed idea of observing the little hammerhead underwater, I have been urged by everybody—from scientists to fishermen—to forget it. The one- to two-foot underwa-ter visibility of the shark's habitat simply keeps it hidden from divers, they say.

I climb aboard the pirogue with its captain and two other Trini fishermen, and we putter down the jungle river a few hundred yards to where it empties into the ocean, past a small family of red howler monkeys swinging in the tallest coconut palms. The hull, plain white on the outside, looks like a lime that has been halved and fiberglassed within. Beyond the river mouth, we crash into a steady line of whitecaps, headed into open seas outside the windbreak of the high, foliage-covered bluff that curls protectively toward the village like a prehensile tail.

When Castro isolated the golden hammerhead here for study, he had to start virtually from scratch. Historically, most of the little sharks had been examined by taxonomists back in museums long after being caught and preserved in alcohol. Not only was there scant connection between the animal and its real-world habitat, but its intense colors had usually broken down to a dull gray or chalk white.

Alive, S. tudes was "one of the most beautiful elasmobranchs," Castro found. But more spectacular than its beauty was how it was acquired. Born live in broods of six to twelve in the shallow, shrimp-rich nurseries under the waters of Manzanilla and adjacent Matura Bay, the young hammerhead pup was unspectacular—colored mouse-gray with a pale yellow belly. But by the time it reached 55 to 70 centimeters in size (21 to 27 inches), it had turned an intense metallic yellow. Then, by maturity, its glory was gone. Its gold had faded to a dull, splotchy yellow.

In analyzing the stomach contents of over one thousand sharks, Castro discovered a local marine catfish and its eggs—both a dull yellow—when the shark's colors were muted, and a bright yellow shrimp (Xiphopenaeu kroyeri) when they were the most vibrant. The connections seemed obvious.

A half mile offshore, Charlie throttles down the outboard and we cork over gentle five- and six-foot swells as his men begin pulling in an 800-foot-long gill net set here last night. Fewer than a dozen bony fish two and three pounds each come up in the twenty minutes it takes to retrieve the net. By now, the heavy mono is stacked waist-high inside the lime-green hull like a giant backlash from a fishing reel.

From here, we run parallel to the wild Matura coast of isolated coves, palms, and jungle for another hour before Charlie turns the pirogue in toward the beach. The boat rocks precariously as one fisherman lets out the seine, hand-over-hand, setting it perpendicular to shore. When he is done, we are barely one hundred yards off the beach in six to eight feet of water, the pirogue rising and falling on the crest of each breaker.

A few degrees to the left or right and we would be swamped, maybe swimming over the muddy bottom with the yellow sharpo and his crustacean fodder ourselves. But Charlie, laconic and slow-moving back on shore, is a fine boatman with quick reflexes, and we are again headed safely back out to sea.

Harvested mainly as an incidental by-catch, like other sharks here, the bottom dwelling *S. tudes* is one of the smallest Caribbean elasmobranchs. Castro found it maxes out at 122 centimeters (four feet), but averages closer to only 108 centimeters (3.5 feet) and 6.4 kilos (14 pounds). Except for its color and size, it could be easily confused with the scalloped hammerhead, which grows much larger and ranges up the eastern seaboard of the United States.

It is not size, though, or even its unique biotransference of pigments that ultimately may distinguish *S. tudes*—but the reason it needs to turn gold. Castro speculates its coloration is "protective," a costume that helps the small shark blend in with the clay-colored silt to avoid larger predators during a vulnerable time of its life cycle. "It is possible the diet is used for camouflage," Castro says. "Quite often pigments are used for that reason."

The startling difference, of course, is that while other animals—including many dramatically striped and spotted sharks—also use pigmentation to their benefit, they often do so because of eons of mutation, natural selection, and adaptive change. In contrast, the gold of *S. tudes* is not a generational fait accompli, handed it on a genetic platter simply because its species was so encoded. Unlike the spotted whale shark and the horned shark, the cat and the blue, this pint-sized elasmobranch has to eat his way into the yellow range of the color spectrum. In this way, it is more like the flamingo, which without its shrimp-rich diet would be closer to white.

As the tropical sun drops low on the horizon, Charlie turns his pirogue back toward the village. Smoke from the dry-season brush-fires—many of them ecologically destructive slash-and-burn attempts to convert jungle into rice and melon farms—wafts out to sea, mixing with the salt spray. When the rainy season begins, local waters will turn even more silty from the freshwater erosion and runoff, mimicking the regional effects of the Orinoco.

For now, if the weather holds, if the sea stays "plenty much calm," we will be back in the morning atop the cresting breakers to pull the nets, hoping to find a little golden hammerhead.

Dawn breaks in Manzanilla to the braying of goats. Tiger sharks and fish landed earlier are already being filleted, salted, and packed into a huge gray plastic vat that a fish buyer from Port-of-Spain will come for later. Shark fins, collected for export to Japan, are being dried separately. They will bring four to five times the value of the meat. In one of the shacks, an old islander with a white beard is boiling shark livers with a handful of spices over a fire. Later, he will strain and funnel it into empty quart rum bottles to sell as a folk remedy.

Despite the rich storytelling culture of Trinidad, there is no mythology to conjure lore for the golden hammerhead. Most Trinis I have met simply know it as a little fish that is sweet tasting. Unlike the ceiba tree, which sometimes harbors the spirits of jumbies, or the bamboo-poled flags that summon Hindu gods here, the golden hammerhead is seafood that just happens to be gold. It is only science that exalts the species.

It is this unique shark that has come up in the nets of one boat this morning, a single two-foot-long specimen. When Charlie sees me, he tells me of the catch. I follow him to the pirogue where fishermen have left the shark for me to see. Grabbing its tail, I look at it closely, holding the dead animal up so the new sun backlights the gold, making it seem to glow. It is every bit as unreal as I'd hoped.

Scientists at Clemson University who have studied the biochemical makeup of the yellow chapeau have found the color is a carotenoid—a pigment commonly found in plants and vegetables such as carrots. Still unknown, though, is how the carotenoid makes its way from the digestive tract to the skin. If new studies into the biochemistry continue, they will have a sense of urgency that Castro's early work did not have: that's because the yellow hammerhead, badly overfished like many shark species, may be driven to extinction if it is not managed. In all my time here, I have only seen a single gold shark. Yet when Castro was here fifteen years ago, he reported seeing them in the villages in large piles as they were being off-loaded from the pirogues.

If the hammerheads are the most recently evolved of all the sharks, with less than twenty-five million years to experiment with their wide-slung, hydrodynamic lobes, then perhaps this is one of the "newest" and most specialized sharks of them all. As bronze as the waters in which it lives, *S. tudes* could be a breakthrough in adaptive behavior, the only shark known to truly become what it eats. And then again, it could be an evolutionary dead end, restricted to a rarefied environment with regional boundaries that are being daily changed and exploited by man.

Whatever its destiny, the fate of this single specimen is clear. In a few rapid movements of a sharp fillet knife, the golden hammerhead loses all that makes it so. And *Sphyrna tudes* is now a small pile of clean, white meat to be iced and packed with other fish not nearly as esteemed. It is only the charcomas that still worry with the gold, pecking and pulling at the orange skin at the edge of the dark tidal mud.

The Turtle People
of the Miskito Coast

Waiting to Exhale

The photographer folds his tripod, rests it on his shoulder like a
weapon, and joins me in the dirt main street of Puerto Cabezas just
before midnight. We are headed for the butcher's house in the cool
tropical blackness of the remote Miskito Coast of Nicaragua, where
green sea turtles will be filleted for market.

Somewhere in the distance, a gunshot and then another rings out.
Braziers cut from oil drums spit sparks into the night, tended by old
women hunched like wood storks, selling tiny lobes of fish, chicken
for *just a few córdobas, Señor.* We march as if we do this every night,
come to watch the butcher rip the shells from the massive greens,

overturned on their back like half moons under the stilts of his wood and tin-roofed home.

Nicaragua had a civil war not so long ago, and the United States, eager as always to assert itself in the business of others, intervened on behalf of wealthy Nicaraguans who did not much like how land reforms were threatening their fiefdoms. The wealthy Nicaraguans, who established their own government-in-exile in Miami, were called the Contras. To destabilize the economy of Nicaragua, the United States funded the Contras, mined the harbor at the capital of Managua where most of the country's trade goods were delivered, and banned trade. By the time it was all over, no one, really, had won, but the economy was fully in shambles. It had become the second poorest country in the hemisphere, after Haiti. There was almost no funding to help biologists better understand—and help care for—natural areas like parks and preserves.

Most money, like power itself, remained on the Pacific, the high and dry coast from which the Spanish colonists had historically ruled Nicaragua. Here, on the remote Miskito Coast of the Caribbean, a low and wet and malaria-ridden place, there was no cash to build schools and hospitals or even to train and arm policemen.

When shots ring out in the night, as they are doing now, it is usually because someone is shooting someone else, or trying to, and while there are laws about such things, there is no one to enforce them. *Vigilancias* are more common than *policía*.

In front of us, on the dirt street, a few men come tumbling out of the Discoteca Jumbo, pushing and shoving each other. Only one, a solidly built man in his early twenties, is sober enough to even notice the two gringos, and, ignoring the others, he stands feet apart in the middle of the road, glaring, fixing for a fight. We give him a wide berth, moving deftly around him while also trying not to show fear, and this seems to work okay.

We cross a low wooden bridge and walk through a narrow path

bounded by high grasses. By now we are away from the town, into a more wooded area where houses are up on stilts, surrounded by breadfruit and mango trees and the big thick leaves of plantains. It is all dark here at this hour, only the butcher's house marked by the amber glow of a single low-voltage incandescent light in the backyard. The light hangs over a table of driftwood laid out with rusty knives, just the edges sharpened and gleaming like razors. The butcher nods at us—we have already made arrangements to be here, and there is nothing more to say. Two large boys grasp a hefty green sea turtle, *Chelonia mydas,* by its flippers and haul it out from under the house, its carapace scraping like a sled on the hard dirt. The butcher is a lean Miskito Indian, his brown skin as finely lined as an old porcelain vase. The turtles are two hundred to four hundred pounds each, as old as he is, maybe older. They will have a lot of meat.

The butcher hesitates, telling me that he is waiting for the turtle to exhale, otherwise the kept air will sour its meat. Then, suddenly, he slams a sledge hammer into the head of the animal. She lets go with a deep *whooosh,* the sound of wind being sucked into a vortex, a final mortal sigh. Skilled hands slice the plastron from the soft underbody. Reddish meat with green fat goes into a tub, and the gristle and shell are tossed to the pack of gathering half-feral dogs. The strobe of the photographer's flash fires again and again, burning this vision deeply into my brain. Months later, I can still see it when I close my eyes, as if it just happened a second ago.

I have come to Nicaragua to learn more about sea turtles and the people who hunt them, maybe to try to figure out how it all fits into this modern world. For me, sea turtles seldom fail to evoke a transcendent sense of awe. I have seen adult turtles underwater soaring through the everlasting blue of infinity like some prehistoric bird gliding on muscular wings. I have watched in wonder as baby turtles scuttled about in low-tech native hatcheries off Los Roques, Venezuela, and Isla de Juventud,

Cuba. I have witnessed mature males and females thrashing in mating rites on the surface of the water in Tagus Cove in the Galapagos.

When I first started diving in Florida in 1976, it was considered okay to harass turtles. One West Palm Beach dive operator, before she became a conservationist, was widely known for riding the shells of giant sea turtles, and even had T-shirts printed with the image of her doing just that. Now most divers know it's not even good sense to disturb one when it's sleeping. Or feeding. Or mating.

To get to Puerto Cabezas, I flew from Managua over the rugged central mountain range on La Costeña, a domestic prop service, bumping down on a hard clay airstrip just outside of town. With its population of forty-five thousand, Puerto Cabezas is the largest "city" on the Miskito Coast. Bluefields is the only other settlement here of any size, and it is to the south. Both towns are isolated coastal enclaves, unlinked by roads. To the interior is a dense tropical jungle, a kind of Central American Amazon. Early maps show almost the entire Caribbean coastline of Central America mapped as Miskito or La Mosquitía. The history of this coast is a rich one, for it offered shelter to all the pirates and renegades and castaways who once roamed the Caribbean Sea. Many of these reprobates were British, which explains why English—or a patois of it—is widely spoken, and why there are so many place names—like Corn Island and Sandy Bay—mapped in English.

I have rented a spartan room with bath here for twelve dollars a night. My fellow boarders are all timber men, foreigners who have traveled here to strike exclusive deals to allow them to clear-cut the great wild forests of richly grained tropical hardwoods. *La Prensa*, the daily paper in Managua, has told of others coming, too—some Americans—with the intent to buy the rights to take all the fish and shellfish they want from the healthy waters of the Miskito Coast.

At least six different schemes have proposed allowing barges to dump toxic waste—garbage from Miami, hospital waste from New York, chemical waste from the eastern U.S. coast—in some of the *lagu-*

nas. The government, cash poor, considers all such offers. If it weren't for the civil war, the hustlers would have been here sooner. Oddly, its own conflict has saved Nicaragua from exploiters.

I have arranged to meet Jeanne Mortimer here in Puerto Cabezas. A herpetologist who studied under the renowned naturalist and turtle expert Archie Carr, Mortimer is now a consultant for the Caribbean Conservation Corporation (CCC) based back in Gainesville, Florida. The CCC, which arose from Carr's own work, is a nonprofit that specializes in the conservation of sea turtles worldwide. It has adopt-a-turtle fundraising and educational outreach, and radio-tracking programs in which turtles with small transmitters fiberglassed to their shells bounce signals off of distant satellites. Although sea turtles have been around as a species for some two hundred million years, it wasn't until the 1940s that Carr discovered what a wide range they really had. "In those days," Carr wrote in *Windward Road,* "zoologists even doubted *Chelonia* was a migratory animal."

Now it is clear they routinely travel for thousands of miles, between the beaches where they are born, to places where they feed, and then back again as mature adults to those very same beaches to nest. They navigate in the dead of night, underwater, with no reference point. Scientists think this may have something to with an instinct to read magnetic fields; for me, it is an act so wondrous it approaches a miracle.

I head off down the road on foot to see Mortimer. The smoke of wood and charcoal cooking fires hangs like a haze as giant Russian-made convoy trucks rumble through the streets in ferocious clouds of dust, hauling people and boxes of supplies. In the absence of retail stores, a street market winds for blocks with its piles of pineapple, mangoes, firewood, tobacco, clothes, and shoes. A small hut advertises Carey y Coral Negro—hawksbill jewelry and black coral. A man sitting next to a makeshift table is picking through rice, and when I look closer, I see he is culling maggots from it.

I find what I am looking for. It is a large ramshackle wooden stilt house, vaguely reminiscent of British colonial structures I have seen in Belize City. Under the building are storage rooms with scuba tanks and dive gear, a dilapidated old skiff, a rubber boat chewed into uselessness by rats, and a family of chickens.

The CCC funds this office, salaries for a small staff of Miskito Indians, and owns the *Palpa,* a twenty-one-foot research vessel berthed in a nearby creek at Lemlaya. There is a reason for all of this, and it goes far beyond sea turtles. In fact, the subvention for the office, staff, and boat has come from the U.S. Agency for International Development (USAID), which contracted with the turtle group to help devise a strategy to "manage" a 5,000-square-mile offshore area stretching from here to Honduras. If successful, this will become the Miskito Coast Protected Area (MCPA), and it will be unique because—unlike most state-run programs in Latin America—it will try to engage indigenous people in such plans. Traditionally, preserves and parks and protected areas are simply plopped down in the middle of Indian territory, with little regard for the people living there. Sometimes natural resources, which for centuries have been used sustainably by the Indians, are simply sold for profit to foreigners. The democratic planning for this protected area is an anomaly in Latin America.

Upstairs, a "conference room" features a display of shells and coral specimens on a table and photos of sea turtles on the wall. In the hall, one poster urges people not to harm or kill the local manatee; another advises new mothers on the importance of breast feeding. Here, I finally meet Mortimer. She is lanky, blonde, with healthy good looks; like most biologists who have worked a long time in the field, she has very little pretense.

Mortimer, the sole gringo assigned to the project, tells me she first visited the region as a graduate student in the late 1970s. She has since traveled the world in search of sea turtle information, living in fishing villages in far-flung locales like the Seychelles and Malaysia. Although she is too modest to tell me so, she is now considered a world expert in sea turtles. "Turtles are very political," says Mortimer, smiling. "It's hard to study them without considering the culture and the geography of where they are found."

Politics, certainly, are a big part of the equation here. Plans for "protected areas," even good ones, can quickly backfire if not handled with sensitivity. "If you don't understand what the resource means to the local people, you can't come up with a plan," says Mortimer. "If I come in as this pristine white creature with a Ph.D. and tell them what they should do after two weeks, it trivializes the whole experience for all of us."

Instead, Mortimer, fluent in Spanish, tries to blend in with the locals, listening carefully for what it is they are really saying. Besides more carefully identifying cultural needs, a good rapport may also help reveal a wealth of local information about marine life from veteran fishermen. Although *Chelonia* and its brethren are endangered worldwide, the Miskito fishermen here have been harvesting this animal so long they are known as the "Turtle People." While it may seem brutal to us *norteamericanos,* eviscerating a turtle is no less moral to them than, say, turning a cow into a steak or a lamb into a chop, says Mortimer.

We go for lunch at a little native restaurant, a place where sea turtle eggs are offered for sale. We eat rice and beans and stringy chicken. Mortimer and I figure out a plan. She, along with other Miskito leaders involved in the planning for the protected area, will travel to the remote natural harbor of Sandy Bay, which can only be reached by sea, three hours to the north by motorized boat. There, they will meet with villagers and turtle hunters to encourage their input for the MCPA and, in the best of worlds, to effect a buy-in to the plan. Although this protected area is sanctioned by law, once the USAID grant is gone, it will be up to the ethic and understanding of locals to help make it work. The concept sounds simple—to help villagers appreciate long-term sustainable conservation, in effect, to institutionalize what they have practiced all along.

There are problems, however. Back in Managua, I had talked with the head of all protected areas in Nicaragua, and he seemed nearly overwhelmed by the challenge. "We are a poor country," he said. "People hunt in our parks for food, take trees for firewood. Our police and navy have no money for gas to enforce laws." Bringing locals into the strategy is the only way to make any park work. But the Miskito Indians are suspicious. "For years, they have been only 'spectators' while outsiders exploited their territory. . . . When we first came to them with our plan for the MCPA, they asked us: 'Who is going to get rich from this?' "

Mortimer tells me she and her colleagues will use a large motordriven cayuco for the trip to Sandy Bay, but it is already full, and the photographer and I will have to find our own way. She gives us some leads on a boat and a person to navigate it. The nearshore waters can be dangerous, she adds, especially if the wind picks up. And the entrance to the harbor itself is treacherous, only a tiny cut bounded by ever-shifting shoals.

After lunch, the photographer and I walk around town, hunting down leads Mortimer has given us. Finally, we find a young Miskito— no more than seventeen—who says he has a boat and will take us to Sandy Bay. The boy's name is Clemente. He is brown-skinned and stocky, with a friendly open face. Clemente speaks Miskito, Spanish, and English. We follow him to the beach, which is littered with giant empty turtle shells, bleached white from the sun. Dry palm fronds are hiding the overturned hull of the boat. We uncover it and turn it right side up. A family of land crabs living inside scuttles away. It is a simple hand-built dory, no more than sixteen feet, and has no seats inside. Clemente says this is not a problem; he disappears and comes back with a plank of driftwood. It will be the seat. Now, we must find a motor. Clemente knows of a man who will rent us one. We track down the man and strike a deal for use of the motor for a few days. Then we must find fuel. There is one station selling petrol today—supplies are slim—and we buy twenty gallons, more than enough, says Clemente.

We make plans to meet near dawn the next morning. Then we call it a day.

Clemente and his brother are at the beach when we arrive. The sun has just burned its way above the horizon, already starting to turn the pink sky into a pale blue. Just to the north, near the border of Honduras, is the remote cape that Columbus—after a narrow escape in high seas—named Gracias a Dios. To the south is the village of Waunta and the *laguna* cave where Miskito legend says the mother of all manatees lives. The sea stretches out before us, with waves creating little rolling hills of white on it. No problem, says Clemente. He is from a family of fishermen, and they know these waters well. We load our gear into the boat—we have sleeping bags as there is no guarantee where we will stay—and all four of us drag the boat down to the surf. We are up to our waists in the sea when Clemente finally crawls in and starts the motor, motioning us to quickly join him. We do, and off we go, first straight out through the line of rollers, and then finally running parallel to the shore. Clemente handles the boat well, but out here, the sea is rougher than it first looked, and the hull of the boat crashes down with a bone-rattling thump on every other wave crest. We thump along like this for the entire trip, Clemente happily smiling, and the photographer and I anxiously waiting for the thump that will finally splinter the hull. Every five minutes or so, I crouch in the bottom of the dory and bail using an old plastic milk jug.

We are passing through the heart of what will be the protected area. Onshore, there is nothing but spectacularly wild beach, backgrounded by mangrove and then forest. It is the "Windward Road" of the Caribbean that Carr once wrote of, a place where "the good beaches are the windward ones built up high and clean by the driven surf."

Bill Alevizon, a marine biologist working for the CCC, came here earlier to study this region. After spending hours underwater diving on sites around the offshore Miskito cays, the extensive coral-bank reefs, and the vast, healthy beds of turtle and manatee grass, Alevizon reported a true "underwater frontier" distinguished by a healthy profusion of marine life, from spiny lobster and shrimp to manta rays, bull sharks, snook, and schools of snapper and grunts. The region, reported Alevizon, is "probably the most biologically productive in the Caribbean Basin" and, except for fishing, "is one of the last almost totally unspoiled [regional] ecosystems untouched by tourism, coastal development or commercial exploitation." Certainly, for sea turtles, it is one of the best feeding grounds in the world, another piece of the migratory puzzle that includes Tortuguero, the famous protected turtle nesting beach south of here in Costa Rica.

The mouth to the natural cut at Sandy Bay approaches, announced on land by a break in the thick forest and, at sea, by monstrous rolling waves. We are all soaked to the skin with the seawater by now. Clemente circles the boat once to get a better approach and then zooms in, careening off the edges of the shallow bar, just a heartbeat away from falling into the gully between the rollers. I noticed he has stopped smiling now, for the first time. Finally, we reach a smoother patch of water, just enough surge now to carry us into the narrow mouth of the estuarine bay.

The mouth turns into a creek and then an inland bay, creased with more creeks. We are headed for the village of Tawasakia, a few miles away. As we go, we see a barefoot Miskito Indian in worn shirt and pants, leaning from his small wooden dugout to hack away at a stand of red mangrove. He is gathering dead branches that can be used for firewood or made into charcoal for cooking. The deep, clear tidal water that courses past his dugout moves out toward the sea, enriching the massive bay with bits of mangrove leaf, soil, tiny plant and animal plankton. Tarpon and snook thrive here, feeding on the shrimp that other Miskitos will catch by early evening in small seines, casting to tiny bursts of bioluminescence flashing in the water.

We near Tawasakia, passing a young woman with her shirt hitched up to her thighs, washing clothes at the edge of the water. There are other villages back here, all reached by tidal creeks, separated by marshy savannas. We finally put ashore on a high bank. The forest is more open here, and stilt homes with tin and palm-frond roofs are scattered inside of it. A covey of elementary-age schoolgirls with scraps of paper and notebooks held over their heads titter shyly as they wade back across the river on their way home from the frond-topped *bohío* that is their school. Nearby, a young boy chases a small herd of half-wild ponies through a grove of banana trees, rousting chickens and a gaggle of sharp-nosed peccaries in a frenzy of oinks and squawks. The acrid smell of burning wood drifts from a grove of coconut palms where an older Miskito woman is stirring a pot of turtle meat inside a molded clay kiln. Live sea turtles are scattered everywhere, under other houses, turned on their shells, their legs bound. We offload our gear and stow it in a new stilt house that is still being built by men using claw hammers and hand-saws. It is one big open room with windows, but it has a roof, and we can sleep here under it later tonight.

As we get our bearings, a large sail-rigged wooden dory arrives. In its hull is a 200-pound green turtle and two smaller hawksbills. Milo López, a middle-aged fisherman, is watching from his seat on an over-turned dugout. Turtle, says López, is the cheapest meat, the only meat most villagers can even afford. The green, prized among all turtles for its taste, will bring 150 córdobas—about U.S.$25. The smaller hawksbills, their shells used only for jewelry products, might only draw $12 or $13 each, more if taken by water to Puerto Cabezas, a twelve-hour journey by sail. I ask López why the green sea turtles—considered the tastiest to eat—are so called, since their shell is not at all green. "It is the fat inside," he says. "The fat is green."

The meeting of Mortimer and her Miskito colleagues from Puerto Cabezas with locals is underway, we are told. We learn we are in the village of Ledarka, not Tawasakia, which is another mile or so from here, across the marsh and creek. We shoulder backpacks and head out in knee-deep water in the general direction, looking for a simple wood-frame church where the meeting is taking place. I finally spot it on a higher bluff, slightly above the marsh with its metal roof gleaming. The photographer wanders off looking for things unknown to me, and I go inside and sit quietly in a back pew. The wood has been covered with masonry and is ventilated with large glassless windows, bright yellow shutters thrown open. Outside, young boys play catch with a hard, immature mango, using bent pieces of cardboard as gloves. Nearby, a young woman draws a bucket of water from a shallow well dug into the limestone. On the altar, there is one simple wooden statue of Christ and, inexplicably—since this is springtime—an overturned artificial Christmas tree. The tree, in a village that has no electricity, is trimmed in a string of Twinkle Lites.

Although most villagers speak Spanish, the visitors from Puerto Cabezas are careful to keep all discussion in Miskito, an ancient pre-Columbian language. I find it fascinating to listen to but baffling to understand, and after a half hour of this I wander outside and sit in the shade of a breadfruit tree. During a break, Denis Castro, a quiet young Miskito in a baseball cap with a Los Angeles Angels logo, comes out and joins me. Castro, now part of the planning team, once worked as a fisherman. "The problem we face is to truly reclaim the land for the people," he says, sounding a little like a politician. Then, I realize that it is the politicians who try to sound like him. There are some thirty-four villages inside the proposed protected area, and all must sign on if a real strategy is to work. The Miskitos, says Castro, have been eliminated for centuries from decision-making by governments that either ignored them or, during the thirty-year-long Somoza regime, exploited them as cheap labor for the American and British firms that operated plantations and timber mills here. As a result, villagers are simply not used to being a part of a grassroots process like this one. "They are glad we are here to talk to them," says Castro, "but they are very angry at the government."

Still there is a sense of urgency, now more than ever. Nicaragua, which has never courted tourism very well, lost any cachet it had during its civil war. Its people are restless, expecting change, but unsure what form it will take. And here in the villages, tradition still looms large.

The protected-area plan acknowledges that continuing to hunt endangered sea turtles is not a good thing. At some point, that harvest, even here, will decline, says Castro. Perhaps "ecotourism" might help, wherein nature-minded visitors are boated in to visit the village and see live turtles, guided by ex-turtlers. Perhaps more of the fish in the region can be harvested. There are a lot of "perhapses," and all that is certain is that change will happen. The villagers have seen enough of the outside world to know that they want more than they have. Materialism has a certain seductive appeal. Who can say it does not?

Mortimer comes out and joins us in the shade. A rooster crows off in the distance. She is the first to admit there is a vast cultural void between hunting a species and showing it off to visitors through ecotourism. As the Miskito Coast becomes more accessible, it's just a matter of time before the outside world begins to test the natural limits of any resource and the will of the people who live here. Even if the Turtle People are empowered to control their destiny, little is likely to remain the same. Indigenous peoples may still consume sea turtles, but they do so with great reverence. Indeed, some Miskitos believe in a Great Turtle Mother, an omnipotent spirit who intervenes between the world of animals and humans.

Still, it is not the turtlers who have sent this far-ranging animal to the brink of extinction. What has changed in the thousand or so years they have been eating turtles is the rest of the world. Modern humans are very thorough about how well we have invaded the historic territory of this reptile—catching it incidentally as we trawl for shrimp and seine for fish, polluting the ocean in which it lives, and reformatting the beaches where it has nested for centuries. It's not that we don't like turtles; they simply get in the way of our prosperity. Indeed, in the 1930s, naturalist Carr reported a massive *arribada*—when sea turtles crawl ashore en masse to nest. During this particular one, some forty thousand Kemp

Ridleys arrived on one day on a beach at Rancho Nuevo, Mexico. Today, a single arribada of even two hundred Ridley females is rare.

The meeting comes to an end, and all leave the church. I trudge back through the marsh to Ledarka, two little Indian boys leading the way, giggling good-naturedly at the inability of this gringo visitor to follow a simple path. It is late afternoon now, and a bronze light infuses this remote, heartbreakingly magnificent tropical world. This is still very much a place of timeless legend—a place where mangoes are used as baseballs and the mother of all manatees still lives shrouded in a sea cave.

I think of the turtle butcher back in Puerto Cabezas and how he believed that a sea turtle's last breath, if not released, will ruin its meat. The butcher insisted that, knowing this, the turtle keeps its final exhalation inside as long as it can. By holding its breath, then, the sea turtle prolongs its life for a few more seconds. In some ways, perhaps the Turtle People of Nicaragua's Miskito Coast are doing the same.

Cuba

Warships and Flashlight Fish

in the Abyss

El Uvero is a smattering of thatched-roof *bohíos* tucked away in the creases of the green valley that cradles the Río Macambo. When I go on deck of the research vessel *Seward Johnson* early this morning, Uvero is already there, forming itself from the foglike mist that shrouds the Sierra Maestras, occupying a special cleft both in geology and time. As the tropical sun rises higher in the sky, the cumulus burns quickly away. Only the peak of the mile-high Pico Turquino holds tight to the vapor, disappearing convincingly into a ceiling of white.

From the stern of our oceanographic ship, I can see a roadway curling in and out of the boulder-strewn coast barely a quarter mile away, skirting the edge of the turquoise sea. Fast-lane locales in the Caribbean—the Caymans, Cozumel—might have a coastal lane like this lined with time-share condos and billboards and tourist shops with varnished blowfish wearing little sombreros. But along the road to Uvero, there are only coconut palms and sand and wild tropical foliage, interrupted, momentarily, by a cow out for a stroll.

The *Cristóbal Colón,* the largest and most fearsome of Spanish warships, was sunk nearly a century ago just off this beach during the Spanish-American War—known among nationals as the "War of Cuban Independence." Chased out of the Santiago harbor by American gunships, the *Colón* was grounded by its defeated captain to keep it from being used by the enemy. He need not have bothered: Spain, after being pounded by courageous Cuban nationalists for several years, was already at the tail end of its glory in this New World colony. And the more proficient American ships—newly entered into a civil war for less than honorable reasons—were running circles around the Spanish navy.

We will scuba dive on the *Colón* this morning to see what we can find. I am not certain what our adventure on the shipwreck will turn up for natural science, but it will surely make impressive theater for the documentary we are making, and I, for one, am looking forward to getting a front-row seat. As I gather my gear out of the rubber Tuffy can on deck, our small jet boat zooms ashore with Cuban government Navy observer Ariel Ricardo aboard to get a fix on the wreck site. But as it approaches the boulder-strewn coast, its engine dies, a large wave washes over it, and it bobs helplessly in the rise and fall of the sea.

Up goes a flare to get our attention. I worry that locals—based on the history of the last four decades—might be a bit rattled by gringos shooting off rocketlike devices near their shores. But no one stirs, save a goat, which now occupies the road. The reaction back on the ship is equally underwhelming. "Where is Falco when you need him," cracks one crewmember, evoking the omnipresent Cousteauan TV expedition diver who was always enlisted when a daunting challenge arose.

"Yeah," says sub engineer Jim Sullivan, "I always thought *Falco* was French for 'dumbshit.' Here's a job that could drown you: 'Hey *Falco*, come here.'"

A crane lifts a larger and more seaworthy vessel off its cradle on the ship and sets it down in the water to aid in the rescue. It is a sort of Boston Whaler, but with a large rubber Zodiac-like bumper around it. As it zooms off to shore, another crew member uses a faux French accent to describe the hapless jet boat. "Zee boot, eeet is, how you say, becoming leek a flon-der." All soon return to the ship, the good skiff pulling the bad with a towrope, its passengers soaked but unharmed. As they putter up to the side, underwater producer Al Giddings shouts down to a soggy but smiling Ricardo, informing the official Cuban observer he has just logged his first dive of the expedition.

Back in the conference room aboard ship, Giddings previews the upcoming action with his singular panache: "We'll make an exploratory dive on the wreck, and if it's spectacular, we'll make a film dive later. . . . Okay, now, let's go! It'll be rock-and-roll out there in the water, and don't expect good viz." Indeed, the best visibility off this southern coast is usually from February to June, which are the driest months. It is December now, at the end of the rainy season, and while it is relatively dry, that alone may not be enough.

I load my own scuba gear aboard the larger rubber-sided launch, and five of us head out to the general vicinity of the coastal wreck site. Giddings tells me when he was first here fifteen years ago, a portion of the *Colón*'s deck jutted out of the water, providing an easy marker, but today that wreckage is nowhere to be seen. Seaman Mike Conda drives the whaler up and down the shore, while all aboard—including biologist John McCosker, underwater cameraman Randy Wimberg, and associate producer Karen Straus—peer over the gunnels into the aquamarine sea, searching. The bottom falls quickly here; barely three hundred yards from shore, the depth finder shows four hundred feet of water under us, well outside scuba range.

Conda steers us in, fifty yards or so closer, and the slope rises to one hundred feet. Giddings decides a better view is needed and volunteers Wimberg, who, wearing only mask, snorkel, and fins, is pulled behind us from a ski rope, his long frame skimming like a log through the water. Still no luck. Nearby, on the brown flat beach, what must be most of Uvero finally arrives—nine men, women and children, and one dog. They wave at us. McCosker says he will swim in to the beach and ask if they know where the *Colón* might be.

With that, McCosker jumps overboard and swims ashore. When he returns, he tells us we are very close to the site. As for the once-protruding wreckage, the locals told him it is in their homes and farms—hammered into useful tools and hardware. The people of Uvero are *guajiros,* fiercely independent rural campesinos, making a meager living from livestock and farming, augmented by whatever else comes their way—including the maritime fodder of history. Like the Cubans who keep the ancient American Pontiacs and Studebakers running back in Havana, they have learned to do a lot with a little.

With McCosker back in the boat, Conda starts the engine and we move slowly through the sea until we see the Uveritos waving their arms frenetically when we finally reach the site. Down goes an anchor. Giddings free dives here and returns to tell us that after a surge-churned layer of sediment under the surface, the water clears at around forty feet and the wreck can be seen below that. Then the alpha filmmaker puts together the dive plan on the spot: Giddings, Wimberg, and McCosker will descend to one side of the wreck; Straus and I to the other. Straus is a quiet, handsome woman. Born in South Africa, she is an accomplished underwater still photographer and a dive instructor, as well as a producer. She seems to know exactly what she is doing, and goes about her business of assembling her gear with an unruffled confidence.

With our tanks on, we fall backward overboard, Giddings and team first, and then Straus and I a couple of minutes later. Just under the surface, Straus and I fin over to the anchor line and pull our way down through the surf-churned sediment of the surface, hand-over-hand. Giddings was right—the first ten meters are murky and stiff with current. But once we are beyond the upper layer of surge, the visibility begins to clear and one end—the stern or the bow?—of the once-mighty 300-foot-long *Colón* gradually emerges.

Earlier, in a shipboard briefing, Latin American scholar Richard Fagan, along as a consultant, had given us a "Cliff's Notes" version of the *Colón*'s demise: on July 3, 1898, this armored steel warship steamed westward on the remote Cuban coast out of Santiago Bay, firing 120mm shells at its American pursuers. Realizing he was outgunned, the captain grounded her on the rocks at Uvero and opened the sea cocks. Americans boarded her later and, inexplicably, towed her back out to sea, where—with the plugs pulled—it sank. Later, the *Colón* settled down on the sandy bottom, one end at forty feet, the other below one hundred. And here it has been ever since.

I reach the uppermost tip of the wreck and duck down in its lee as soon as I can to avoid the heavy surge whiplashing back from shore. I am carrying one of Straus's still cameras, which she will use when she exhausts the film in her Nikonos. While the camera is nearly buoyant down here, it is bulky and cumbersome and requires some adjustment to my diving style. It gives me far greater appreciation for what Giddings and Wimberg must have to constantly deal with, for the video housings they carry are each the size of a small TV set. Certainly, holding anything underwater will affect what divers call "trim," the dynamic in which even dangling gauges make movement less efficient.

As we fan out on the wreck, Giddings, Wimberg, and McCosker disappear over a distant edge of the ship. Straus pauses, touches her forefinger to thumb, giving me the OK sign; I respond in kind, and we both fin away to the opposite side, and then sink to ninety feet. The deeper I go, the more the *Colón* reveals itself to me, a slow filmlike dissolve in reverse. Just as Spain once colonized this island, obliterating the indigenous Taino culture with its own, the sea has colonized the *Colón*. Nearly every inch of surface is covered with invertebrates—delicate feathery hydroids and bryozoans, red and yellow sponges molded into fingers and branches, soft corals configured into rods and fans and whips. A newly vacated cowry shell glistens, while tiny blennies the size of a pencil point poke their heads cautiously out of worm holes, ducking back in as I pass over—I must seem like some giant holiday-parade balloon to them.

Time and tide have collapsed the hull in upon itself, ripping holes in the deck as well. I flipper down through a jagged maw of one, shining my light in dark crevices below. Back in one corner, a school of copper-colored glassy sweepers cluster, shy of the light. Thin and discus-shaped, the juveniles in the school are almost transparent. Behind them, a still-round porthole looks out over the seascape and I position myself just inches from it, imagining long-gone Spanish crewmen once pressing their faces up against this same port, a half a world away from home. Perhaps they wondered, as I do now, what will happen next. Nearby, giant gears from the engine room lie askew, as does a metal ladder that must have led to the upper deck. I feel like I am inside a movie set of a wreck.

Straus has been firing off shots with her Nikonos in and around the *Colón;* whenever she does, her camera's strobe immerses everything in a blinding white for a nanosecond, adding to the surreal nature of the experience. She fins over to me, blonde hair suspended above her in the water, points to the camera, and gives me a shrug. It is a wordless message: out of film. We dawdle some more on the bottom, until our gauges show only just enough air left in our tanks for a five-minute safety stop—a precaution against the bends—and we both begin our slow ascent. Soon afterward, we are back aboard the *Seward.*

By early evening, I climb our own metal stairs, up to the captain's bridge. Veteran sub pilot Phil Santos is there, watching the shore through a set of powerful binoculars. Twilight has colored the hills of Uvero bronze. There are now odd geometric incisions on the slopes that I hadn't noticed before. Santos, a personable, good-natured man with a strong Boston brogue, is trying to figure out if the incisions are a trick of light or a hastily constructed message of some kind.

Around us, consoles with a half-dozen computerized screens glow with their own unworldly radiance, reporting radar and sonar and other arcane data, pinging and buzzing with static. As I watch, our submersible ascends to just under the surface with its latest cache of deepwater prizes from two thousand feet, its strong lights making the black sea around it smolder in an electric blue. Aboard is Cuban ichthyologist Rodolfo Claro, and in the collection vat with him will be an apricot bass, a deepwater species first described off Curaçao years ago. A strikingly colored palm-sized member of the grouper family, the little fish sports a large yellow dorsal, with three red blotches and a bronze tail fin. Until this sub dive, it has never before been found in Cuban waters.

It is full dark now. Ashore at Uvero, wood and charcoal fires begin to burn. The golden blur of kerosene lamps flickers from the windows of the *bohíos,* thatched-roof homes that are intimations of the original Taino architecture. With the filter of darkness, the reality of Uvero seems especially fluid, easily existing in the now, or one thousand years before the now. However it appears, I am struck by the proximity of two vastly disparate eras—ashore, a simpler, pre-industrialized past, and at sea, a complex and elaborate techno-future.

Santos, finished studying the terrain, puts down his binoculars. I am curious about what he has seen.

"Trick of light?" I ask, referring to the geometric markings on the hillside.

"Nope," says Santos. "It's a message, for sure."

"What does it say?" A pause. I notice Santos is smiling broadly.

"Send lawyers, guns, and money."

By 9:00 P.M., Cuba has vanished, consumed in the black night—all gone except for a distant flicker of a lighthouse marking the exact place where the mainland has been squeezed into a point of treachery at Cabo Francés. Off the stern of the *Seward,* large red squid—perhaps two-pounders—have been darting about at the surface, invertebrate bodies constantly reforming themselves, as if free-associating not with thought but with form. I put on my wet suit and join biologist McCosker, filmmaker Giddings, and a few of the underwater crew in the skiff for a night dive here.

In the boat are a Honda generator to power Giddings's underwater lights, three hundred feet of heavy insulated cable, and the two eighty-pound high-end digital video cameras with their underwater housings. Add eight people and their dive gear to this and you have a craft with very little freeboard, one that moves sluggishly through the water like a giant wounded animal trying to regain its bearings.

Diving on an oceanographic expedition is challenging all by itself, since the exercise is geared not for the comfort or amusement of the diver but for the pursuit of science, under any depth and weather condition. It is nothing like sport diving. And filmmaking adds another challenge—a search for the compelling, drop-your-jaw sort of image that drives a documentary film, keeps the family glued to the screen instead of surfing 140 other channels. Field science can be risky, but when underwater documentary production is factored into the equation, the process can become downright perilous. Filmmakers like Giddings are audacious and fearless jocks who are very adept at wrestling gear about, hovering motionlessly at great depths while breath-holding and, more often than not, surfacing with little or no air left in their tanks. It is how such documentaries get made, has been ever since Jacques Cousteau invented the original cinematic formula that blended high adventure with marine biology.

But there is an added twist: since funds for marine science are now rerouted by politicians into dramatic rocket-plumed trails of space exploration, the institutions most able to afford pricey oceanographic expeditions are the entertainment corporations. The academics with doctorates who once led such field missions now perform on camera in exchange for the chance to practice taxonomy or to ground-truth new ecological theories. But they do so with varying degrees of enthusiasm.

A new winter front has again cooled the air, corrugating the sea into small waves. As the whaler prepares to push away from the *Seward,* an entire school of flying fish—giant pectorals spread like wings—pull from the water, glide fifty feet over the surface, and then disappear almost soundlessly, as if they are being stitched in and out of invisible seams of the gloomy sea. Giddings's rebreather techie, along on this dive only to schlep gear, makes a gratuitous comment about how the colder night waters are perfect for an encounter with a great white shark. This particularly bothers me because I know he is right. After all, the Cuban shark known as the Monstruo de Cojímar was—at five thousand pounds and twenty-one feet—the largest great white ever caught in the world.

We have been offshore this cape on the southern coast near the Gulf of Batabanó for two days now, delayed not by the weather but by topside producer Jim Lipscomb's concerns that if we were to arrive in Havana by New Year's Eve the entire crew would go ashore and run amok. Something similar had already happened during the Christmas evening we spent a few days ago at the Colony, an old Batista-era lodge on the Isle of Youth. Off a dry ship for the first time—after working sixteen-hour days for three weeks—we succumbed to the sirens' call of *mojitos* and Cristal *cerveza.* At the Colony, a slender young *jinetera,* dressed in a skintight dress scored like a football referee's shirt, had commanded a great deal of attention, eventually leading biologists, filmmakers, and ship's crew in a ragged, drunken conga line. Later, various participants either fell off the boat on the way back to the ship, had to be physically carried like sacks of rice, or threw up in the john. It was comically surreal, right out of the classic Herman Wouk novel on the Caribbean, *Don't Stop the Carnival.* But most of our expedition had been hammered so thoroughly they couldn't be rousted to work until late the next day.

"Everyone liked the 'referee' and that was a lot of fun," Lipscomb had said, in reference to the Christmas night of debauchery at the Colony, "but we need to get some film in the can." Latin American scholar Fagen, along to help us navigate the tricky cultural and political waters during our month of filming here, also realized another concern: "Jim fears that our crew will get in trouble on New Year's Eve (in Havana) and queer Castro's visit." It is a reference to the expectations we all have for *El Jefe* himself to finally materialize when we dock next to the old colonial-era city at an extension of the Malecón. It's taken over a year to get permission to film here, and, even now, Castro—never fully comfortable with the idea of North Americans rooting around where he couldn't see them—is said to be edgy about us bringing in a four-man deep-diving sub.

Underwater exploration that could have taken place off Havana in the final days can as easily be done here, Lipscomb has reasoned. But, we need some science—contrived or otherwise—to perform for the cameras. When McCosker suggests the availability of deep water and a late-rising moon will allow us to hunt for the elusive and peculiar "flashlight fish" at scuba depths, Giddings seizes it as an occasion for a night film dive.

The map shows a sudden drop-off here, marked as *La Furnia*, where the shallow platform holding Cuba does odd things—first plunging steeply into nothingness, then sending up 1,200-foot tall pinnacles to within fifty and sixty feet of the surface. I had asked Cuban scientist Pedro Alcolado—who is aboard with us for the entire trip—for a meaningful translation of *furnia* and he says the closest it comes in English is "drop-off," although "abyss" might also work.

Earlier today, I watched the wind pick up, tearing apart the high clouds like shredded Cuban flank steak, *la ropa vieja*, in the sky. Ashore, I could see the low coast restructure itself into a series of arid escarpments, announcing the arrival of the isolated westerly peninsula of Guanahacabibes, the place where the pre-Columbian Tainos known as the Guanahatabeys made their last stand against the brutal conquistadors.

Now here we are, preparing to penetrate the Tainos' black sea. As we gear up on the bucking whaler, McCosker tells me a bit about the fish we will be searching for—*Kryptophanaron alfredi,* the Latin genus name for "hidden lantern" and the species for Alfred Mitchell, who originally collected a dead specimen off the coast of Jamaica. Our quarry, one of four known species of flashlight fish, is the only one found in the Caribbean. "It has a set of bright bioluminescent organs under each eye—and when it needs to 'turn off the lights' to avoid predators, it retracts them by rotating the organ downward . . . like the way the headlights of a Porsche 914 retract." Adults, which max out at four inches, spend their days inside caves and crevices at depths of three hundred feet or more. At night, they emerge and can be found skittering along in water as shallow as ninety and one hundred feet—if you know where to look.

"It's a classic synergistic relationship between the fish and the millions of tiny bacteria that live in organs under each eye. The fish provides the bacteria with housing and nourishment, and the bacteria provide light." The luminescence is notable because—unlike many of the jellies and other inverts that only use light for one specific purpose—the flashlight fish alternatively uses its "headlights" to find and attract prey, communicate, and to confuse predators.

Despite the abundant life glowing in the night sea, such a specimen should be easy to find because it will be one of the brightest lights of them all, McCosker promises. In context, several of the little fish together will look like "a rally of little Volkswagens on a dark country road."

Surely there is great novelty here. But *Kryptophanaron* also holds a more promising biomedical potential than most fish because competing bacteria aren't able to invade its light organs—indicating a very effective immune system that can ward off unwanted foreign attacks. Moreover, no species has ever been recovered live off Cuba. If we can collect several healthy specimens, we can even donate them to the National Aquarium in Havana in a great public display of international fish diplomacy.

McCosker and I drop overboard at the point where the sonar shows pinnacles rising from a steep bottom and begin our descent. The whaler putters a few hundred feet away to where Giddings's crew will set up their bright HMI underwater lights near a shallow ledge at a depth of about sixty feet. The plan is for McCosker and I to free-fall in slow motion with our lights off until we sense we are close to one hundred feet, an act signaled by the constant clearing of pressure on our ears from the increased depths. At that point we will search for the fish, and once we spot them, we will turn our lights on.

I have dived with McCosker before, and I know that as a marine biologist he is intrepid, going far beyond routine sport-diving limits to chase after what could be new species of fish—some of which he has found as deep as three hundred feet. His tenacity and his eye for detail have been rewarded: he has discovered—described, really—scores of fish never before identified, a feat that terrestrial-bound scientists in this known, modern world find impossible to duplicate with their own animals of choice—birds, reptiles, mammals. Fish live in a place where we can stay no longer than a tank or two of air will allow: practicing ichthyology is not a walk in the woods. Especially off the coast of Cuba, at night.

Although I am along on this expedition as a writer, I will serve as a biological technician on this dive; as such, I carry a large glass specimen jar under my arm. "It'll be blinded by the light," McCosker promised, of the flashlight fish. "You can literally pick it up and put it in the jar." Thus containerized, *Kryptophanaron* will then be transported over to the impromptu underwater film set, where the Klieg-like illumination will turn the unassuming little fish into a documentary star.

Down we go in the dark, bioluminescence flashing around us everywhere—blue light in tiny muted firefly blinks, in long exploding skyrocket trails, and, occasionally, in distinct outlines marking the silhouette of a large fish or sea turtle swimming past us. McCosker, a slow breather, only reveals himself to me by the exhalation of his scuba bubbles, each flush of air effervescing as miniature sapphire spheres. Mc-Cosker has assured me that the light of the fish will make my jar glow like a lantern, once we herd it inside, and the notion is both exciting and vaguely nostalgic. It reminds me of summer nights I spent as a kid in lonely country fields collecting lightning bugs to turn other jars into lanterns. Between my eager anticipation, the sparkling luminescence, and the nitrogen in my system from the depth, I am no longer an impassive observer of the sea—I have become a living part of it, as inextricably woven into it as the school of flying fish.

The weight of the sea pushes more firmly on my body, and my exhaust actually sounds different, somehow tinnier, both signs that I am in deep. Finally, I turn on my light to read the digital computer gauge on my wrist. The numbers that show depth are scrolling rapidly as I continue to drop: 100, 104, 108. I shine my light down and see that I have missed the edge of the cliff we were aiming for. Below me, the beam of my little light seems pitifully meager as it disappears into the 1,200-foot void of La Furnia, down into the interminable veil of the abyss.

This is definitely not a good thing. I splay out my fins to stop my descent, and then raise my light to where I think McCosker ought to be, but he is not there. Slowly, weightlessly, I rotate 360 degrees in the water with my light and still I see nothing—no McCosker, no pinnacle, no bottom, and sure as hell, no *Kryptophanaron*. A small part of logic in my brain tells me McCosker may have descended on another side of a pinnacle earlier in the dive, and now, with the current, I likely have washed somewhere away from that rock, into deep open water.

I remember the submersible dive I made with biologist Edie Widder to two thousand feet a few days ago, recall her telling me that by night, the primitive ancestors of life living much deeper in the sea—the mesopelagics—rise to the surface to feed. I wonder what else could be there among them, beyond the siphonophores and the ctenophores and the medusas, animals million of years older than my own puny mammalian form.

The warm fuzzy of the nitrogen meets head on with a strong surge of adrenaline, creating a sort of midroad psychic collision. A tiny voice tells me that I am somewhere off the coast of Cuba in the middle of the night and that I am likely as lost as I have ever been. It strikes me that I urgently need a new plan. I hold tightly onto my glass specimen jar, figuring if I drop it, it will signal the end of my presumptive role as a cine-science explorer and reinsert me directly into the food chain.

I switch my light back off, and rotate once again, this time looking for the scantiest shard of light from Giddings's HMIs. The incandescence from the plankton in the water is so rich that each time I exhale, my own exhaust sends an upwelling of tiny blue aureoles across my mask, obscuring my vision. Widder's magical cool blue light, seen so safely from the dry interior of the JSL, has now swallowed me whole.

I turn in the water once again, this time more slowly, trying to control my breathing so that I don't panic. I am at least one hundred feet beneath the sea. High above, the surface is choppy and if I ascend, I could be lost in the wave gullies and carried off by a current to God Knows Where. Merchant ships, which might offer some random downstream hope of surface rescue, are virtually absent because this, after all, is Cuba, and political voodoo has kept the country poor and the wave troughs free of such vessels. I am left to fin through the ocean at fifteen fathoms, hoping ardently for some faint trace of dead reckoning to kick in.

At last, I see a glimmer of light slightly brighter and more steady than the natural blue flashes around me. I check my air and see that, while my initial adrenaline rush sucked up more than usual, I have enough for another ten minutes if I swim up to sixty feet and, from there, try to find my way back. Up I go, my eye on the distant light. At sixty feet I level off, and then start to carefully swim toward what I most earnestly hope is the film crew and the safety of the boat. I fin slowly, single-mindedly, trying not to alert my conscious mind that I am in a heap of trouble—just another North American out for a casual night dive in your average Cuban abyss. But after finning in that direction for five minutes, the light doesn't seem to be getting any closer.

It suddenly occurs to me that maybe the moon has finally risen and what I am seeing is its reflection in the sea. I try to get my mind around some real questions: have I actually been swimming in the wrong direction, away from the boat? Is my dive buddy spiraling below me somewhere in La Furnia? And what previously extinct apparition from some distant geological epoch is preparing to rise and feed? When you are lost and alone under the tropical sea at night, your mind can imagine you as a gulp away from most any reality—up to and including any sea monster Odysseus may have encountered.

A tiny cognitive shard settles down on my mind, reminding me it was McCosker, after all, who co-authored a book on the great white shark. In it, he suggested that if the *Carcharodon megalodon,* a ferocious ancestor of today's great white still existed today, it would likely be somewhere in the abyss of the ocean—in the same sanctuary where the "extinct" coelacanth was found living back in the 1930s. Fossilized seven-inch-long teeth of *megalodon* have been found in Cuba, big enough to support a shark that stretched sixty to eighty feet from end to end—as long as a line of ten Volkswagens on a dark country road. It would be large enough to simply open its mouth and inhale me without missing a stroke. I think that, were it not for the cobwebby comfort of the nitrogen buzz, the bold hope that I will actually find my way back safely might also vanish into nothingness.

I promise to give myself another five minutes worth of finning toward the distant light at depth, and if that source does not then prove to be real, I will at last surface and, from there, take my chances. On I go, with my light still off and the jar still clenched tightly under my arm. Although this is the Caribbean Sea, it is December and, at this depth, it is cold. Despite my quarter-inch-thick wetsuit, I am shaking, but I don't know if it's because of the chill or the grim realization of my condition. Just as I figure my final five minutes are about up, the light becomes markedly brighter. I steady myself, trying not to become overly excited at the prospect that I have found my way back.

Soon I find myself at the edge of a man-made aura of HMI-induced sunshine, and my relief is clearly audible—I exhale with a sigh of great existential joy into my regulator. Nearby, the underwater film crew is hovering in the black water; they seem like small space capsules with running lights, navigating over the surface of some distant planet. I spot Giddings, who is fiddling with one of his underwater digital cameras, housed inside a console as large as a desktop computer.

I feel like Odysseus just returned from some horrific mythological voyage—or Joseph Campbell's heroic traveler back from the brink. But when I approach, Giddings looks up and points to the jar, which I am still cradling under my arm. I realize my entire life-and-death quest is unknown to him, and he is simply asking where the flashlight fish is. I shrug—who knows?—and ascend to the decompression line trailing from under the whaler.

There, I am elated to find McCosker, who apparently has been hanging onto the rope for some time now. We both blow off nitrogen on the line until our air is almost gone and then fin up twenty feet to the surface. I take off my fins and weight belt and tank, hoist myself over the side, and then help McCosker in.

Finally, Giddings and crew are all aboard the dive boat and we are headed back to the *Seward*. I climb the ladder onto the larger ship, shed my wet suit, and stow my dive gear. Then I head below deck, climb into the tiny shower stall in my cabin, and let the warm water wash over my cold skin.

McCosker is already in his bottom bunk by the time I climb into my upper. Ironically, it was his fearless savoir faire attitude about diving into the abyss with our lights off that helped convince me of the relative wisdom of such exploration.

Unable to sleep, I stretch out on the bunk and read a reprint of an article McCosker wrote about flashlight fish in *Scientific Ameri-*

can. In it, he observes, the fish are so seldom seen—even by diving ichthyologists—for good reason:

> The rarity of these fishes must be attributable to the habitat they
> presumably prefer, namely reefs that are below the depths where
> most scuba divers go and rocky areas that are relatively inaccessible to
> collection with nets.
>
> I might add on the basis of personal experience that for sane
> biologists deep diving in tropical seas on dark nights with one's diving
> light turned off is rarely practiced and never enjoyed.

I roll over, switch off my reading light, and shut my eyes. The last thing I consider before I fall sleep is a mental shrug of expeditionary proportions: *Now he tells me.*

The Florida Everglades

Searching for Mr. Watson

Just minutes after I leave my home in northeastern Florida to drive
down to the Everglades to search for Mr. Watson, I zip past a wood
stork. It is standing at the side of the entrance ramp to the busy
interstate, looking at once noble and woefully misplaced—like a
lonely chess piece on a checkerboard.

The 'Glades, with its vast subtropical wilderness, is a good five
hours away at the other end of the state. But the stork is here anyway.
It is knee-deep in a drainage ditch—cars whizzing by on their way to
Disney World without a notion of *whatever can it be*—and it is doing
what wading birds like it have done in Florida before anything like a
human or a theme park arrived. It is sweeping its curved beak through
the cloudy water, hoping to connect with something alive there.

My friend Terry, an old college pal who will paddle the other end of the canoe, misses the bird altogether, not because he is obtuse, but because he lives on the opposite rim of the country and his senses are already saturated with local exotica. It will take a mighty dose of melodrama to jar him.

"Wood stork," I say, pointing with one hand and driving us onto Interstate 4 with the other.

"Is that a rare bird?" asks Terry earnestly, and I tell him that it is. I say I am both heartened to see it but disturbed it has ranged so far outside its natural home. Not so long ago, this bird with the head that seems fire-charred—this "iron head"—was so integral to the 'Glades it was considered a barometer of its health. But the Everglades are on the brink, have been for a while now. The wood stork is trying to roll with this change, ranging far outside its historic territory.

Terry is from three decades' worth of my past, a fraternity brother and ex-jock, a reformed party animal like myself seeking redemption in the solitude of distant natural places. Individually, we have struggled to unravel the jumble of civilized threads to get at the nugget of ourselves buried inside. From its discovery, we have come to learn that this nature offered solace, living Whitmanesque lessons in the values of singularity and tolerance.

And so Terry hikes east of Los Angeles, back into places like Death Valley and Borrego Springs and camps there. I live in Florida and kayak on any wild body of water I can find—the St. Francis Dead River, the Blackwater Creek, the Mosquito Lagoon.

Now we are headed together to the 'Glades, to canoe deep into its distant western boundary in a hunt for the "Watson Place," a pre-Columbian Calusa midden mound. It is a forty-acre composite of shell and stunted tropical foliage, a thread between us and the time-wronged desperado who once lived here.

Like the 'Glades and the wood stork, we too are on the brink, aging jocks ranging beyond what is safe and known. In this way, we sweep through the experiences that still lay out before us, hoping to connect with something alive and vital. All we are sure of is we have come to appreciate wilderness for the way it lays itself down on the soul.

Unlike other men who seek solace in this way, we don't carry traditional props; we are not hunters or dapper L.L. Bean campers. I carry a set of old binoculars to watch for avifauna, but the truth is, beyond raptors and tropical wading birds, I'm lost unless a species appears clear and unobstructed in the scope. As for our gear, it is jerry-rigged and stuffed into duffels and garbage bags and PVC buckets.

Instead of giant foil pouches of official freeze-dried camp food, I have brought Noodles-in-a-Cup and tins of tuna and chicken. We have granola bars that look and taste like Oreos compressed into little rectangles. I imagine Jack Kerouac, when he went up on Desolation Peak out west, might have packed like this.

I do place a lot of significance, however, on a compass and the correct nautical map to lead me in and out of untamed places like this. Each tiny paper squiggle, each logarithmic degree corresponds to something tangible—an oxbow or bar or tiny islet. Once ground-truthed, these coordinates can sometimes nudge the senses, linking near-meaningless geographic names to remarkable places on the landscape. Ahead in the 'Glades, my map promises Pavilion and Buzzard Keys, Chokoloskee and Rabbit Key Passes, Lostman's and Chatham Rivers.

I have tucked both compass and map inside a waterproof Seal-Lock Baggy I will carry on my lap when we finally reach our canoe. Also in the baggy is a paperback copy of Peter Matthiessen's novel *Killing Mr. Watson.* As I drive south on I-95, this idea amuses me, as if the immediacy of the adventure will require me to be ready at any time to understand direction, latitude, and literary metaphor. Nevertheless, this book and its sequels are the thread that has re-linked Terry and myself after all these years, something real our adult selves respond to that goes far beyond the retelling of old locker-room jokes and keg-party stories.

After all, we twisted the party gauge to its edge, and then kept on pushing. When we quit playing sports midway through school, we developed a sort of restless enmity, a condition that could end in a fistfight, a brawl, a mindless round of punching holes in doors—the old kind, made of solid wood. The truth was, we were athletic, but we weren't typical monosyllabic jocks; nor did we fit the supercilious frat boy mold, either. Restless, without a real belonging or focus, we became known in the parlance as "bad actors." And we did all we could to live up to that label. Once established, our respective reputations had lives of their own, and they lasted long after the deeds were done.

Like me, Terry had read the three Matthiessen novels on Watson's life and demise. Like me, he felt a kinship with Watson—a complex soul who existed far outside the monotone of local myth. Matthiessen may have "reimagined" Ed Watson's life, but in doing so, he admits the retelling probably "contains much more of the truth of Mister Watson than the lurid and popularly accepted 'facts.'"

In *Watson, Lost Man's River,* and *Bone by Bone,* Matthiessen uses the real life and death of renegade cane grower Ed Watson to re-create a wild place and a maverick culture special to southwest Florida. But if his books are about a vanished time, they are also about the social evolution of perception, about how the realities of a richly embroidered moment—or a mystifying personality—can be spun down into simpleminded slogans. Time has treated both the 'Glades and the strong, passionate man who was E. J. Watson this way, turning the magnificent Everglades into a swamp and the complex E. J. into "Bloody Watson."

Searching for Mr. Watson is not a walk in the woods, however. The 'Glades is a sprawling subtropical territory larger than the state of Delaware; ranger stations and interpretive boardwalks dot the outer edges, but inside, sawgrass stretches to the east and mud-rooted mangroves to the west, leaving little dry land in between. It is, as Matthiessen has observed, a "labyrinthal wilderness," and its sheer lack of accessibility has been the secret to keeping it so. Or, as *Lost Man's* character Speck Daniel puts it: "What the hell kind of tourist would beat his way three to four miles back up a mangrove river to take a picture of some raggedy ol' lonesome place."

Down we go on the notorious I-95 into Miami, the car-jacking, drug-shuttling, neon-rocker-paneled, middle-finger-in-the-air conduit, finally turning west near the Latino bustle of Calle Ocho. From here, we drive through block after block of urban landscape that barely half a century ago used to be freshwater marl prairie, bristling with great fields of sawgrass. Today it is colonized by espresso shops and *santería botánica*s, 7–11's and Texacos hugging every available square inch.

"Man," says Terry, shaking his head. "Talk about sensory overload." I run this gauntlet for an hour until we are safely west of the city, headed out across the northern boundary of the 'Glades. Open space and dwarfed cypress and sawgrass command the geography now, with great white cumulus billowing overhead, fed by the wet, feral terrain. There may be two more contrary realities this close to each other somewhere else in the world, but I'm not aware of them.

We are safely atop the Tamiami Trail now—a word squeeze of "Tampa-to-Miami." It is the road that first splayed the 'Glades in two when it was built, water-spitting draglines and dredges crunching their way through the limerock in the 1920s.

Water-driven, the 'Glades is at the mercy of the kindness of strangers upstream. And this trail we are driving serves as a massive dam across it. The lazy but deliberate sheet flow of water that once swept down across southern Florida from just below Orlando is now squeezed under us through a series of mechanical gates, giant Erector Set–like devices built for flood control. Man plays god with the upland rainfall and water now, and as gods go, he has proved to be a baleful, selfish sort, a minor Old Testament deity with more ambition than wisdom.

Soon, we arrive at SR 29, the narrow southerly road that trails past "Panther Crossing" signs and dead-ends six miles south in Everglades City, the fishing village now being transformed into an RV tourist mecca on the far western tip of the park. The freshwater sweeping down from the easterly sawgrass meadows meets the coastal mangrove buffer a few miles inland from here. Everglades City is our jumping-off point for our quest.

Clinging to shards of a hardscrabble pioneer culture still tended by a handful of stone crabbers and mullet fishermen, this little town on the edge of the park now teeters precariously toward a fun-house-mirror version of "ecotourism." Anything alive, it seems, is fair game: airboat rides and canned "Safaris" and "Jungle Boat Tours" (Gators Guaranteed!) are everywhere, as are boutiquelike souvenir shops painted peach and green, with incongruous names like "Jungle Erv's." The natural rhythm—of place and people—has been squeezed and massaged and marketed in a heavy-handed attempt to catch up to the trendiness that has homogenized much of Florida's coast.

As I watch a gaggle of tourists board an air-conditioned park-service pontoon boat for a guided excursion onto Chokoloskee Bay, my only thought is how white and spanking clean everyone is. The outlaw plume hunters and gator poachers, turtlers and contraband smugglers—the bona fide heirs to the Watson legend and time—have died, trickled away, tried to grow up. *Lost Man's River,* set in the past, foretells this gentrification: "Beaten flat, [it] would disappear beneath the tar and concrete, the tourist courts and house trailers, the noisy cars of vacationers with their red faces, sun hats, candy-colored clothes."

We are eager to get to the former Watson homesite as soon as we can. But it is now late in the day. Faced with spending a night in a motel here or paying an outfitter to ferry us and our canoe back to the old Watson mound by motorboat, we choose the latter, planning to use the time saved to more thoroughly explore the creeks and sloughs of the backcountry on our five-day paddle back.

A slight young man named Justin wearing white rubber fisherman's boots has brought us to the threshold of the Watson site in his go-fast fiberglass outboard, expertly twisting and turning the wheel behind the center console to deliver us through the look-alike puzzle of mangrove islands and tidal rivers.

Justin's new girlfriend has come along for the ride, and, on our trip here, I overhear her asking him who this Watson was. Either Justin had not read the Matthiessen books, or he didn't feel like re-creating the complexities of them. He gives her the shorthand folk version, the one locals have been giving to tourists for years. "He was a guy who lived back up here and grew cane . . . and when it came time to pay his hired help, he would kill them instead."

The "Watson Place" is one of several dozen primitive campsites in this odd park; most are docklike "chickees" built where there is simply no dry land to be found. But a few, like this one, are high mounds of shell and bone constructed first by the Calusas and later colonized by farmers, fishermen, and assorted renegades. It arises from the dark tannin of the Chatham River like a high natural bluff, fringed at one edge with a thick cover of snake plants—a hardy, spiky ornamental that settlers cultivated in their yards in Florida a century and more ago. It is an odd relief, back here in this mud-driven monoculture of red and black mangrove, an exotic harbinger of other surprises yet to come.

It is 4:30 P.M. and the early spring sun is dipping down toward the top of the tall black mangroves just across the Chatham River. Justin is anxious to get back to the marina at Everglades City before dark. We quickly unload our canoe and supplies on a narrow wooden dock. The ferocious saltwater marsh mosquitoes—"Swamp Angels" to the settlers—seem to be marshaling their forces for sundown; their humming from back in the tangle of truncated tropical jungle at the edge of the clearing produces a low-grade static. It is early April, at the wane of an El Niño winter in which a few mildly colder months have barely kept a lid on the hatch of bloodsucking insects. We are as concerned about getting our mosquito-flapped tents set up as Justin is to get home to his warm bed.

As Terry and I sort through our pile of gear, Jason cranks the motor up, eases his boat away from the dock, and disappears in a meringue-like froth around the corner of Chatham Bend. I think of Ed Watson's old gasoline launch, the *Brave,* and how he puttered slowly down the Chatham to Chokoloskee Island in it one last time on October 24, 1910, the distinctive *pop-pop-pop* of the ancient motor announcing his arrival to a gathering mob of islanders who would murder him in broad daylight. Watson had scared them with his reputation one too many times, and he finally paid for it.

Finally alone now, we establish priorities: first, we douse ourselves with repellent, then we hurry to set up camp in the scant half-acre or so of open, weedy land. At the clearing's edge, an entangled jungle has colonized the rest of the forty-acre mound, slender trunks and boughs of native gumbo limbo and manchineel gridded together like spiderwebs, along with lime and guava and avocado left from the Watson era, all feral and wild now.

After I work up a light sweat assembling my tent, I stop and look around, letting the reality of being atop the former Watson homestead settle in. The quiet back here is complete, so full it seems to have measurable weight. At the edge of the Chatham River, several large red mangroves, bowlike roots arching into the oyster-shell mud, frame the water. The sun dips down below them to the west. "You think ol' Ed trimmed back those mangroves to give him a good view of the sunset?" Terry asks, and I figure he probably did.

This Watson Place is the largest shell mound for miles in any direction. The Calusas shucked oysters and clams here, discarded bones from bear and panther, manatee and deer for at least two thousand years. Spiritually complex and savvy to nature, they understood its power—especially the water-thrashing energy of tropical hurricanes—and did all they could to literally rise above it.

In his time, Ed Watson painstakingly hauled timber in by boat to build a substantial two-story frame farmhouse here, flanking it with flowering red royal poinciana trees. It was said to be the finest of its type inside the great uncivilized wash between Ft. Myers and Key West. Since Watson's death, the home had been used by hunters and fishermen and squatters. Hurricane Donna damaged the house in 1960, and the park service—looking for any excuse to clear old private structures from public land—razed it soon afterward.

I ask Terry if he's ready to look for Ed's homesite in the jungle, and he says he is. It is a Friday night now, a weekend evening in the middle of the Everglades, darkness coming fast. A large, unseen gator bellows out a mating call from the edge of the Chatham—or perhaps it is a territorial warning. I can't imagine being in a place more removed from the superfluous collegiate atmosphere under which Terry and I met. He must think the same of me, for we both exist far outside the social conventions that first bound us.

Off we go on a narrow trail back into the wall of stunted tropical foliage, ducking under low branches. Terry has on long pants and a T-shirt sporting an E.T.-like extraterrestrial, a large Bowie-type knife strapped to his belt. I am in jeans and T-shirt, wearing a baseball cap that reads "Jung." Under the thick canopy back here, the sun barely penetrates—by day, it is sepia-tinted; in the early evening, it is downright gloomy. At the edge of the trail lies a skull and skeleton, a small mammal of some sort, about the size of a raccoon, like the wild-eyed coons I have been seeing clattering about on the bow roots, dark stripes bleached almost white by salt and sun.

We are in the midst of the insect static now, and despite our repellent, the swamp angels blanket us—hanging on for dear life, waiting for the chemical to wear off. Settlers, like Watson, virtually lived in the black smoke of smudge pots, which they kept burning day and night; when they had window screens, they rubbed crankcase oil on them to keep the insects from smothering the grid.

Just off the trail, I see what looks like knee-high concrete boundary markers, scattered haphazardly. I look closer and realize they are the original foundations Watson once built his fine house upon, raising it up a couple feet for ventilation. They are made of a tabby, crushed limerock and shells of the sort the Calusas left behind. From the elegant trunks of the gumbo limbo trees, tissue-thin patches of red-amber bark curl like the skin of a sunburned tourist, pineapple-like bromeliads tucked away in the crooks.

Just when the buzzing seems enough to drive us mad, I notice a mysterious structure peeking out from the thick jungle just ahead. It is made of the same tabby material as the foundations, except it is rectangular, as large as a room-sized funeral vault. The park service has built a wooden cap atop it to keep people and animals from falling in. "It's Ed's Cistern," I say, "where he gathered rainwater." Weathered by a century of tropical heat and rain, the tabby walls look more like the sides of an ancient Spanish mission. A gumbo limbo, far bigger than any of the others, grows from a corner of the cistern, happy for the fresh water still inside. Nearby, Ed and his family slept and dreamed. Of what, I wonder?

The swamp angels, perhaps a mutant breed, are starting to bite now, and we move as fast as we can back to our camp. I fire up my gas lantern, and as I do, an easy breeze picks up from the Chatham, enough to hold the insects at bay. We concoct a dinner swill over a one-burner stove, and as we eat, the scarlet sky turns gray, then full black. Fireflies, a rarity in ChemLawned Florida nowadays, dart the edge of the jungle with their green-blue light.

I look overhead to see Venus hanging itself just under the sliver of new moon; minutes later, the sky is as full of stars and constellations as any I have ever seen. I turn down the lantern and Terry and I sit in silence, watching meteors streak through the darkness like distant flares, as if underscoring our own sense of awe. From the Chatham, mullet leap and splash, joyous ghosts water-skipping in the night.

It is too warm for a sleeping bag so, when I crawl into my tent, I lie on top of the bag, using it for a mattress. Above, the bright stars burn a soft glow through the thin fabric. From the river, I hear a deep humanlike exhalation, the sound of a bottlenose dolphin surfacing to blow. From back up the trail, a chuck-will's-widow calls its own name over and over, waiting for an answer that doesn't come. Everywhere, unseen critters rustle and gurgle in the isolation of the Everglades darkness. Instead of distressing me, it has a remarkably calming effect, as if the mound itself is exuding the timeless exhalations of all who have come here before me, the Calusas, the renegades, Ed Watson. And now, into the collective dreams of the mound I also go.

The new morning is fresh, dew on the tent and the wild grass in the clearing. After a quick breakfast, we walk the edge of the jungle, find what must have been a farm plow in the weeds, metal wheels dark red with rust. Back in a few yards, we discover the frame of an old truck, rubber and wood long gone. Terry takes my photograph sitting on it. Out near the shell-encrusted shore of the river, we see the 150-gallon iron kettle where Watson rendered down his cane, still mounted inside a waist-high concrete and brick pedestal. Instead of cane syrup, the kettle holds stagnant rainwater, green now with algae, tadpoles swirling back and forth just under the surface. I run my hand on the concrete rimming the kettle, realize someone once took the trouble to round and smooth the edges, a remarkable act of civilization in such a place.

Watson, as Matthiessen wisely guessed, was ambitious, a person who cared about how the world was ordered around him. He was, after all, the only white man to live on this mound more than a year or two—farming it for nearly two decades before he was killed in 1910. I reach down to the ground, pick up a piece of metal, maybe a ladle, iron corroded beyond recognition. Watson's presence here is nearly palpable: I think of him laying down this tool ninety years ago on the edge of the smooth concrete rim, going down to Chokoloskee to take care of business, just for the afternoon.

We have spent three days here now, using the Watson mound as a base to explore local waters, segueing up into tight canopied creeks, including one that wasn't even on our map. Once back there, we paddled for almost a mile, until the tide ebbed finally out from under us, reshaping our path into an impassable slough of foliage and roots. Stoic, we rested, drank tepid water and ate granola bars, listened to the coon oysters spit, watched the mangrove crabs nervously scuttle over the mud like black mice. Terry, gracious, named the creek Belleville. From there, I saw my first swallowtail kite of the season, newly arrived from Brazil, joining the frigates soaring overhead like untethered origami. In three days, we encountered only five other boats, and all were fishermen hunkered down, coming or going to or from Florida Bay.

Each night on the mound, the chuck-will's-widow sang his sweet sad song, a four-note serenade of all he has ever seen and cannot fully say, and the stars fell, inexorably marking mortal time. One evening, I slept next to the water and Venus rose under a crescent moon, laying down a trail of pale light that connected me to it, a planet too distant to imagine, yet able to touch me in these Everglades.

Now, with our canoe loaded to the gunnels, we are pushing away from the mound one last time for our two-day paddle back to Chokoloskee and Everglades City. Terry began to sketch and paint several years ago, waiting for each image to "push" its way out, allowing his unseen self to become less so on paper, healing old wounds. I try to do much of the same with words, a mechanism to remind me of what I have experienced. And now, in our coming back together after all this time, we grasp onto the tangible around us, discuss it with great joy, and then let it sink back into ourselves, waiting to see what it will finally reveal.

Upstream we go on this fine river, one eye on the tree line and the sky above, the other on the map and compass. Mangroves surround us on all sides, and from a distance, they seem like a diminutive northern forest. Up close, though, the land under them is ephemeral, water and detritus-fueled mud, rich nursery grounds for the same critters—redfish, trout, snook, tarpon—the fishermen hunt. Neither fully land or water, this Everglades has long placed a hold on the imagination of visitors, spooking them with its mystique.

The early Spanish conquistadors, at once superstitious and brutal, first charted this territory as La Laguna de los Espíritus Santos, the Lagoon of the Sacred Spirits. As we bear down today against a building wind and outgoing tide, I think of this place in that way, a terrain with a pulse and a heart, able to breathe. Right now, its breath is sun-warmed mangrove leaves and sea purslane, a dusky perfume of salt and chlorophyll and sap.

Up the Chatham we go, following the more narrow branch that meanders to the west, once almost running aground on a shoal that mysteriously appears in the middle of the river where eight and nine feet of water should be. Instead of working our way north through Last Huston and Huston Bays, we sneak around the lee sides of mangrove islands, crouching as close to shore as we can get to avoid the wind-driven thrash of the waves that will pile up in two-foot-high whitecaps. Sometimes the water is so clear we can see blue crabs scuttling across the seagrass bottom, needlefish flashing iridescent at the surface. Other times it is soil-brown, a moving organic soup.

As I paddle, I pay careful attention to direction, to the spin of a little sliver of metal locked inside glass, gauging how the world of mangrove and marl unfolds around us, curious how it matches up to my nautical chart.

Suddenly, the air is filled with scads of sulfur-wing butterflies, the color of pale planet light, fresh from a new spring hatch. We paddle through them for a mile until, finally, they vanish as quickly as they appeared, a rainshower of butterflies. Up to the southerly forks of Huston Bay we go, and then down again into an unnamed branch leading to the Huston River. It empties us into House Hammock Bay, named for an old clan that once homesteaded here, collecting buttonwood mangrove for charcoal like Watson did, fishing and hunting.

House Hammock is barely two and three feet deep, and as I dip and draw my paddle it touches mud as often as not. Ospreys are nesting everywhere, young chicks just large enough to raise up and squawk now from their huge beds of twigs. Mother birds fly over us, small mullet in their talons, headed for home. In the distance gators, bodies as black and corrugated as large truck tires, thrash in the water and mud to flee this odd apparition, a log with two moving heads.

Ahead, we will spend a night on the wooden dock chickee at Sunday Bay, and then, surf-rolling breakers, back out of its broad lagoon. As we do, we will ride an easterly wind beyond Barnes and Crooked Creeks, into the lee of the shoal-filled Cross Bays where we run aground, using our paddles as poles to finally push away. From there, we skim the conflux of Hurddles Creek and the Turner River, an intersection deep enough to hold giant half-ton manatees, up from Florida Bay to frolic like giant children, flukelike tails out of the water, bodies rolling and churning the water in some outsized mammalian ecstasy, safe at last from motorboat props. We sit at a distance and watch in quiet obeisance, then push on toward Chokoloskee under a bright tropical sun.

Once, just after a flock of white ibis fly low across the mangrove tops, I blunder somewhere off the map, getting lost as thoroughly as I have ever been. When I tell Terry of the mistake, I joke that we must be in such a state before we can ever truly be found, and he smiles and says gently, I know what you mean, bro.

Safely back on track, we finally enter Chokoloskee Bay, windswept and sparkling in the sun, the end-game in sight now. I wonder what secrets are still hiding from us. In the end, I decide it doesn't much matter; this lagoon of the sacred spirit and its ghosts will be here, whether I want them to be or not.

Still, there is this: I think one last time of Ed Watson and how Matthiessen treated him more generously than life ever did. And I wish the same for the 'Glades itself. I wish it in my heart for Terry, for me, for us all.

Jungle Dreams

From *Swiss Family Robinson*

to Tangled River Bends

Jungles have always held a fascination for me, long before they were
given more accurate—or politically correct—names like tropical
rainforest or hardwood swamp or emergent aquatic community.

There's something about the way the crowns of the trees
droop overhead like giant canopies, foliage rising up in thick,
impenetrable green walls, vines weaving in and out of it all like
something alive—freeze-framed for the moment you see it before
it returns to its endless writhing. It is a riot of photosynthesis,
untrimmed and untamed, doing what plants have always done when
the latitude feeds them generously with moisture and heat, looking

now like they did before man was not much more than something small and furry, howling in the treetops.

This jungle seems gothic, imaginary almost, like the impractical design in which an unbalanced, teetering architecture of spires and vaults and arches expresses the wildest shards of human imagination—in a time before architecture became pragmatic and boring and useless to the soul.

But if these jungles deliver themselves in great bursts of rococo imagery, it is far more than just form and style that make them so. It has something to do with the dance of shadows and the dim amber reckoning of daylight filtering down through the gridwork of wood and leaf, bouncing from the veined acetate of beetle wings, to the ovary of an orchid bloom, to the shiny varnish of a tiny mandible.

Light in the jungle is changed, muted by what it flows beyond to reach the floor. It is light that carries organic memory of its journey with it. I think of it as I do the illumination that reaches a deep reef in the sea, rendered not just less by the distance it travels from the surface but refracted by the near-invisible plankton it must pass into and out of—the spawn of the lobster and fish and coral, the tiny microalgaes and the plants yet to be. It is light energized and changed by its passage. No longer bright and cheery and incandescent, it is dim and ocher and enigmatic, charged with the remembrance of where it has been.

A place like this is heavily cloaked in its geography, a bas-relief of landscape, rising and falling to the swales and berms of earth and rock just under its skin of leaf humus. It is the inaccessibility of this wild geography that also helps protect it. Far beyond the range of routine travel, a jungle is thankfully free of industrialized sounds and rigid angles and people moving in quick and jerky Western motions, aiming to fix something or tear it down. There is no critical mass of consumers here, insisting on expediency. Leaf cutter ants or howler monkeys have little need for FedEx. Steam rises, rain falls, life goes on.

When there are humans here at all, their movements seem un-rushed, stoic, the natural rhythm of a bough swaying in a light breeze, locomotion imitated from the flow of the jungle itself, barefoot and careful and light. The indigenous people of this jungle are not dissimilar from the other living beings that occupy this same place. Like birds, mammals, reptiles, even insects, they are cryptic, their presence woven into the moist tropical fabric. They seem to amass rather than merely appear, as if molecules are assembling themselves a particle at a time. When they leave, they do so as if dissolving into ether, the sound of their departure absorbed by the thick and wet of the forest. The worlds of the spiritual and secular, the exterior and interior meld, coalesce here at the seat of the very soul.

If these jungles I love are made mystifying by their refracted light and foliage castles, their existence also portends something secretive and obscure: it is the promise this gridwork of nature has to hold mystery close to its heart. Unlike open savannas or mountains, you cannot see very far at all in a jungle, and every tree trunk, every vine-clogged pathway, every bend in the swampy river conceals a new discovery. Each step taken moves you farther inside this puzzle—leading you on a journey back through time, recapturing that genetic epoch before our own ancestors first launched themselves upright, prehensile hearts and minds still entwined around a branch, a vine, a slender mossy trunk. Safe back here, no need to move.

I first experienced these jungles vicariously as a child in story-books like *Swiss Family Robinson,* in which an entire shipwrecked household washes ashore somewhere off New Guinea. Here, the mother, father, and four young boys built a small cottage in what I have always thought to be a banyan tree, shooting nutria, fishing and gathering cassava root and bananas for food. While the parents longed to return to Europe, the youngsters seemed "perfectly intoxicated with joy" at the prospect of the tropical island wilderness. After I read that book, I asked my dad if we could abandon our ranch-style home and go and live in a tree house in a jungle somewhere, and he looked at me quizzically.

Later, I studied the real-life visions rendered in the astonishing pen-and-ink drawings of Frederick Catherwood, who traveled to the farthest reaches of the Maya in Mesoamerica in the 1800s. Here, long before Chichén Itzá or Uxmal had been cleared from the forest and restored, Catherwood sketched half-seen temples and ballcourts and observatories still shrouded by the near-impenetrable vegetation of the Yucatan, tamarind trees sprouting out of sacrificial altars and vines reclaiming limestone archways and sacred chambers. These were so unlike the linear, sterile neighborhoods I knew in North America, and I knew one day I would go off in search of them.

Now as an adult when I travel—to the Miskito Coast of Nicaragua, the Darién of Panama, the *cayos* of Cuba's lee shore, the upstream tributaries of the Amazon, the rainforest of northern Queensland—I have the chance again to relive the mystery I knew as a child. Now I can add my own twist to these nascent fairy tales. I learn the names of the giants of the rainforest—the towering ceiba and jacaranda and fig—and come to understand how and why they buttress themselves in giant fluted wedges to withstand the inundation of the seasonal floods. I know the difference between lianas that grow up and aerial roots that trail down. I understand why the orchids and the bristling mosses with the spiked flowers, the *epiphytes,* do so well because they absorb moisture from the humid air.

Safe in the dim light, under a protective ceiling of green, the ferns—ancient plants from a Devonian epoch when mammals were only a glint in the eye of the cosmos—still endure here, supple prehistoric remembrances you can touch with your fingertips. Indeed, nurtured by the warm and the wet, everything that grows or scampers or crawls in this jungle simply does so in far greater varieties than back in more temperate zones. Certainly, jungles are reservoirs of biological diversity, storehouses where yet-undescribed lifeforms commingle, tiny details that function like cogs in a larger set of wheels, each turning with its own diminutive purpose and speed.

And the greater whole—what of it? Beyond the value and inter-dependence of each specimen of biology, there is a more astonishing raison d'être, and I have finally come to appreciate that, too. It is the way a jungle functions as a mammoth lung for the earth, the manner in which it cleans our air—inhaling carbon dioxide and exhaling fresh oxygen. Scientists describe large forested tracts like jungles as a "carbon sink," a sponge so vital to the respiration of the rest of our planet that it should be conserved for that reason alone.

If I have learned something about the natural history of the jungle, so too have I begun to understand the breadth of its cultural ecology—what we now label as ethnobotany. I have done so by being introduced to some of the many plants that indigenous peoples use to prevent and cure disease, to ignite powerful magic, to celebrate their lives and the sacred places in which they live. I have hiked and paddled dugouts and ridden broken-down river boats, vehicles that transported me to the villages of the Emberá of Panama, the Cocomilla of the Peruvian Amazon, the Makushi of Guyana's Rupununi. For them all, the forest is a vast natural pharmacy, a storehouse of promise and dreams and even nightmares, and the information of its utility and myth has been passed tribally from generation to generation for centuries.

It had been this way for the "Indians" who were here to greet the first Europeans when they landed—the Timucua and Tequesta and Calusa of Florida, the Taino of the Caribbean, and all the tribes vanquished from the New World before their names were even known.

It is, in fact, such a connection that can still keep humans intimate with their own place, help them sustain the vital bond between spirit and earth. It is a connection many of us sophisticated Westerners are just now beginning to appreciate, and as latecomers, we often do so as a lament: we have, after all, worked very hard to distance ourselves so far from our own landscape, to conquer or rule or transform it. We are just now emerging from a swoon of technology, as if awakening from a long odd dream where material shards of our lives swirl about at random, teaching little but confusion, mentored by an unconscious not yet able to fully process it all.

What did my grandfather tell my own father about the terrain around him? What did his grandfather tell him? What will I tell my own grandson? If it was not important to us, will we remember anything about the earth under us at all? Or will we just retain information about the contrivances that sit atop it? Do we even know—or care— what predominant natural features first drew others to the places where we live today? And if we do, will the stories of it all make us more whole as humans, more integrated and complete, or will it simply make us mourn for the loss?

Because of my affection for these jungle things, I have lived in Florida most of my adult life, and not in the Florida that most tourists—or even new residents—see or experience. It is an old Florida, where a cracker-style house is assembled from cypress wood, up a few feet off the ground under gables and overhanging eaves and metal roof. It is beneath magnolia and water oak and sugar hackberry, inside a sprawling yard of bamboo and cereus cactus, guava and citrus, vines with red and blue flowers, and wisteria rising, purple and pungently sweet in the spring. I let it grow wild, almost anywhere it wants and never spray poisons on any part of it. Butterflies visit here often—the zebra wing that naturalist William Bartram first noticed when it drifted up from the tropics, the giant tiger swallowtail, the intrepid monarch. They feed on the nectar of wildflowers, competing with hummingbirds who hover about in preposterous blurs of color and light.

There are hardy sabal palms in this yard, as well as several large queen palms, their more tender palmate fronds a gentle contrast to the stiffer foliage of the sabal. I cherish the queens, even though I know a good freeze will likely burn them back one day in this more northern

Florida latitude. More durable is the coontie, the knee-high cycad left from some distant geological time when ferns were preeminent and volcanic vents blew out sulfurous air and large cold-blooded reptiles had not yet come to be. Confused about its destiny—or perhaps intent on keeping its identify instead of fully climaxing into a palm—it became a fusion of tree and fern. As a result, this little coontie now ornaments itself with both spores *and* seeds. In this way, at least, it is a throwback in time, not unlike my own childhood jungle dreams, still-remembered visions of clarity and deep implication that even middle age won't compromise.

This homestead where I live is nothing close to a real jungle, except when compared with the nervous structure of extruded suburbs with walled subdivisions. And then it is a mighty jungle indeed. Just beyond my dirt road, a whole world rages on to something else, something new and fast and clamorous. But here time seems thankfully elastic, stretching itself back into tranquillity and nuance, the scent of old wood, the view through window glass veined by imperfection, the discarded skin of a cicada on a wren's nest under the porch.

There are other such home sites in Florida like this, and in a few cases, they are even cherished—the "cracker" cottage where Marjorie Kinnan Rawlings once lived in Cross Creek is now protected as a state historic site. But the Rawlings house is preserved for its *celebrity*, a commodity in high demand in our society. Most cracker homes are simply too retro to be useful to a rootless, fast-growing state like Florida, and as a result, they and the landscape they occupy are disappearing at an alarming rate.

The nostalgia of something once cherished and revered is still thick here in my homestead, as palatable as the sweetness of the wisteria: the dust-covered cane poles with string and rusty hooks, stored in the garage after the boy who once lived here put them away one last time, back in the 1950s and then, having grown up, never touched again. The glass marbles embedded into the mortar between the coquina rocks of the little man-made pond, now cracked and empty of goldfish and lily pads and frogs. The wood and tin chicken coop crumbling behind the stand of bamboo, ghosts of hens and roosters left to scratch in the white Florida sugar sand. It is a jungle of wistfulness, expressed by a longing ache for a simpler time.

All of it stitches itself into my own fiber, emblematic of my inexorable search for meaning, nothing less than the revelation of life's mysteries, the enigmatic vine-woven authority of nature and the sacredness of place. "Tell me the landscape in which you live, and I'll tell you who you are," wrote the Spanish philosopher José Ortega y Gasset once. He might have added: *Tell me your dreams of the earth.*

I dream it as a jungle, I would say, moist and hidden, enchantment somewhere inside a thick hammock of trees. Just beyond the deadfall of wood in the animal trail. Somewhere around the next river bend.

Illustration Credits

Map
"Map of Sites" drawn by Mary Estes Kenyon.

Introduction
My parents, Kathleen and Bill Belleville Sr., on a remote beach on the Eastern Shore of Virginia, not far from where they met. This was taken before I was born.

The Sacred Cenote of the Taino
A pre-Columbian Taino pot recovered by archaeologists from the sacred cenote of Manantial de La Aleta in the Dominican Republic. Photo by Bill Belleville.

Guyana
Kaieteur Falls in the isolated interior of Guyana. Photo by Bill Belleville.

The Sunken City of Port Royal
The shore of the peninsula of Port Royal, Jamaica. Photo by Bill Belleville.

The Suwannee
An Ogeechee tupelo on the banks of the upper Suwannee River. Photo by Bill Belleville.

St. Lucia's Parrot Man

Tropical bird conservationist Paul Butler next to the Jacquot Express on St. Lucia. Photo by Bill Belleville.

Cat Island

Limestone monastery hand built by Franciscan priest Father Jerome in the 1940s on Cat Island in the Bahamas. Photo by Bill Belleville.

Sir Francis Drake in Panama

The ancient Spanish coral-rock fortress of Santiago de la Gloria at Portobelo, Panama. Photo by Bill Belleville.

The Amazon's Pink Boto

A river village on the Rio Marañón, upstream from the main stem of the Amazon. Although I took this picture in 1999, it could have been taken a couple of centuries ago. Photo by Bill Belleville.

Turks and Caicos

Biologist Catherine Dyer holds a large mature queen conch, which has relaxed enough to extend almost its entire body from its shell at the "Caicos Conch Farm." Photo by Bill Belleville.

Blue Springs

Cypress trees at the edge of the St. Johns River near Blue Springs. Photo by Bill Belleville.

Florida Keys

A section of the Florida Keys with the Overseas Highway bridging it, as seen from the air. Photo by Florida Keys Tourist Development Council. Used with permission.

Galapagos Journal
An endemic land iguana suns itself on rocks in the Galapagos Islands of Ecuador. Photo by Bill Belleville

Coral Spawning
A porkfish (grunt) over an assemblage of hard and soft corals. Photo by Andy Dalton. Used with permission.

Trinidad
The rocky eastern shore of the continental island of Trinidad. Photo by Bill Belleville.

The Turtle People of the Miskito Coast
Miskito Indians net a large green sea turtle for food on the Miskito Coast of Nicaragua. Photo by Bill Belleville.

Cuba
Juvenile hawksbill turtles at the Isla de Juventud in Cuba. Photo by Bill Belleville.

The Florida Everglades
Alligators in the Florida Everglades. Photo by Bill Belleville.

Jungle Dreams
Hardwood swamp around the remote Blackwater Creek, where I love to paddle in northeast Florida. Photo by Bill Belleville.